I0026538

Islam & Muslims in the 21st Century

By Abdus Sattar Ghazali

Title Design by
Khalid Saeed, Sacramento CA

ISBN   978-0-9909766-2-2

© All Rights Reserved

No part of this book may be reproduced or transmitted in any form or by any means, electronic or mechanical, including photocopying, recording, or by any information storage and retrieval system without the written permission of the author, except where permitted by law.

Dedicated to my grand children:

Dr. Sara, Sabah, Imaad, Farhad, Humza, Danial & Hira

Also by Abdus Sattar Ghazali

American Muslims in Politics (2015) revised version (2017)

Islam & Muslims in the Post-9/11 America (2012 republished 2014)

Islam & the West in the Post-Cold War Era (1999) Clash of Civilization or Clash of Interests

Islam & Modernism (2000) Religious reconstruction and moral regeneration

Hegemony of the Ruling Elite in Pakistan (2000) Subversion of the constitution & Generals in politics

Islamic Pakistan: Illusions & Reality (1996) A political history of Pakistan

Islam in the 21st Century: Challenges, Conspiracies & Chaos

About the author

The author is a professional journalist, with Master's degree in Political Science from the Punjab University. Started his journalistic career working in local newspapers in Peshawar, Pakistan. Served as a News Editor in the Daily News, Kuwait from 1969 to 1976.

Joined the English News Department of Kuwait Television as a News Editor in December 1976. Retired in 1998 as the Editor-in-Chief of the Kuwait Television English News.
Also worked as the correspondent in Kuwait of the Associated Press of Pakistan (APP) and the Daily Dawn, Karachi, a leading Pakistani newspaper. Also worked briefly as editorial writer in the Daily Dawn, Karachi.

He is the author of Islamic Pakistan: Illusions & Reality (1996), Islam & the West in the Post Cold War Era (1999), Islam and Modernism (2000), Hegemony of the Ruling Elite in Pakistan (2000) and Islam & Muslims in the Post-9/11 America.

Contributed a chapter on Civil Rights to "Blessings of Liberty: Individual Rights," published in April 2012 by Perfect Learning, Clive, Iowa. The book is for the K-12 educational market.

Contributed to "At Issue: How Does Religion Influence Politics?" published in 2010 by Gale Cengage Learning, Farmington Hill, Michigan.

Contributed a chapter - Why the US image declined in the Muslim World? - to "US Foreign Policy Towards the Muslim World - Focus on Post 9/11 Period," published in 2010 by University Press of America, Inc., Lanham, Maryland.

He has written extensively on the Middle East, South Asia and American Muslims which is published widely by the media in the Middle East, India, Pakistan and the United States.

Currently working as free lance journalist, the Executive Editor of American Muslim Perspective (www.amperspective.com) and the Chief Editor of the Journal of America (www.journalofamerica.net)

Islam in the 21st Century: Challenges, Conspiracies & Chaos

Introduction

The Islamic states are part of the so-called Third World that is dominated by the West. The Western dominance is of a multi-dimensional nature, not just military or political hegemony. Economic and intellectual forces are important components of the dominant power that the West wields.

The dominant countries of the West have not only penetrated the Third World, particularly, the Islamic or Arab countries in economic and political terms but also in very significant cultural areas.

This hegemonic or dominant role is exercised by certain Western countries because of the ascendant position they occupy in the world market and the community of nation states buttressed by military and technological superiority. According to Robert Keohane, author of After Hegemony: "The theory of hegemony, as applied to the world political economy, defines hegemony as preponderance of material resources. Four sets of resources are especially important. Hegemonic powers must have control over raw materials, control over sources of capital, control over markets, and competitive advantages in the production of highly valued goods."

The global sweep of late capitalism has been seen by many cultural critics to be wedded to the view that modernity and Westernization are the best goals for all peoples, individually and corporately. So, Western views of the world and the West's hegemonic structures and processes are seen to work hand in hand, one supporting the other in a vast co-optative system embracing everything from production-consumption, pop culture, the exportation of human rights and democracy, to the maintenance of "friendly" political regimes and the preservation of the status quo in power relations between the East and the West.

The dominant Western systems were created to enforce the rules of an international economic order, the main purpose of which was to promote the interests of the dominant powers. The international economic system is heavily tilted in favor of the industrialized West. This imposes severe restraints on the modernization and development processes in the developing countries. In economic terms, growth and modernization are key concerns of the so-called liberal philosophy. But it is more concerned with increasing the size of the cake than distributing it fairly and equitably.

Western policy, based on a single principle, i.e. self interest, is pursued brutally

No doubt, every country's policy serves its self interest however western policy, based on a single principle, i.e. self interest, is pursued brutally.

The Western policies towards the third world - that includes the Islamic world - are primarily determined by the analysis of economic and power interests, not by the evaluation of a religion. These policies are single- mindedly pursued by Western self-interest, at times brutally, with little regard for the lives of people there. It is a question of power politics and control.

In his top secret Policy Planning Study 23, Mr. George Kennan, in 1948 outlined the US policy: "we have about 50% of the world's wealth, but only 6.3% of its population....In this situation, we cannot fail to be the object of envy and resentment. Our real task in the coming period is to devise a pattern of relationships which will permit us to maintain this position of disparity....To do so, we will have to dispense with all sentimentality and day-dreaming; and our attention will have to be concentrated everywhere on our immediate national objectives....We should cease to talk about vague and...unreal objectives such as human rights, the raising of the living standards, and democratization. The day is not far off when we are going to have to deal in straight power concepts. The less we are then hampered by idealistic slogans, the better. ... We should recognize that our influence in the Far Eastern area in the coming period is going to be primarily military and economic. We should make a careful study to see what parts of the Pacific and Far Eastern world are absolutely vital to our security, and we should concentrate our policy on seeing to it that those areas remain in hands which we can control or rely on." [1]

Not surprisingly, in its annual Human Development Report 2013, the UN said that gross inequalities between rich and poor countries are worsening, with the richest one percent of the world's population owns about 40 percent of the world's assets, while the bottom half owns no more than one percent. The UN report says that income inequality has increased by 11 percent in the developing countries between 1990 and 2010. A significant majority of households in developing countries – more than 75 percent of the population – are living today in societies where income is more unequally distributed than it was in the 1990s. A The UN report pointed out: Although the world is globally richer than ever before, more than 1.2 billion people still live in extreme poverty. The world is more unequal today than at any point since World War II. [2]

Interestingly, alarming figures of rich and poor gap was confirmed by an Oxfam survey of January 16, 2017 which found that the combined wealth of the world's richest 8 people is now equivalent to that owned by half of the world's population – or 3.6 billion of the poorest people. As decision makers and many of the super-rich gather for this week's World Economic Forum (WEF) annual meeting in Davos, the charity's report suggests the wealth gap is wider than ever, with new data for China and India indicating that the poorest half of the world owns less than previously estimated. Oxfam, which described the gap as "obscene", said if the new data had been available before, it would have shown that in 2016 nine people owned the same as the 3.6 billion who make up the poorest half of humanity, rather than 62 estimated at the time. In 2010, by comparison, it took the combined assets of the 43 richest people to equal the wealth of the poorest 50 percent, according to the latest calculations. [3]

While many workers struggle with stagnating incomes, the wealth of the super-rich has increased by an average of 11 percent a year since 2009, Oxfam pointed out. Oxfam bases its calculations on data from Swiss bank Credit Suisse and Forbes. The eight individuals named in the report are Gates, Inditex founder Amancio Ortega, veteran investor Warren Buffett, Mexico's Carlos Slim, Amazon boss Jeff Bezos, Facebook's Mark Zuckerberg, Oracle's Larry Ellison and former New York City mayor Michael Bloomberg. [3A]

Robert Weissman, author of "Grotesque Inequality: Corporate Globalization and the Global Gap Between Rich and Poor" in 2003 wrote:

"There is something profoundly wrong with a world in which the 400 highest income earners in the United States make as much money in a year as the entire population of 20 African nations-more than 300 million people. Global inequalities persist at staggering levels. The richest 10 percent of the world's population's income is roughly 117 times higher than the poorest 10 percent, according to calculations performed by economists at the Economics Policy Institute, using data from the International Monetary Fund. This is a huge jump from the ratio in 1980, when the income of the richest 10 percent was about 79 times higher than the poorest 10 percent. Exclude fast-growing China from the equation, and the disparities are even more shocking. The income ratio from the richest 10 percent to the poorest 10 percent rose from 90:1 in 19S0 to 154:1 in 1999." [4]

In 1980, median income in the richest 10 percent of countries was 77 times greater than in the poorest 10 percent. By 1999, that gap had grown to 122 times greater. In December 2006, the United Nations released a report titled "World Distribution of Household Wealth," which concluded that 50 percent of the world's population now owns only 1 percent of its wealth. The richest 1 percent own 40 percent of all global assets, with the 37 million people making up that 1 percent all having a net worth of $500,000 or more. The richest 10 percent of adults own 85 percent of global wealth. Under current conditions, the debts of the poorer nations can never be repaid but will just continue to grow. Today more money is flowing hack to the First World in the form of debt service than is flowing out in the form of loans. By 2001, enough money had flowed back from the Third World to First World banks to pay the principal due on the original loans six times over. But interest consumed so much of those payments that the total debt actually quadrupled during the same period. [5]

The World Distribution of Household Wealth

According to The World Distribution of Household Wealth published in February 2008, globally, wealth is more concentrated than income both on an individual and national basis. Roughly thirty percent of world wealth is found in each of North America, Europe, and the rich Asian-Pacific countries. These areas account for virtually all of the world's top 1 per cent of wealth holders. [6] There has been much recent research on the world distribution of income, but also growing recognition of the importance of other contributions to well-being, including those of household wealth. Wealth is important in providing security and opportunity, particularly in poorer countries that lack full social safety nets and adequate facilities for borrowing and lending. We find, however, that it is precisely in the latter countries where household wealth is the lowest, both in absolute and relative terms. Globally, wealth is more concentrated than income both on an individual and national basis. Roughly thirty percent of world wealth is found in each of North America, Europe, and the rich Asian-Pacific countries. These areas account for virtually all of the world's top 1 per cent of wealth holders. On an official exchange rate basis India accounts for about a quarter of the adults in the bottom three global wealth deciles while China provides about a third of those in the fourth to eighth deciles. [7]

The wealth share estimates reveal that the richest 2 per cent of adult individuals own more than half of all global wealth, with the richest 1 per cent alone accounting for 40 per cent of global assets. The corresponding figures for the top 5 per cent and the top 10 per cent are 71 per cent and 85 per cent, respectively. In contrast, the bottom half of wealth holders together hold barely 1 per cent of global wealth. Members of the top deciles are almost 400 times richer, on average, than the bottom 50 per cent, and members of the top percentile are almost 2,000 times richer.

About 34 per cent of the world's wealth was held in the US and Canada in the year 2000, 30 per cent was held in Europe, and 24 per cent was in the rich Asia-Pacific group of countries. Africa, Central and South America, China, India and other Asia-Pacific countries shared the remaining 12 per cent. The location of top wealth-holders is even more concentrated, with North America hosting 39 per cent of the top global 1 per cent of wealth-holders, and Europe and rich Asia-Pacific having 26 per cent and 32 per cent respectively. The high share of top wealth-holders in North America is particularly disproportionate, as this region contains just 6 per cent of the world population.[8]

This disparity continues. In its annual Human Development Report 2008, the UN says that gross inequalities between rich and poor countries are worsening. According to the poverty levels in 2005, 5.58 billion people live on less than $1.00 a day while Almost half the world — over three billion people — live on less than $2.50 a day. [9] The poorest 40 percent of the world's population accounts for 5 percent of global income. The richest 20 percent accounts for three-quarters of world income. [10]

The GDP (Gross Domestic Product) of the 41 Heavily Indebted Poor Countries (567 million people) is less than the wealth of the world's 7 richest people combined. The poorest 10% accounted for just 0.5% and the wealthiest 10% accounted for 59% of all the consumption. [11]

Not surprisingly, the richest 1% of the world's population are getting wealthier, owning more than 48% of global wealth, according to the Credit Suisse global wealth report of October 2014. The report pointed out, a person needs just $3,650 – including the value of equity in their home – to be among the wealthiest half of world citizens. However, more than $77,000 is required to be a member of the top 10% of global wealth holders, and $798,000 to belong to the top 1%. "Taken together, the bottom half of the global population own less than 1% of total wealth. In sharp contrast, the richest decile hold 87% of the world's wealth, and the top percentile alone account for 48.2% of global assets," said the annual report. Its findings were seized upon by anti-poverty campaigners Oxfam which published research in January 2014 showing that the richest 85 people across the globe share a combined wealth of £1 trillion (approx $1.6 trillion), as much as the poorest 3.5 billion of the world's population. "These figures give more evidence that inequality is extreme and growing....In poor countries, rising inequality means the difference between children getting the chance to go to school and sick people getting life saving medicines," said Oxfam's head of inequality Emma Seery. *[The Guardian - October 13, 2014]*

However, despite this yawning disparity the problem is the growing military power of many states in the so-called Third World, who could escape Western dominance. The problem is that a widening circle of states reserve the right to use their power as they fit. This is a dreadful nightmare for the West. The countries in question should, hence, behave in a manner that the Western countries 'see fit' and not as they themselves 'see fit.' Therefore, if any country's policies are found contrary to the Western interest, it is dubbed as against the international law and world peace. Islamic Republic of Iran is the best example of this. Not surprisingly, Iran has been labeled as a "rouge" state because it was resisting the western hegemony. President Saddam Hussain of Iraq and Col. Moammar Gaddafi of Libya were also labelled as rouge regimes. Iraq was invaded by US in 2003 and President Saddam Hussain was executed while Colonel Gaddafi was removed by the invasion of western countries in 2011. Col. Gaddafi was assassinated brutally.

The brutal removal of Saddam and Gaddafi was aimed at sending a stern message and warning to other Muslim and Arab leaders to toe the Western dictated policies otherwise they may face the same fate.

Western civilization - based on the Jewish-Christian ethos - is promoted as "the universal civilization"

The term civilization is usually used in the singular to mean modern Western civilization which since the eighteenth century has been in the West as the civilization; one that has set about to destroy and obliterate systematically all other civilizations including the Islamic. It is being done in the name of a world order which is completely based on the modern, Western ethos.

There is a tendency in the West to consider its own tradition alone as rational and scientific and denigrate other traditions as mere propaganda, religious obscurantism or superstition. Global cultural development is often measured by comparison with the Western culture. Consequently, modernity is not considered a characteristic of Islamic societies. Instead, it is seen as an integral part of a universal process of becoming civilized.

According to this scheme, the West is progressive, rational, enlightened and secular. Islam is backward, fanatical, irrational and fundamentalist. What is interesting is that it is not Islam and Christianity that are contrasted, or the West and the East, but Islam and the West, a religion and a geographical area. Furthermore, it is clearly very important for the West to feel superior and to see Western culture as the 'best' and 'most progressive.'

The view which the Christian and the post-Christian West had of themselves in the past, as being endowed with a universal mission of redemption, is in many respects the same. Whereas it was earlier deemed necessary to 'win the world for Christ,' now 'modernization' - that is, adherence to the model of the West - is exported and preached with almost evangelical fervor as a sure means of redemption.

The West concentrates on Islam as a religion which is made out to be responsible for countless political, cultural and social phenomena in Islamic countries. And it is clearly Islam as a religion that generates such fear in Western culture, a fear of religion that the West thought it had banished from its enlightened societies. To quote Reinhard Schulze: The West appears to re-enact, indeed to prove its own enlightenment and its own independence from the power of religion by comparison with the Orient. This is surely also because doubts have arisen about the victory of the world over religion, or of reason over irrationality in the West itself. [12]

The so-called Islamic or cultural resurgence is complex and multifarious

The so-called Islamic or cultural resurgence is a broad based, complex, multi-faceted phenomenon which has embraced Muslim societies from the Sudan to Sumatra. It is a manifold, multifarious occurrence that is religious, socio-economic and political in character. It is impossible for any single framework to capture it or provide a meaningful comprehension. The phenomenon of Islamic resurgence has been variously described by analysts as the 'fundamentalism,' 'renewal,' 'revival' or 'repoliticization' of Islam, Islamic 'radicalism' and as 'militant Islam.'

The way to understand the Islamic revival as a modern phenomenon must be through an understanding of the modern milieu in existing Muslim societies -- their economies, politics and cultures in the broad senses of the term. The modern political religious movements are apparently the outcome of the distorted process of modernization to which Islamic societies were exposed, of the economic crisis that capped their encounters with the Western-dominated economic and political system, and of the crisis of identity engendered by the cultural encounter with the so-called modernism.

The point to be made here is that both external factors, the Western domination of global economic and political system, and the internal factors have produced this phenomenon. Islamic or cultural resurgence in the modern Muslim world is a socio-religious and political movement that represents social interests, perhaps those of the alienated petty bourgeois mass and its proletarian extension. During the first decade of the new millennium, the Muslims feel that because of the strategic location of the Middle and Near East, they have been under siege for nearly two centuries. When faced with such a continuing and often over-whelming force, they have taken recourse to what is easily and immediately available.

Because adherence to the Islamic Shariah brought so much glory to the seventh century Islam, many Muslims genuinely feel that their present plight can be explained largely because of their failure to practice and follow certain clear and rigid principles and institutions of the Quran and the Sunna.

However, one can discern several types of responses on the part of Muslims to what they term Western dominance and neo-imperialism. It has given rise to a variety of voices and expressions, that have been unrelenting in pursuing their major goal, which is to alter or supplant (some of) the existing culture and society either through legal peaceful means or revolutionary methods.

In every Muslim society in which Islam is followed by a substantial proportion of the population different political or ideological manifestations of Islamic traditions will be discernible. Three broad types of Islamic orientation may be identified: ultra-conservative or orthodox, conservative or traditionalist and moderate or secular. A moderate wishes to preserve Islamic culture and norms, but without taking this to the political arena. He believes in reforming the Islamic society on modern lines and argues that religion should not be invoked in political, legal and economic matters which should be conducted in the context of the present-day world (example: Turkey). Islamic revival or fundamentalism in its ultra-conservative aspect seeks to interpret Islam as a reform movement and is opposed to modernistic interpretations of Islamic teachings which are attempted by modernist and liberal-minded Muslims (example: Saudi Arabia). A conservative or traditionalist interprets Islam in legalistic-ritualistic terms that helped the ruling elites to use Islam as a political instrument. (Example: General Ziaul Haq of Pakistan 1977-1988)

References

[1] George Kennan, U.S. State Department Policy Planning, Study #23, February 24, 1948.

[2] "Humanity Divided: Confronting Inequality in Developing Countries" was launched by Helen Clark, UNDP Administrator in January 2014.

[3] Reuters report of January 16, 2017.

[3A] Ibid.

[4], Grotesque Inequality: Corporate Globalization and the Global Gap Between Rich and Poor by Robert Weissman – 2003.

[5] Enslaved By Debt: The Shocking Truth About Our Money System And How We Can Break Free by Ellen Hodgson Brown 2007 - P-263.

[6] The World Distribution of Household Wealth by James B. Davies, Susanna Sandström, Anthony Shorrocks, and Edward N. Wolff - February 2008

[7] Ibid.

[8] Ibid.

[9] World Bank Development Indicators – 2008 Cited by Anup Shah - Poverty Facts and Stats

[10] 2007 Human Development Report (HDR)

[11] World Bank Development Indicators 2008

[12] R. Schulze, lecture in Cologne, September 1991

Chapter I
The Islamic World today

* Arab and Islamic summits
* Arab League expels Syria over 'failure to end bloodshed'
* Arabs invite the West to invade a sister Arab state, Libya*
* Most Arab states backed the US invasion of Iraq in 2003
* U.S. troops leave as Iraq declines immunity
* Legacy of US occupation: Sectarian politics and violence
* The real reasons for US invasion of Iraq: Stupid it was dollar and oil
* Iraq invades Kuwait: The first Gulf War in 1991
* Was Saddam tricked to invade Kuwait?
* Egyptian-Israeli peace agreement weakens the Arab World
* President Sadat's assassination
* Normalization of Egypt-Israel ties unlikely: Morsi
* Israeli attack on Gaza (2012)
* President Morsi arrested by army
* Muslim Brotherhood declared a terrorist group by Egypt and Saudi Arabia
* Egyptian judge sentences hundreds to death in mass trial
* Social media curbed
* Abdul Fattah al-Sisi elected president
* Fast forward to March 2016 - Morsi supporter hanged
* Egypt closes 27,000 mosques
* Egyptian kangaroo court confirms 20-year-prison sentence on Morsi
* Extra-judicial killing of Muslim Brotherhood leaders

The 20th century will be remembered in the collective Muslim memory as a period of failure and humiliation. Today, at the beginning of the second decade of the 21th century, there are around 1.6 billion [1] Muslims living mostly in their independent states which are grossly under-developed. With adherents spread all over the globe, Islam is the world's second largest religion after Christianity. Muslims constitute majorities in 57 countries, from Asia to Africa to the Middle East and Far East. Though Muslims living in 57 member states of the Organization of Islamic Cooperation (OIC) constitute 22.8% of the world's population, they account for less than 11% of the globe's gross economic product, despite owning 54% of the world oil revenues which are worth trillions of dollars. Economically and politically weak, they are still dependent upon and followers of the Western powers. Not one of the 57 Muslim states is capable of standing on its own feet. [2] None of the Muslim 57 Muslim states is capable of standing on its own feet. [2] None of the Muslim countries has now any international importance, not even the status of a second-rate power.

Today the position is that Muslim countries without a single exception are merely autonomous and are by no means the master of their destiny. Nearly two thirds of the Muslim countries fall into the category of the poorest nations and nearly all the recent famines have occurred in countries with largely Muslim populations, among them the Sahel countries of Africa, as well as Somalia, Sudan and Ethiopia. Out of the world's 48 LDCs, 21 are OIC countries almost all of which depend for their growth and development on the exports of a few non-oil, mostly agricultural, primary commodities. [3] Thanks to oil money only a few countries, mostly with small populations, (such as Kuwait, Saudi Arabia, the UAE, Qatar, Oman, Brunei) have income levels comparable to those of the developed countries. The per capita GDP based on purchasing power parity (PPP) in the richest member country was 17.1 times higher than the average of the OIC countries in 2010. [4]

Due to the unequal distribution of population and resources, the Muslim world is divided into two groups of nations -- the low income economies like Pakistan, Egypt, Bangladesh, and high income oil exporters like Kuwait, Saudi Arabia, Iraq and Libya. The low income Islamic economies constitute amongst themselves nations with the lowest per capita income, lowest life expectancy, lowest adult literacy and highest infant mortality rate. The high income oil economies have higher life expectancy, higher per capita income and all indicators relating to quality of life indicate better standard of living. The marked difference between the two groups of Islamic nations can be appreciated if one sees the per capita GNP which averages $270 for the low-income Muslim world and $13,500 for the high income Muslim world. More than 600 million people live below poverty line. The failure of the Muslim world to embrace modern technology and spreading education is obvious with only 500 PhDs being produced annually as compared to 3,000 in India and 5,000 in the UK.

Mass poverty in Islamic countries is a result of exploitative and oppressive global economic and political systems. [5] This state of affairs is partly due to the fact that a majority of the Muslim countries had been colonized and exploited over the recent centuries, and their culture and economic development neglected. Today the Muslim states like other developing countries find themselves in a debt trap. More than one-third of their gross national product (GNP) now equals their external debt. [6] The Muslims are excluded from the advanced technological society which will shape the political future of the world, condemned to be passive spectators rather than active participants.

Equipped with knowledge, technology, exploitation of economic resources of other societies [7] and as Huntington said, the use of brutal and indiscriminate force, [8] the Europeans have dominated the world for the last 400 years. The scientific revolution formulated the new experimental mathematical method of acquiring knowledge about the social, political, economic, cultural, psychical, physical, biological, geographical and cosmic world. This method is empirical and observational. This method acknowledges no authority except empirically and experimentally proven facts and theories. Most of the knowledge we live by today has been acquired through this method largely in the last 300 years. The non-Western world, including the Muslim bloc, has contributed very little to this knowledge. Even the very rich Muslim-ruled Arab countries spend insignificant amounts on acquiring knowledge. Though they are among the largest buyers of the products of latest science and technology. Being mostly consumers and insignificant producers of knowledge, the Third World pose no threat to the dominance o f the industrialized West. The Western world employs over three million scientists and engineers, whose only job is to create new knowledge and exploit the same for the development of new goods, services and new weapons systems.

According to 2012 CRS Report for US Congress - Conventional Arms Transfers to Developing Nations, 2004-2011 - developing nations continue to be the primary focus of foreign arms sales activity by weapons suppliers. During the years 2004-2011, the value of arms transfer agreements with developing nations comprised 68.6% of all such agreements worldwide. More recently, arms transfer agreements with developing nations constituted 79.2% of all such agreements globally from 2008-2011, and 83.9% of these agreements in 2011. The value of all arms transfer *agreements* with developing nations in 2011 was over $71.5 billion. This was a substantial increase from $32.7 billion in 2010. In 2011, the value of all arms *deliveries* to developing nations was $28 billion, the highest total in these deliveries values since 2004.

Recently, from 2008 to 2011, the United States and Russia have dominated the arms market in the *developing world*, with both nations either ranking first or second for each of these four years in the value of arms transfer *agreements*. From 2008 to 2011, the United States made nearly $113 billion in such agreements, 54.5% of all these agreements (expressed in current dollars). Russia made $31.1 billion, 15% of these agreements. During this same period, collectively, the United States and Russia made 69.5% of all arms transfer agreements with developing nations, ($207.3 billion in current dollars) during this four-year period. [9]

In 2011, the United States ranked first in arms transfer *agreements* with *developing nations* with over $56.3 billion or 78.7% of these agreements, an extraordinary increase in market share from 2010, when the United States held a 43.6% market share. In second place was Russia with $4.1 billion or 5.7% of such agreements. In 2011, the United States ranked first in the value of arms *deliveries* to *developing* nations at $10.5 billion, or 37.6% of all such deliveries. Russia ranked second in these deliveries at $7.5 billion or 26.8%. [10]

In worldwide arms transfer agreements in 2011—to both developed and developing nations—the United States dominated, ranking first with $66.3 billion in such agreements or 77.7% of all such agreements. This is the highest single year agreements total in the history of the U.S. arms export program. Russia ranked second in worldwide arms transfer agreements in 2011with $4.8 billion in such *global* agreements or 5.6%. The value of all arms transfer agreements worldwide in 2011 was $85.3 billion, a substantial increase over the 2010 total of $44.5 billion, and the highest worldwide arms agreements total since 2004. [11]

In 2011, Saudi Arabia ranked first in the value of arms transfer agreements among all developing nations weapons *purchasers*, concluding $33.7 billion in such agreements. The Saudis concluded $33.4 billion of these agreements with the United States (99%). India ranked second with $6.9 billion in such agreements. The United Arab Emirates (U.A.E) ranked third with $4.5 billion. [12]

World's total nominal R&D spending was approximately one trillion dollars in 2010 with US spending 405.3 billion dollars on R&D. Top ten spender on R&D, besides US were: China ($153.7b), Japan ($144.1b), Germany ($69.5b), South Korea ($44.8b), France ($42.2b), United Kingdom ($38.4b), India ($36.1b), Canada

($24.3b), Russia ($23.1b) and Italy ($19.4b). [13] According to R&D Magazine, in 2014, ten countries were expected to spend about 80% of the total $1.6 trillion invested on R&D around the world; the combined investments by the U.S., China and Japan will account for more than half of the total. Together, the U.S., China, Japan and Europe account for about 78% of 2014's $1.6 trillion total. [14]

Interestingly, most Middle East countries were expected strong GDP growth in 2014, but were constrained by weak R&D infrastructure—with exceptions such as Israel and Qatar. [15]

The peculiar manner in which political development has taken place in the Muslim countries have created elite groups which control all the economic resources and sources of power and, in their own interest, sustain dictatorships. They impose systems of education, economy, social institutions and mores to perpetuate the stranglehold they have established over the entire area of national life.

To borrow Khalid bin Sayeed the author of Western Dominance and Political Islam, most of the Muslim countries are ruled by vicious 'friendly' tyrants, [16] surrounded by a predatorial narrow elite group. All the West has to do is to enter into private deals with tyrants; pamper the elite groups and leave the rest to them. The latter would do most of the exploiting and present wonderful profits on the platter to the particular great power. Convergence of interests between the First World's own gainers and the Third World dictators and elites lead to collusive deals between the two that are facilitated by the government of the developed nations which are ever ready to play power games. [17] Muslim countries have the fewest democracies in the world. In most of the Muslim countries, the head of government rose to power through force -- his own or someone else's. The result is instability and a great deal of internal coercion to control his own people. Governments are largely un-representative and mostly unresponsive to public opinion which is easily manipulated. Ruling cliques in league with vested interests exercise power without accountability. Islam is used often as an instrument for preserving and perpetuating status quo.

The West (and once the USSR) has for generations helped repressive and often incompetent regimes hang on to power. In this way, instead of contributing to the resolution of problems they have helped to aggravate and perpetuate them. Internal stagnation, the failure of ruling elites and prolonged economic misery is therefore, the destiny of people in the Middle East, closely connected with the West's predominance in the region. This perception may be exaggerated at times, and may also be dressed up as a conspiracy theory, but it is essentially appropriate. It is hardly surprising then that in the long term a considerable potential for resistance would build up in the Middle East, which would be directed not only against the dictators there but also against the men behind them - the West. [18]

In many Middle Eastern countries the ruling elites have long promised economic development, independence and a solution to the Palestinian problem, to mention but a few examples. Yet they have increasingly proved themselves incapable of resolving even a fraction of the problems of their countries, and instead have only pursued the interests of power, and in the process not uncommonly amply lined their own pockets. Western countries (and earlier to a certain extent the Soviet Union) have played an important contributory role in this. They have collaborated with the ruling elites, and in some cases even helped them to hold on to power artificially. Often, there has been a community of interests between Western governments and Middle Eastern dictatorships (the region being brutally free of democracy) against the people of Middle Eastern countries. [19]

Author Dr. Ziaul Haq wrote the following about the conditions of the Muslim World in 1992 but it is true today after more than two decades: "The modern Muslim society is living under semi-feudal, tribal, rural and capitalist social formations. After its integration into the world capitalist system it now stands polarized into a small minority of powerful elites and a vast majority of powerless and poor masses. These ruling elites, in league with the Western capitalists have been maintaining the exploitative systems of semi-feudalism and neocolonialism. They block all social change, since any change in favor of the poor masses will weaken and eliminate the control of these elites on power and privilege, economics and politics. The economic and political systems of the Muslim societies in general cater to the needs of the elites. During the 1960s and 1970s the western capitalists themselves had initiated development plans to create these elites in the Muslim societies. The evolutionary method of brining change through political pluralism and parliamentary democracy has also been monopolized and distorted by the elites. They always capture power through alignment with different groups within these elites, and through rigging elections and with all sorts of clever maneuvers." [20]

French author, Oliver Roy, wrote in 1994 with great insight on the politics of the Muslim states: "Their politics cannot be explained, as Seurat aptly demonstrates, without reference to the concept of the asabiyya, to segmentation and esprit de corps, which is to say to the establishment of clientele networks more concerned with their own prosperity than with that of the state. But these networks do not represent the permanence of a tradition behind a mere facade of modernity. The structures of the traditional asabiyya were dismantled by urbanization, by the shuffling of society, by ideologization: they rebuilt themselves along different lines (political patronage and economic mafias), but they may also disappear. The modern asabiyya are re-compositions of the esprit de corps based on the fact of the state and the globalization of economic and financial networks; they are translations of a traditional relationship of solidarity into the modern realm. The modern asabiyya are not merely the permanence of tribalism or religious communalism: they may be reconstituted on the basis of modern sociological elements (the new intelligentsia versus the old families), but they function as predators and perpetuate themselves through matrimonial alliances. Their space is no longer the grandfather's village but the modern city. The militia of Beirut may function as old urban asabiyya -- the futuwwa, brotherhoods of bad boys who ensure order and "protection" in the areas poorly patrolled by the palace -- while political parties may function as patronage networks around important notables. [21] In Syria and Iraq, power is held by asabiyya, solidarity groups founded on ethnicity, clan and family. After the riots of October 1988 in Algeria, the sole strategy of the ruling FLN (National Liberation Front), was to stay in power, which it did through multiple manipulations of electoral law. In Pakistan, both the conservative party (the Muslim League) and the Bhutto family's People's Party were arms of large families with industrial and land holdings. [22]

In the present era, the Islamic countries are witnessing the eruption of great political fervor in the form of revolutionary and reformist movements which call for the Islamization of state and society. At the bottom of such an upsurge is the problem of harnessing the development of society -- which has been in a state of flux ever since the inertia was shed by the coming independence -- with an appropriate bridle. In this expedition, the search for a cogent ideology engages all competing social forces. This invariably involves questions about democracy, modernization and socio-economic reforms. [23]

Perhaps in every Muslim society in which Islam is followed by a substantial proportion of the population different political or ideological manifestations of Islam will be discernible. Three broad types of Islamic orientation may be identified: ultra-conservative or orthodox, conservative or traditionalist and moderate or secular. A moderate wishes to preserve Islamic culture and norms, but without taking this to the political arena. He believes in reforming the Islamic society on modern lines and argues that religion should not be invoked in political, legal and economic matters which should be conducted in the context of the present-day world. Islamic revival or fundamentalism in its ultra-conservative aspect seeks to interpret Islam as a reform movement and is opposed to modernistic interpretations of Islamic teachings which are attempted by the so called modernist and liberal-minded Muslims. A conservative interprets Islam in legalistic-ritualistic terms that helped the ruling elites to use Islam as a political instrument.

Islamic resurgence, as a ultra-conservative or orthodox religio-political movement, essentially means going back to the origin sources and roots of Islam. It advocates adherence to the original beliefs of Islam in their liberalist interpretations as fundamental and basic principles thus transcending all social, economic, political and cultural transformations which span a period of fourteen centuries. The original sources of Islam are the Quran and Hadith which are revolutionary in the sense that they give broad and universal values, ideals and principles (of equality, brotherhood and freedom) to change any iniquitous and unjust social system.

Muslims feel that because of the strategic location of the Middle and Near East, they have been under siege for nearly two centuries. When faced with such a continuing and often over-whelming force, they have taken recourse to what is easily and immediately available. Because adherence to the Islamic Sharia brought so much glory to seventh century Islam, many of Muslims feel that their present plight can be explained largely because of their failure to practice and follow certain clear and rigid principles and institutions of the Quran and the Sunna. [24]

Though the Muslim countries share the poverty and backwardness of the Third World as a whole, they differ from the rest of that world by virtue of their dynamic faith, and a glorious history of past accomplishments that inspires them. They have a deep-seated sense of brotherhood, and of sensitivity to the fate and fortunes of Muslims everywhere. The spark of the Islamic faith, and of the vision of a revived Ummah, is there, and inspires a growing number of Muslims all over the world. [25]

The political, utopian goal of recreating the Muslim empire and the return to a mystical golden age holds the greatest attraction. It is the dream of magically transforming their weak, impotent and subordinate position in the world into one of domination. Although no one has yet explained how this transformation would occur simply by applying the Sharia. It is quite clear that the main preoccupation and sole purpose of these modern Muslim mass movements is instant utopian glory, unlimited worldly power in a project which is designed to recreate a cherished past. [26]

High hopes were raised of a great Arab revival in the Middle East at the turn of the 20th century following the collapse of the Ottoman Empire. Hopes of a great cultural and political awakening were raised again following the discovery and exploitation of oil. But as the century ended, the Arabs found themselves as weak and dependent on outside powers as when it began. At the root of this is the gloomy fact of the Arab world's dismal political and economic failure. The early hopes that oil revenues would fuel an economic boom which would catapult the Arab nations into the industrial era were quickly dashed as these revenues tended to be squandered uselessly on arms or on inefficient industrial projects which themselves became a burden on the economy. Associated with economic failure is the political failure. The Arab political order created by the colonial power has remained virtually unchanged. This was a largely artificial order. As a result nearly all Arab states exist today either by direct violent repression of their people or by the threat thereof and few can claim to rule by the consent of the populace. Quite apart from the Arab states' internal political bankruptcy, the living proof of Arab failure and impotence came with the establishment of the state of Israel and the displacement of hundreds of thousands of Palestinians across the Middle East. [27]

"The early Arab political response to the bewildering changes in the world and in the region was the formulation of Arab nationalism. This is a political creed which borrows heavily from Western sources and mixes this with images taken from Arab history yearning to recreate a mythical golden age based on the early Islamic Empire of the 7th-9th centuries. The most elaborate of the Arab nationalist sects is Ba'thism, which believes in a certain glorious, mystical destiny for the Arabs in the contemporary world and calls for unity of all Arabs "from the Gulf to the Atlantic." This Arab state would then become the third superpower (in a world where there were still two). The man in the Arab street responded with great fervor to the claims and promises of nationalism, seemingly unaware that a modern superpower is more than a large land mass and a sizable population. Nevertheless the vision was powerful and captivating, for all fantastic nature of the claims were either lost to them or subconsciously denied. The outrageous claims of the Arab nationalists were completely shattered in the 1967 Arab defeat by Israel. Far from attaining a superpower capability, three Arab armies were roundly defeated by the "Zionist entity" (the term used by the Arab media of the time), a mere client state of the US. As a result, Nasser, the most prominent Arab nationalist of the time, lost all credibility." [28]

Arab nationalism is now largely a vanished cause. Once it aspired to unite Sunni, Shi'a, and Christian Arabs under a secular banner. It is the official ideology of the Ba'ath party in Syria. In June 2003 after the invasion of Iraq in 2003, the US outlawed the Ba'ath Party in Iraq. Sectarian differences between Arabs are seen as more important than common language and culture. The Ba'ath Party was founded in 1947 by Michel Aflaq, a Syrian teacher, whose brand of radical Arab nationalism won supporters across the region. In Arabic, ba'ath means renaissance or resurrection. It functioned as a pan-Arab party with branches in different Arab countries, but was strongest in Syria and Iraq, coming to power in both countries in 1963. The party's early slogan "unity, freedom, socialism" attracted a generation of Arab political activists who wanted to overthrow the western-client governments of the Middle East and create a modern industrial economy.

Today in January 2015, the Muslim world and the Arab world are in chaos and disarray. It is divided horizontally and vertically. Pan-Arab and Pan-Islamic organizations in a bid to bring cohesion, fraternity and unity failed miserably because the main actors of the Arab and Muslim world served the interests of their western masters while failing to respond to the aspirations of their people and ignoring their national interests.

Arab and Islamic summits

Not surprisingly, the Arab and Islamic summits and meetings reflected these sharp divisions and differences. In March 2014, an Arab summit was held in Kuwait amid sharp differences on the major issues confronted by the Arab world. The Western fomented and supported Syrian civil war; Qatar's conflict with Saudi Arabia and the United Arab Emirates over Qatar's support of the Egyptian Muslim Brotherhood that has been declared as a terrorist organization by the Saudis.

The BBC enumerated the following sharp differences as the Arab leaders gathered in Kuwait on March 25-25, 2014 [29]:

- Iraq has accused Saudi Arabia and Qatar of seeking to destabilise the country by supporting insurgents in Iraq's Anbar province.

- Relations between Egypt and Qatar are strained over the Muslim Brotherhood issue.

- Like the USA, Saudi Arabia has designated the the Muslim Brotherhood a terrorist group.

- Saudi Arabia, the UAE and Bahrain have withdrawn ambassadors from Qatar because of the latter's support for the Muslim Brotherhood in Egypt and elsewhere. They are furious about Qatar's refusal of their requests for an end a stream of pro-Brotherhood propaganda broadcast by Doha-based al Jazeera television.

- Egypt, which has also Muslim Brotherhood as a terrorist organization, has also designated Hamas a terrorist group to isolate Gaza. Hamas is the ruling party in Gaza Strip.

- Syria, embroiled in a civil war with outside backing, has accused Saudi Arabia and Qatar of seeking to undermine the country.

- Saudi Arabia and Qatar are supporting different factions of the Syrian opposition.

- The Arab Gulf states, Egypt and Jordan accuse Iraq of acting as an agent of Shia Iran and allowing Iranian arms to reach Syria - and of marginalising the Iraqi Sunni community.

- Saudi Arabia and Bahrain accuse Iran of meddling in their internal affairs by stoking unrest within their Shia communities, while Oman has recently hosted the Iranian foreign minister on an official visit. Oman also angered other GCC states by brokering secret talks between Iran and the United States on the nuclear issue.

Like George Orwell's Animal Farm, the Arab leaders recognize the importance of exploitation and manipulation of language and words as political and power strategy to control the masses. Hence the final communiqué of the Arab summit used crafty language full of empty rhetoric. The only point of consensus was the issue of Palestine and the Arab-Israeli conflict. Arab leaders said they would never recognize Israel as a Jewish state, blaming it for a lack of progress in the Mideast peace process. "We hold Israel entirely responsible for the lack of progress in the peace process and continuing tension in the Middle East, the summit communique said. "We express our absolute and decisive rejection to recognizing Israel as a Jewish state."

On the crucial issue of Syria, the summit failed to take a decisive stance. Syria was expelled from the Arab League in 2011. Its seat remains vacant since many Arab states oppose giving this to the Syrian opposition. However, a Syrian opposition leader, Ahmad-al-Jarba, the head of the "National Coalition for Revolutionary and Opposition Forces" was invited to speak at the summit. Ironically, Qatar and Saudi Arab back different opposition groups involved in the Syrian war.

The Arab leaders failed to agree on a final communique at the end of the summit. Instead a long "Kuwait Declaration" was issued which reflected the stance of the Western countries on the Syrian issue. Blaming the government of President Bishar Al Assad for the current crisis, the Arab leaders called on the Syrian regime to immediately halt all military action against the Syrian people and put an end to the bloodshed, while strongly denouncing the mass killings carried out by the Syrian troops against innocent people, including the use of internationally-outlawed weapons. They also expressed support of the national coalition of revolution and Syrian opposition as the legitimate representative of the Syrian people. [30] The Kuwait Declaration, UAEInternet.com

Arab League expels Syria over 'failure to end bloodshed'

In November 2011, an emergency session of its 22 member states was held in Cairo to discuss the Syrian bloodshed. The league decided to expel Syria for government crackdowns of anti-government demonstrators. Using a diplomatic language, the Arab League said: the league decided to exclude Syria until it implements the terms of an earlier agreed peace deal to stop the violence.

Lebanon and Yemen opposed the expulsion of Syria.

The league also agreed to impose economic and political sanctions on Syria over its failure to stop the violence and appealed to its member states to withdraw their ambassadors from Damascus.

In February 2012, the six-member Gulf Cooperation Council (GCC) announced: "Members have decided to withdraw their ambassadors from Syria and ask at the same time for all the ambassadors of the Syrian regime to leave immediately." The GCC includes: Saudi Arabia, Oman, Bahrain, Kuwait, Qatar and the United Arab Emirates (UAE).

The decision comes a day after the US closed its embassy in Damascus and pulled out all remaining staff. The UK, France, Belgium, the Netherlands, Spain and Italy have also recalled their ambassadors.

As in the case of Libya, the imperialist powers were relying on the Arab League to legitimize intervention in Syria. [31]

Not surprisingly, Syria was also expelled by the 57-member Organization of Islamic Cooperation in August 2012. An extraordinary summit was called in Mecca, Saudi Arabia to discuss the Syrian issue. "The conference decides to suspend the Syrian Arab Republic membership in the OIC and all its subsidiary organs, specialized and affiliated institutions," the closing statement said. It was not a unanimous decision since Iran bitterly opposed the OIC decision. [32]

Arabs invite the West to invade a sister Arab state, Libya

Collaborating with the Western designs to remove the government of Col. Moammar Gaddafi, the Arab League on March 12, 2012, called for the U.N. Security Council to impose a no-fly zone over Libya.

The 22-member Arab bloc, which had already barred Libya's government from taking part in League meetings, said Gaddafi's government had "lost its sovereignty." It also said the bloc would establish contacts with the rebels' interim government, the National Libyan Council, and called on nations to provide it with "urgent help." In a statement, the Arab League asked the "United Nations to shoulder its responsibility ... to impose a no-fly zone over the movement of Libyan military planes and to create safe zones in the places vulnerable to airstrikes."

As Asia Times Online has reported, a full Arab League endorsement of a no-fly zone is a myth. Of the 22 full members, only 11 were present at the voting. Six of them were Gulf Cooperation Council (GCC) members, the US-supported club of Gulf kingdoms/sheikhdoms, of which Saudi Arabia is the top dog. Syria and Algeria were against it. Saudi Arabia only had to "seduce" three other members to get the vote. Translation; only nine out of 22 Arab countries voted for the no-fly zone. [*The US-Saudi Libya deal By Pepe Escobar - Asia Times, April 12, 2011*]

Five days later, the United Nations Security Council imposed a no-fly zone. The UN resolution, introduced by France, was supported by ten of the 15 members: Bosnia and Herzegovina, Colombia, Gabon, Lebanon, Nigeria, Portugal, South Africa, and

Five days later, the United Nations Security Council imposed a no-fly zone. The UN resolution, introduced by France, was supported by ten of the 15 members: Bosnia and Herzegovina, Colombia, Gabon, Lebanon, Nigeria, Portugal, South Africa, and permanent members France, the United Kingdom, and the United States. Brazil, Germany, and India, and permanent members China and Russia abstained, with none opposed. The UN SC resolution acknowledged the importance of the Arab League role in invited the UN to impose a no-fly zone that was a code word for giving go-ahead to the Western nations to invade Libya. The Anglo-French-American consortium and NATO, impatient to invade Libya, launched its military operation on March 19. Shame for Arabs, three Arab countries, Jordan, Qatar and the UAE sent token forces to participate in the Western invasion of Libya.

On October 20, 2011, Col. Moammar Gaddafi was brutally killed in mysterious circumstances. He was the second Arab ruler to meet his end as a result of Western invasion in this new century. President Saddam Hussein was executed by the US occupation forces on December 30, 2006.

The brutal killing of Gaddafi was a chilling warning to other Muslim/Arab leaders that they will meet the same fate if they refused to implement the Western imperialistic agenda.

Most Arab states backed the US invasion of Iraq in 2003

On March 19, 2003, the United States invaded Iraq on the pretext that President Saddam Hussein has developed Weapons of Mass Destruction (WMD). The initial invasion saw cluster bombs, white phosphorus, highly carcinogenic depleted uranium and a new kind of napalm — what we might call weapons of mass destruction — dropped in dense urban areas.

On March 1, less than three weeks before the Anglo-American invasion of Iraq, the Arab leaders gathered in the Egyptian port resort of Sharm el-Skeikh on the Red Sea for their 15th regular summit. The summit proceedings well illustrated where the interests of Arab rulers lay as they all knew that the invasion of Iraq was part of a series of wars to come in America's "long war."

As Mahdi Darius Nazemroaya of Global Research reported: On the eve of war the Arab League adopted a set of resolutions calling on members to refrain from assisting in the Anglo-American invasion of Iraq. The rulers of Saudi Arabia,

Kuwait, Bahrain, Qatar, and the U.A.E. however utterly ignored the resolution in practice by assisting, supporting, and hosting the invading Anglo-American forces with critically important military facilities. The American and British troops, vehicles, tanks, and warplanes that were preparing to attack Iraq did so in the territories and waters of these absolute monarchies of the Arabian Peninsula. Saudi, Jordanian, Kuwaiti, Qatari, and Emirati airspace was also used throughout the invasion and in the occupation phase of the war against Iraq. All this took place against Iraq without the slightest protest from the rulers of these Arab states. [33]

Nazemroaya says the transcripts of the gathering in the port of Sharm el-Skeikh are in a way a form of indictment that exposes the culpability of the leaders of the Arab World in the bloodbath that has become occupied Iraq. In an all too familiar gesture of war, the U.A.E. and the Arab Sheikdoms of the Persian Gulf personally blamed Saddam Hussein for the Anglo-American war preparations and aggression against Iraq. Iraq the victim was being blamed for the actions of the aggressors, America and Britain, and their Arab accomplices. . [34]

When the Arab summit ended, the Information and Culture Minister of the U.A.E., Sheikh Abdullah Bin Zayed Al-Nahyan, who represented the U.A.E. at Sharm el-Sheikh told reporters that a U.A.E. initiative to support the U.S. and Britain in demanding the removal of Saddam Hussein was backed "on the record" by Saudi Arabia and Kuwait. The Emirati official also told reporters that there was broader, but secretive, support amongst Arab rulers for the Anglo-American invasion of Iraq: "We [also] got support off record from other [Arab] countries, but unfortunately they do not want to discuss it on camera. All the Arabs agree that Saddam should go, but none have the courage to say it publicly." [35]

This doublespeak and secretive approach has been a trademark of the autocratic Arab regimes.   Not surprisingly, days after the US-British invasion of Iraq, on March 25, 2003, the Arab League ministers meeting in Cairo passed a resolution declaring the war on Iraq to be a "violation of the United Nations Charter and a "threat to world peace." They demand an unconditional withdrawal of US and British forces from Iraq. The resolution is adopted unanimously by the 22-member League except for a key US ally Kuwait. [36]

U.S. troops leave as Iraq declines immunity
The US occupation of Iraq formally ended in December 2011 when the last American troops left Iraq. On August 19, 2010, U.S. President Barrack Obama

announced that all U.S. combat operations would end on 31 August. However, 50,000 troops would stay in an advise-and-assist role. Having failed to secure a guarantee of legal immunity for remaining US troops, Obama ordered their withdrawal in December 2011.

While the troops have left, a 1,000-man Office of Security Cooperation-Iraq based at the US embassy remains, including both US military personnel and contractors. It has managed hundreds of military sales contracts amounting to over $9 billion since the end of the occupation. US contractors, most of them ex-special operations troops, remain "embedded" with Iraqi forces as "advisors."

The U.S. Embassy in Baghdad is the largest in the world, the size of Vatican City. America has consulates in Basra, Irbil and Kirkuk as well as other locations around the country where contractors will train Iraqi forces on U.S. military equipment they're purchasing. About 5,000 security contractors and personnel will be tasked with helping protect American diplomats and facilities around the country, according to the State Department.

Legacy of US occupation: Sectarian politics and violence

In May 2006, the U.S. installed Nouri Al-Malki, a Shiite, as Prime Minister after clearance from the CIA. Not surprisingly, al-Maliki government has pursued an openly sectarian agenda, ruthlessly purging leading Sunni political figures, using the security forces to crack down on the Sunni population of Anbar and branding protests against these abuses of power as acts of 'Al Qaeda' terrorism.

Maliki has worsened the situation by allowing and encouraging purges of Iraqi politicians in the name of de-Baathification. He has systematically marginalized prominent Sunni politicians such as former Vice-President Tariq al-Hashemi who fled to Iraqi Kurdistan in December 2011 to avoid arrest on murder charges. The Central Criminal Court of Iraq convicted him and sentenced him in absentia to death in September 2012. Hashimi is living in Turkey. In My 2012 Turkey said that Hashmi will not be extradited despite an international arrest warrant.

The U.S.-trained Iraqi Special Operations Forces, also known as the "dirty brigade," have carried out summary executions, searches and kidnappings closely echoing the U.S.- trained death squads on Cold War-era in El Salvador and Guatemala.

US last year provided a hundred and fifty-two Hellfire missiles and more than two dozen Apache attack helicopters to crush anti-government Sunni militias. [37]

Nearly nine years of US military occupation of Iraq has unleashed a sectarian bloodbath. People in Iraq continue to die from the sectarian violence and militia fightings.

More than 8,000 people were killed in Iraq in 2013, according to the U.N. estimates -- most of them innocent civilians caught up in the tempest of violence that grips their country. At least 4,000 people reported killed in 2014 till the end of May. In a protracted surge in bloodshed, a suicide bombing at a Shia mosque in Baghdad, killed 27 people on May 27, 2014. A suicide bomber blew himself up at the entrance to a Shia mosque in central Baghdad's Shorja neighborhood as worshipers were performing ablutions ahead of mid-day prayers. In another incidence, at least 19 people were killed and 34 wounded in the blast at the Abu al-Timan Husseiniyah, in Baghdad. [38]

According to New Yorker, "the resurgence of Iraq's Shiites is the greatest legacy of the American invasion, which overthrew Sunni rule and replaced it with a government led by Shiites—the first since the eighteenth century. Eight years after Maliki took power, Iraqis are sorting through the consequences." [39]

The real reasons for US invasion of Iraq: Stupid it was dollar and oil

President George Bush gave the Iraqi Weapons of Mass Destruction as a rationale for the US invasion of Iraq in 2013. However, the real reason for the US invasion was different. According to John Chapman, a former Assistant Secretary in the British civil service, there were only two credible reasons for invading Iraq: control over oil and preservation of the dollar as the world's reserve currency.

Explaining his argument, Chapman pointed out: "Saddam controlled a country at the centre of the Gulf, a region with a quarter of world oil production in 2003, and containing more than 60% of the world's known reserves. With 115bn barrels of oil reserves, and perhaps as much again in the 90% of the country not yet explored, Iraq has capacity second only to Saudi Arabia. The US, in contrast, is the world's largest net importer of oil. Last year the US Department of Energy forecast that imports will cover 70% of domestic demand by 2025." [40]

"Control over Iraqi oil should improve security of supplies to the US, and possibly the UK, with the development and exploration contracts between Saddam and China, France, India, Indonesia and Russia being set aside in favour of US and possibly British companies," said adding: "Overseeing Iraqi oil supplies, and maybe soon supplies from other Gulf countries, would enable the US to use oil as power. In 1990, the then oil man, Dick Cheney, wrote that: "Whoever controls the flow of Persian Gulf oil has a stranglehold not only on our economy but also on the other countries of the world as well." [41]

The British official further argued: "In the 70s, the US agreed with Saudi Arabia that Opec oil should be traded in dollars. American governments have since been able to print dollars to cover huge trading deficits, with the further benefit of those dollars being placed in the US money markets. In return, the US allowed the Opec countries to operate a production and pricing cartel. In 1999, Iran mooted pricing its oil in euros, and in late 2000 Saddam made the switch for Iraqi oil. In early 2002 Bush placed Iran and Iraq in the axis of evil. If the other Opec countries had followed Saddam's move to euros, the consequences for Bush could have been huge. Worldwide switches out of the dollar, on top of the already huge deficit, would have led to a plummeting dollar, a runaway from US markets and dramatic upheavals in the US." [42]

The US invasion of Iraq placed the second largest reserves of oil in the world under direct American control. It was also aimed at sending a very clear message to any other oil producers just what will happen to them if they do not stay in the dollar circle.

As Oil Industry analyst, Antonia Juhasz said, "Prior to the 2003 invasion and occupation of Iraq, US and other western oil companies were all but completely shut out of Iraq's oil market. But thanks to the invasion and occupation, the companies are now back inside Iraq and producing oil there for the first time since being forced out of the country in 1973." [43]

As Professor Michael T. Klare, author of Resource Wars, explains, one of the main objectives of the Bush administration in invading Iraq stems from the analysis made by Vice-President Dick Cheney in 1990, when he made clear that "Whoever controls the flow of Persian Gulf oil has a stranglehold not only on our economy. but also on that of most of the other nations of the world." [44]

The Iraqi constitution of 2005, greatly influenced by US advisors, contains language that guarantees a major role for American and British oil companies.

The world's leading Western oil companies have been expanding Iraq's giant southern fields - Rumaila led by British Petroleum, West Qurna-1 run by Exxon and Zubair operated by Eni of Italy and the southern field of Majnoon, led by Shell.

A group led by BP will receive $2 billion per year to develop Iraq's Rumalia field and a Shell-led group is to get $913 million per year. An Exxon-led group is to get $1.6 billion per year, Bloomberg News reports. .....The only area of Iraq where oil firms fare better than fee-for-service work is in the northern Kurdish autonomous region (KRG) where businesses including Norway's DNO International ASA are pumping crude under production-sharing agreements "not recognized by the central government," Bloomberg reports. Hunt Oil Co., of Dallas, Tex., clinched a separate deal in Sept., 2007, with Iraq Kurdistan Regional Government.[45]

The Kurdistan Region sits on some 45 billion barrels of oil reserves and more than 110 trillion cubic feet of gas. It has granted oil and gas concessions to some of the world's biggest energy companies, including ExxonMobil, Gazprom Neft, Total and Chevron.

In 2013, the Kurdish enclave also signed a multibillion-dollar energy package with neighboring Turkey, which includes construction of a second oil pipeline and one for gas.

The genocidal invasion and preceding sanctions killed three million Iraqis, including half a million children, and totally destroyed a relatively advanced developing country whose people were largely prosperous. Close to five million Iraqis were displaced by the invasion out of a population of 31 million, and five million Iraqi children became orphans. Women suffered the greatest losses in education, professions, child care, nutrition, and safety. More than one-fourth of Iraq's population died, became disabled, or fled the country as refugees. [46]

Iraq invades Kuwait: The first Gulf War in 1991

On August 1, 1990, Saudi-mediated talks between Iraq and Kuwait held at Jeddah, Saudi Arabia, collapse when Kuwait reportedly refused Iraq's demands, which included reduction in Kuwaiti oil production, compensation of $2.5 billion for oil produced in disputed territory, forgiveness by Kuwait of about $15 billion in debts accumulated during war with Iran, control of Bubiyan and Warba islands giving Iraq direct access to Arabian/Persian Gulf for its oil exports. [47]

The next day, on August 2, 1990, Iraqi forces occupied Kuwait which has a tiny force of about 15,000 men of all cadres. For the Iraqi army it was just a walkover. The ruling Sabah family fled to Saudi Arabia overnight. Only the younger brother of Amir, Sheikh Fahad Al Sabah, was left behind. He was killed in an encounter with the Iraqi forces outside the Dasman Amiri palace. [48]

The United States President George H. W. Bush assembled a coalition of forces to evict Iraq from Kuwait, consisting of soldiers from 39 countries: Afghanistan, Argentina, Australia, Bahrain, Bangladesh, Belgium, Canada, Czechoslovakia, Denmark, Egypt, France, Germany, Greece, Honduras, Hungary, Italy, Kuwait, Morocco, the Netherlands, New Zealand, Niger, Norway, Oman, Pakistan, Poland, Portugal, Qatar, Saudi Arabia, Senegal, Sierra Leone, Singapore, South Korea, Spain, Sweden, Syria, Turkey, the United Kingdom, the United Arab Emirates and the United States. [49]

The Gulf War began with an extensive aerial bombing campaign on 17 January 1991. President Bush ordered 110,000 air sorties against Iraq, dropping 88,000 tons of bombs, nearly seven times the equivalent of the atomic bomb that destroyed Hiroshima, according to a report sent to the Commission of Inquiry for the International War Crimes Tribunal. [50]

Depleted Uranium was used in the war in tank kinetic energy penetrators and 20–30 mm cannon ordnance. Many have cited DU use as a contributing factor to a number of instances of health issues in the veterans and surrounding civilian populations. [51]

On the night of 26–27 February 1991, some Iraqi forces began leaving Kuwait on the main highway north of Al Jahra in a column of some 1,400 vehicles. A patrolling E-8 Joint STARS aircraft observed the retreating forces and relayed the information to the DDM-8 air operations center in Riyadh, Saudi Arabia. These vehicles and the retreating soldiers were subsequently attacked, resulting in a 60 km stretch of highway strewn with (dead bodies and) debris.. [52]   This was dubbed as the Highway of Death.

The cost of the war to the United States was calculated by the U.S. Congress to be $61.1 billion. About $52 billion of that amount was paid by other countries: $36 billion by Kuwait, Saudi Arabia and other Arab states of the Persian Gulf; $16 billion by Germany and Japan (which sent no combat forces due to their constitutions). [53]

On February 27, 2991, US forces enter Kuwait City and President Bush declared Kuwait officially liberated from - seven months - Iraqi occupation.

A Report by the former US Attorney General, Ramsey Clark and Others to the Commission of Inquiry for the International War Crimes Tribunal provides a graphic picture of the indiscriminate US bombing causing thousands of civilian and military casualties and destroying Iraq's economic infrastructure. According to the charges filed in the International War Crimes Tribunal against President George H. W. Bush, Vice President J. Danforth Quayle, Secretary of Defense Richard Cheney, Gen. Norman Schwarzkopf Commander of the Allied Forces in the Persian Gulf, and others:

President Bush ordered the destruction of facilities essential to civilian life and economic productivity throughout Iraq. Intentionally bombed and destroyed civilian life, commercial and business districts, schools, hospitals, mosques, churches, shelters, residential areas, historical sites, private vehicles and civilian government offices. The United States used prohibited weapons capable of mass destruction and inflicting indiscriminate death and unnecessary suffering against both military and civilian targets. The United States killed soldiers seeking to surrender and killed Iraqi soldiers and destroyed materiel after the cease fire.

For example, on March 2, 1991, two days after the ceasefire came into effect on, U.S. 24th Division Forces engaged in a four-hour assault against Iraqis just west of Basra. More than 750 vehicles were destroyed, thousands were killed without U.S. casualties. A U.S. commander said, "We really waxed them." It was called a "Turkey Shoot." One Apache helicopter crew member yelled "Say hello to Allah" as he launched a laser-guided Hellfire missile. [54]

The United States reports it flew 110,000 air sorties against Iraq, dropping 88,000 tons of bombs, nearly seven times the equivalent of the atomic bomb that destroyed Hiroshima. 93% of the bombs were free falling bombs, most dropped from higher than 30,000 feet. Of the remaining 7% of the bombs with electronically guided systems, more than 25% missed their targets, nearly all caused damage primarily beyond any identifiable target. Most of the targets were civilian facilities. The intention and effort of the bombing of civilian life and facilities was to systematically destroy Iraq's infrastructure leaving it in a preindustrial condition. [55]

Was Saddam tricked to invade Kuwait?

Enumerating the factors leading to President Saddam Hussein's occupation of Kuwait, Dr. Hussein El Najjar, the author of The Gulf War: Overreaction & Excessiveness (Amazon 2001), said the position of the Bush administration encouraged Iraq to invade Kuwait without worrying about any serious consequences. He quoted Khalid Bin Sultan, the commander of the Saudi force in the war as saying:

Throughout 1990, particularly during the climax of the crisis in July, the United States never warned Iraq explicitly not to use force to settle its disputes with Kuwait. When John Kelly, the U.S. Assistant Secretary of State for Near Eastern Affairs, visited Baghdad in February 1990, he expressed the American indifference concerning the Iraqi-Kuwaiti disputes. On July 24, 1990, the State Department spokeswoman, Margaret Tutwiler, stressed that the U.S. had no defense treaty with Kuwait and no special defense commitment to it. The same statement was reiterated by John Kelly on July 31, 1990. These statements must undoubtedly have encouraged Iraq to invade Kuwait. [56]

Not surprisingly, the International War Crimes Tribunal report charged: The United States engaged in a pattern of conduct beginning in or before 1989 intended to lead Iraq into provocations justifying U.S. military action against Iraq and permanent U.S. military domination of the Gulf. When Saddam Hussein requested U.S. Ambassador April Glaspie to explain State Department testimony in Congress about Iraq's threats against Kuwait, she assured him the U.S. considered the dispute a regional concern, and it would not intervene. By these acts, the U.S. intended to lead Iraq into a provocation justifying war. [57]

On January 26, 2011, US Congressman Ron Paul recorded the following statement for Congressional Record. It was posted on the Veterans Today website: "It had been long assumed that the United States Government, shortly before Iraq invaded Kuwait in August of 1990, gave Saddam Hussein a green light to attack. A State Department cable recently published by WikiLeaks confirmed that U.S. Ambassador April Glaspie did indeed have a conversation with Saddam Hussein one week prior to Iraq's August 2, 1990, invasion of Kuwait.

"Amazingly, the released cable was entitled, "Saddam's Message of Friendship to President Bush." In it, Ambassador Glaspie affirmed to Saddam that "the President had instructed her to broaden and deepen our relations with Iraq." As Saddam Hussein outlined Iraq's ongoing border dispute with Kuwait, Ambassador Glaspie was quite clear that, "we took no position on these Arab affairs." There would have been no reason for Saddam Hussein not to take this assurance at face value. The U.S. was quite supportive of his invasion and war of aggression against Iran in the 1980s. With this approval from the U.S. Government, it wasn't surprising that the invasion occurred. The shock and surprise was how quickly the tables were turned and our friend, Saddam Hussein, all of a sudden became Hitler personified.

"The document was classified, supposedly to protect national security, yet this information in no way jeopardized our security. Instead, it served to keep the truth from the American people about an event leading up to our initial military involvement in Iraq and the region that continues to today." [58]

Egyptian-Israeli peace agreement weakens the Arab World

Egypt and Israel signed a peace agreement on March 26, 1979, the first of its kind between an Arab country and Israel. [59] This peace treaty ended the state of war between the two entities but weakened the unity and strength of the Arab camp in its efforts to resolve other issues involving Israel. In the Arab world, Egyptian President Colonel Anwar Sadat was branded a traitor. The Arab states suspended all official aid and severed diplomatic relations. Egypt was expelled from the Arab League, which it was instrumental in founding, and from other Arab institutions. Saudi Arabia withdrew the funds it had promised for Egypt's purchase of American fighter aircraft. The Arabs felt betrayed and dismayed that the Palestinian issue, the core of the Arab-Israeli conflict, would remain an unresolved, destabilizing force in the region. The Arab apprehensions were true.

Today in April 2015, the Arab front remains weak and the Arab-Israeli conflict remains unresolved with Israeli massacre of people in Lebanon and occupied Palestinian territories.

President Sadat's assassination

On October 6, 1981, while observing a military parade commemorating the eighth anniversary of the October 1973 War, Sadat was assassinated by Lieutenant Colonel Khalid al Islambuli who was sentenced to death and executed by firing squad in April 1982. Whereas a number of Western leaders, including three former United States presidents, attended Sadat's funeral, only one member of the Arab League was represented by a head of state, Sudan. Only two, Oman and Somalia, sent representatives.

Sadat's handpicked successor, vice president Air Marshal Husni Mubarak succeeded Sadat. In a speech to the People's Assembly in November 1981, Mubarak pledged that the peace treaty with Israel would be honored. In April 1982, the Israeli withdrawal from Sinai took place as scheduled.

For many years, Egypt, the Arab world's most populous nation, remained officially frozen out of Arab dealings because of its peace agreement with Israel. But an Arab League summit meeting in Amman, Jordan, in November 1987 allowed the Arab countries to resume diplomatic relations with Egypt. In January 1984, Egypt was readmitted unconditionally to the Organization of Islamic Cooperation (OIC).

Fast forward to June 24, 2012, when Mohammad Morsi from the Moslem Brotherhood was elected president in the first fair election held in the aftermath of deposition of President Hosni Mubarak on February 11, 2011. Interestingly, after 30 years of autocratic rule President Mubarak did not transfer power to Vice President Omar Suleiman but to the Supreme Council of the Armed Forces.
Mohammad Morsi was the first person in Egypt's very long history who was able to say that he was elected by a majority of voters. However Israel and the United States were alarmed at Morsi's election that has weakened the power of their axis in the region. Nothing less than a pure client government in Egypt was strategically acceptable for the US and Israel. [60]

Normalization of Egypt-Israel ties unlikely: Morsi

In an extensive interview with Al Jazeera TV on April 21, 2013, Egyptian President Mohamed Morsi dismissed the likelihood of a thaw in relations between Egypt and Israel until Tel Aviv continues its violation of the Palestinians rights. "We must always talk about reality, not imagine future things which are impossible as we observe reality," Morsi said in response to a question about the likelihood of normalization of ties with Israel.

The Egyptian president also noted that he wouldn't visit Israel, nor would he host an Israeli leader as long as no real peace is achieved between Israel and Palestinians. Morsi pointed to Egypt's commitment to the 1979 Camp David Accord with Israel, but noted that true peace cannot be achieved as long as Palestinians are denied their rights. "The peace treaty [with Israel] clearly states: 'just and comprehensive peace for the nations of the region.' I refer to the Palestinian people. Where is just and comprehensive peace for the Palestinian people?" he asked. [61] Morsi also said that Israel is responsible for a systematic information campaign aimed at demeaning Egypt and justifying decades-long Israeli expansion.

Since the removal of President Hosni Mubarak's pro-Israel autocratic rule, the Egyptians have held several massive protests across the country, calling on the government to sever all the existing ties with Israel. In September 2011, Egyptian protesters stormed the Israeli embassy in Cairo, forcing its staff to evacuate the building.

Israeli attack on Gaza (2012)

During the US-backed Israeli operation in Gaza in November 2012, President Mohammad Morsi's government issued the sharpest rebuke, recalling its ambassador from Tel Aviv a few hours after the first Israeli air strike, which killed the military commander of the ruling Hamas group, Ahmed Jabari.

Egypt's Muslim Brotherhood, which has close ties to Hamas, called for a severing of relations with Israel in response to the offensive. But Morsi, who had been among the leaders of the movement until he was elected Egypt's president, said only that the Israeli attacks must cease. "The Israelis must understand that we do not accept this aggression, which could lead to instability in the region," he said in televised remarks.

Israeli sources said that Egypt threatened that Israeli operation in the Gaza would endanger the peace treaty between Egypt and Israel. According to the Israeli source, Egyptian President Mohamed Morsi refused to speak directly with Israeli representatives during the cease-fire negotiations, despite the US urging him to do so.

As the ceasefire took effect on the 21st of November 2012, Israeli missiles, bombs, and artillery shells rained down hard on the citizens of Gaza, killing and wounding hundreds. According to press reports, over 160 Palestinians, including women and children, were killed and about 1,200 others were injured and more than 1,500 targets were hit across the Palestinian enclave during the eight-day Israeli assault.

Hundreds of global protests condemned Israel's naked aggression. Many thousands across the Middle East, Europe, North America, and elsewhere denounced Israel's cold-blooded premeditated murder of innocent Palestinians.
Gaza has been blockaded since June 2007, following 2006 sweeping victory of Hamas in legislative assembly election. The Israeli blockade has caused a decline in the standard of living, unprecedented levels of unemployment, and unrelenting poverty. The Israeli regime denies about 1.7 million people in Gaza their basic rights, such as freedom of movement, jobs that pay proper wages, and adequate healthcare and education.

The Israeli assault on Gaza came one month after the US and Israel joint war games which were described as the largest in Israeli history. According to Prof Michel Chossudovsky of the Global Research, the objective of the war games was to test Israel's missile air defense system against attacks from far and near, namely from Iran, Hezbollah and Hamas.

Israeli Prime Minister Netanyahu hoped the Gaza operation will ensure his re-election on January 22, 2013. Also at issue was subverting Palestine's November 29, 2012 UN non-member observer status bid. Israel and Washington were going all out to sabotage it. [62]

During his tenure, President Morsi strengthened ties with Iran. Their diplomatic relationship has been strained since Egypt signed a peace treaty with Israel in 1979. He attended the 16th Summit of the Non-Aligned Movement in Tehran at the end of August 2012, in a visit that could resume normal relations for the countries.

In February 2013, President Morsi hosted the Islamic summit in Cairo attended by leaders of 57 Muslim nations.

In a bid to consolidate power, President Morsi, in August 2012, ordered the powerful head of the army and defense minister, Field Marshal Hussein Tantawi, and several senior generals into retirement and canceled constitutional amendments issued by the military restricting presidential powers. Morsi also sent into retirement the chief of army staff, General Sami Anan, and appointed him as a presidential adviser.

Field Marshal Tantawi was the head of the Supreme Council of the Armed Forces (SCAF), which ruled the country after Hosni Mubarak was toppled as president in February 2011. He was defense minister for nearly two decades under Mubarak. General Abdul-Fatah al-Sissi was appointed to replace Tantawi as defense minister and the general commander of the army.

President Morsi arrested by army

On July 3, 2013, General Sisi arrested the country's first democratically elected president, Mohamed Morsi and suspended the Constitution. At a televised news conference, Gen. Abdul-Fattah al-Sisi said that the military had no interest in politics and was ousting Mr. Morsi because he had failed to fulfill "the hope for a national consensus." At the White House, President Obama urged the military to move quickly to return Egypt to a 'democratically' elected government, saying, "We are deeply concerned by the decision of the Egyptian Armed Forces to remove President Morsi and suspend the Egyptian Constitution." The New York Times pointed out that the president notably did not refer to the military's takeover as a coup — a phrase that would have implications for the $1.3 billion a year in American military aid to Egypt. [63] The armed forces were against President Morsi because they were the beneficiaries of the annual 1.3 billion dollar handouts from US as reward for turning a blind eye to Israel's conspiracies in the region.

Plot to crush the democracy movement was not something unexpected. Conspiracy has been set in motion the day Morsi was elected President. Morsi had only one disqualification that he was supported by the Muslim Brotherhood. [64]

Immediately after the detention of President Morsi the armed forces launched a crackdown on the Muslim Brotherhood. Since the coup Morsi supporters have been holding continual protests demanding his reinstatement. They were met by a fierce security crackdown that has killed hundreds of people and arrested thousands of Brotherhood members and supporters. According to Reuters report of Sept. 6, 2013, since July 2013, they have killed more than 900 of Morsi's supporters and arrested most of the movement's leaders, including Morsi, on charges of murder or inciting violence against anti-Brotherhood protesters.

Muslim Brotherhood declared a terrorist group by Egypt and Saudi Arabia

Egypt's military-backed interim government declared the Muslim Brotherhood a terrorist group on December 25, 2013, criminalizing all its activities, its financing and even membership in the organization, from which the country's President Morsi hails. Deputy Prime Minister Hossam Eissa said that those who belonged to the group, financed it or promoted its activities would face punishment.

The 83-year old Brotherhood had been banned under President Hosni Mubarak, who ruled from 1981 to 2011, and under earlier Egyptian regimes. However, it continued to be grudgingly tolerated as a mass movement sending legislators to sit in parliament as independents. The Muslim Brotherhood claims to have around a million members. In March 2013 it was registered as a NGO called the Muslim Brotherhood Association. The Brotherhood also has a political wing, the Freedom and Justice Party (FJP), which was set up in 2011 as a "non-theocratic" group after the uprising that forced President Hosni Mubarak from power.

Founded in 1928 by an Egyptian schoolteacher, Hasan Al Banna as a reaction to the abuse at the hands of British colonizers, the Brotherhood quickly became one of the largest Muslim organizations in the world, and branches were established in other countries, each of which operated largely independently.

On March 4, 2014, Egyptian military government also banned Palestinian group Hamas. An offshoot of Egypt's Muslim Brotherhood, Hamas has frequently been a secondary target of a crackdown on the Brotherhood since the overthrow of President Mohamed Morsi on July 3, 2013. Hamas and Egypt formed a tight alliance during the tenure of the ousted Egyptian president Morsi, largely due to Hamas's historic links to Morsi's Muslim Brotherhood.

Following Egyptian move, Saudi Arabia formally designated the Muslim Brotherhood a terrorist organization on March 7, 2014. The Saudi designation is also likely to have ramifications for Hamas, the Brotherhood-affiliated group that rules the Gaza Strip and which both the United States and Israel have designated a terrorist organization.

Egyptian judge sentences hundreds to death in mass trial

As the crackdown on Muslim Brotherhood continued, on April 28, 2014 a judge sentenced to death 683 supporters of the country's ousted president, including the Muslim Brotherhood's spiritual leader. [65]

Among those convicted and sentenced to death was Mohamed Badie, the Brotherhood's spiritual guide. If his sentence is confirmed, it would make him the most senior Brotherhood figure sentenced to death since one of the group's leading ideologues, Sayed Qutb, was executed in 1966.
According to lawyer Ali Kamal, the hearing lasted only eight minutes. Security forces surrounded the court building and blocked roads, preventing families and media from attending the proceedings.

According to the Associated Press, some 16,000 people have been arrested since the military ousted Morsi in July 2013, including most of the group's top leaders. [66]

On March 24, 2014, an Egyptian court sentenced 528 supporters of ousted President Mohammed Morsi to death. They were convicted of charges including murdering a policeman and attacks on people and property. According to the BBC, the group was among some 1,200 Muslim Brotherhood supporters on trial, including senior members.

Social media curbed

On April 28, 2014, another Egyptian court banned the April 6 youth movement that helped engineer the 2011 uprising that led to the ouster of longtime autocratic President Hosni Mubarak.

The Cairo court ruled in a suit filed by a lawyer who demanded the banning of the youth group over allegations it "tarnished the image of the Egyptian state" and conspired against the country's national interests. Leaders of April 6 – Ahmed Maher and Mohammed Adel – have been jailed for violating a new protest law that requires that any demonstration must have a police permit.

That ruling was seen by activists as part of a government– orchestrated campaign to stifle opposition and dissent. [67]

In June 2014, the Interior Ministry, in charge of police, announced plans to set a new surveillance system over the Internet to monitor social networking sites for a wide range of forms of dissent, as well as for extremist activity. Social media were one of the main vehicles for the 2011 anti-Mubarak uprising.

An Interior Ministry document on the plans published by the pro-military newspaper Al-Watan listed a wide variety of "grave and dangerous security challenges" on social media that must be monitored, including expressions of "contempt for religion," "spreading rumors and tarnishing facts," "humiliating mockery" of officials, as well as incitement to "extremism, violence, rebellion, rallying for demonstrations, sit-ins and illegal strikes."

Abdul Fattah al-Sisi elected president

On March 26, 2014, Field Marshal Abdul Fattah al-Sisi announced that he has resigned as Egypt's military chief in order to stand for the presidency. Egypt's interim president Adly Mansour on January 27, 2014 promoted General Abdel-Fattah El-Sisi, the army chief and minister of defense, to the rank of Field Marshal.

The 59-year-old Sisi was widely expected to win the vote, and restore a tradition of presidents from military background that Egypt had for all but one year presidency of Morsi since 1952.
The presidential election in Egypt took place between 26 and 28 May 2014. On June 3, the election officials announced that Field Marshal a-Sisi had received 96.9% of the vote and his sole challenger, Hamdeen Sabahi, only 3.1%.

Muslim Brotherhood, crushed by a massive crackdown, had boycotted the polls.

Al-Sisi was sworn-in President on June 8, 2014. Al-Sissi now restores a chain of five Egyptian presidents of military background since the 1952 coup against the monarchy — with Morsi the sole exception.

The White House said it hoped to advance its strategic partnership with Cairo and the "many interests" the countries shares.

Fast forward to March 2016

Egypt closes 27,000 mosques [68]

In March 2015, the Egyptian Ministry of Religious Endowment closed down 27,000 mosques on the pretext of fighting terrorism. The move raised questions about the fate of mosques in many Egyptian villages, the grounds of which are usually less than 80 square meters. Opponents of the government decision such as the Salafist Nour Party said that closing down of mosques without providing a larger alternative serves to further bolster extremist ideology. Supporters of the decision such as intellectuals and scholars claimed that those mosques are time bombs that threaten national security.

An estimated 400 permits were issued to Imams, who pledged not to use Friday prayers for political purposes. A follow-up committee was formed by the ministry in February 2015 to oversee new imams during Friday prayers, cancel their permits and initiate legal proceedings against them if they failed to abide by their agreement with the ministry, as well as permanently bar them from taking the pulpit of any mosque in the country.

Egyptian kangaroo court confirms 20-year-prison sentence on Morsi [69]

Amid mounting anger against the US-client government of Field Marshal Abdel Fattah Al-Sisi because of tax rises, soaring food prices, inflation and cuts in state subsidies, a kangaroo court in Cairo in October 2016 confirmed a 20-year prison sentence against Mohamed Morsi, the first democratically elected President who was deposed by Al-Sisi in July 2013. In April 2015, a Cairo court had sentenced Morsi to 20 years in prison for inciting violence against protesters who had staged a sit-in outside the Ittihadiya presidential palace in December 2012, when Morsi was still in power.

Twenty-year jail sentences were also confirmed against other senior figures from Morsi's Muslim Brotherhood, including Mohamed el-Beltagy and Essam el-Erian.

The men were convicted in April 2015 on charges including kidnapping, torture and the killings of protesters during unrest in 2012. Morsi, elected in 2012 and overthrown in 2013, is facing several trials. After a controversial trial, he was sentenced to death in May 2015 for allegedly participating in violence against the police during the 2011 uprising against former President Hosni Mubarak, but his court appointed lawyers have appealed that verdict. An Egyptian court cancelled the life sentences Oct 25, 2016 handed out to former president Mohamed Morsi and Muslim Brotherhood chief Mohamed Badie along with 15 other leaders of the banned group in an espionage case and ordered a retrial.

The court also cancelled death sentences handed out to 16 other Muslim Brotherhood members, including top leaders Khyrat el-Sharer and Mohamed el-Beltagy Ahmed Abdel Aty. Thirteen of the 16 were sentenced in absentia. The defendants were accused of spying, funding terrorism and disclosing national security.

Turkey's president, Tayyip Erdoğan, had criticized the death sentence for Morsi and accused the west of hypocrisy. "The popularly elected president of Egypt, chosen with 52% of the vote, has unfortunately been sentenced to death," Erdoğan said at a rally in Istanbul. "Egypt is turning back into ancient Egypt," he said, referring to the Pharaonic rule of the land that ended more than two millennia ago. "The west, unfortunately, is still turning a blind eye to Sisi's coup," he added. "While they abolished the death penalty in their own countries, they just look on as spectators at this execution in Egypt."

Morsi, who has also been sentenced to 25 years in prison after being convicted of leaking state secrets to Qatar, has not appointed a lawyer to defend himself and has refused to recognize the legitimacy of the court proceedings, saying he remains Egypt's legitimate president.

The Muslim Brotherhood has been blamed for the unrest in Egypt, which has resulted in the death of hundreds of people. Al-Sisi's government designated the Muslim Brotherhood a terrorist group in December 2013, making even verbal expressions of support punishable by imprisonment.

Hundreds of people have been sentenced to death in a crackdown following Morsi's overthrow. Seven have been executed, including six defendants sentenced to death by a military court for allegedly participating in militant attacks.
On October 29, 2016, an Egyptian kangaroo court sentenced two Muslim Brotherhood supporters to life in prison and 16 others to 15 years in jail for an alleged violent assault on a Cairo neighborhood in 2013 after the ouster of president Mohamed Morsi.

Reuters news agency reported since deposing Morsi, the authorities have held mass trials for thousands of Muslim Brotherhood supporters, with hundreds receiving death sentences or lengthy prison terms. The agency said that the 104 defendants in October 29 case were part of a pro-Brotherhood march held two days after sit-ins supporting the group. The march was violently dispersed leaving hundreds dead. The defendants were tried on a range of charges that included murder, assault, joining an armed gang, resisting arrest, damaging public and private property, and possession of firearms.

Extra-judicial killing of Muslim Brotherhood leaders [70]

In October 2016, Two Muslim Brotherhood leaders have been killed in suspicious circumstances by the Egyptian security forces. A ministry statement carried by the official MENA news agency said 61-year-old Dr. Mohammed Kamal, a physician by profession, was killed along with Yasser Shahata Ali Ragab in an exchange of gunfire as police tried to arrest the two late on Monday, Oct 3, 2016, night.

But a Brotherhood statement posted on its official website shortly after reports of the shootout surfaced said Dr. Kamal had been arrested by police, suggesting he was killed after being taken into custody. The statement went on to say: Here's our reply to your heinous crime, to the murderous military junta. "..We announce it, as also the founding Imam Hassan Al-Banna announced it: "To die for the sake of God is our highest aspiration".

London-based Brotherhood leader Mohamed Soudan told Turkish news agency Anadolu: "Authorities announced the death of Kamal and Shehata shortly after

local media reported that they had been arrested. This means that both leaders had been liquidated," he said.

Dr. Kamal was twice sentenced in absentia to life in prison on charges of setting up an armed group and setting off an explosion near a police station, while Ragab was sentenced in absentia to 10 years in jail.

Dr.Kamal was one of the most prominent leaders of the Muslim Brotherhood and a member of the Guidance Bureau. He was previously in charge of the supreme Administrative Committee, known as the youth committee. He was accused of planning the June 2015 killing in Cairo of Egypt's chief prosecutor, Hisham Barakat. Dr. Kamal was also accused of master minding the assassination attempt on Egypt's former mufti, Sheikh Ali Gomaa, in Cairo in August 2016. Tellingly, Ansar Beit al-Maqdis claimed responsibility for the attack.

Gomaa was a key supporter of the military's 2013 coup. In public speeches, he has been advocating the use of force against the Muslim Brotherhood.

References

[1] The world's Muslim population is expected to increase by about 35% in the next 20 years, rising from 1.6 billion in 2010 to 2.2 billion by 2030, according to population projections released by the Pew Research Center's Forum on Religion & Public Life in January 2011. If current trends continue, Muslims will make up 26.4% of the world's total projected population of 8.3 billion in 2030, up from 23.4% of the estimated 2010 world population of 6.9 billion. According to the Pew report, as of 2010, about three-quarters of the world's Muslims (74.1%) live in the 49 countries in which Muslims make up a majority of the population. More than a fifth of all Muslims (23.3%) live in non-Muslim-majority countries in the developing world. About 3% of the world's Muslims live in more-developed regions, such as Europe, North America, Australia, New Zealand and Japan. [2] The OIC annual economic report 2011

[3] Ibid.

[4] Ibid.

[5] The West controls the economic and political system since Western nations: 1. Own and operate the international banking system. 2. Control all hard currencies. 3. Are the world's principal customer. 4. Provide the majority of the world's finished goods. 5. Dominate international capital markets. 6. Are capable of massive military intervention. 7. Control the sea lanes. 8. Conduct most advanced technical research and development. 9. Control leading edge technical education. 10. Dominate access to space. 11. Dominate the aerospace industry. 12. Dominate international communications. 13. Dominate the high-tech weapons industry. (Clash of Civilization by by Samuel P. Huntington p-81)

[6] According to the recent World Bank classification, 22 OIC countries are still classified as Heavily Indebted Poor Countries (HIPC), of which 18 countries are also classified as Least Developed Countries (LDCs). The total external debt stock of the OIC countries showed an increasing trend during the period 2005-2009. In 2009, the total external debt of the OIC countries amounted to $903 billion. (OIC annual economic report 2011)

[7] Explaining the Rise of the West and the Decline of the East, J.W. Smith, writes: "The Christian and Muslim worlds were relatively equal until the West stole all the gold and silver that the American Indians had mined over several thousand years. This provided greater wealth for the West and drove down the value of the East's gold and silver. The East (the Muslim East) now had far less money and the West (Christians) far more money. The West could now outspend the East in both war and technology. In the 16th-Century Luther broke with Roman Catholic Christianity and the West started its slow (yet incomplete) evolution to democracy and freedom. The big breaks toward liberalism and democracy: the American and French Revolutions came late in the 18th-Century. The crushing of the feudal Muslim East was imminent just 100 years later. As Jared Diamond outlines, control of the world's resources and technology—and expansion of societies through financial, technical, and military superiority—is not only as old as history, it is history.3 The building by the West of the Suez Canal and what railroads there were in the East is evidence of the West's technical, financial, and military superiority. Add the wealth being plundered from the Americas, Africa, and Asia to that being taken from Muslim regions and the Muslim East was obviously in for the rapid decline relative to the Christian West that history records."

...... So long as they are denied equality in technology and trade, the wealth of the East will flow to the West. Muslims retreating into the protection of their religion remains the last bastion of protection for Muslim culture. *(The Deeper History Behind the September 11th Terrorist Attack On America by J.W. Smith - Institute for Economic Democracy Press 2005)*

[8] The West won the world not by the superiority of its ideas or values or religion (to which few members of other civilizations were converted) but rather by its superiority in applying organized violence. Westerners often forget this fact; non-Westerners never do. (Clash of Civilization by Samuel P. Huntington p-51)

[9] Richard F. Grimmett, CRS Report for Congress; Conventional Arms Transfers to Developing Nations, 2004-2012, August 24, 2012

[10] Ibid.

[11] Ibid.

[12] Ibid.

[13] 2011 Global R&D Funding Forecast by the Business of Innovation.

[14] Global Funding Forecast for 2014 by R&D Magazine, September 2013

[15] Ibid.

[16] The regimes, particularly those friendly to the United States, are not very strong politically and very often the United States has to prop them up, knowing full well that they are autocratic. Such regimes have been designated in a recent work as Friendly Tyrants. "The most important of all Friendly Tyrants for the United States is Mexico .... Washington would undoubtedly be prepared to do much more to keep a Friendly Power in power there than elsewhere if the alternative were viewed as being much worse from the perspective of US interests. Certainly it would be more willing to keep an unfriendly tyrant from taking power there than anywhere else in the world." When one considers that the Persian Gulf supplies nearly 60 to 70 percent of Japan's oil needs, over 50 percent of Europe's and above all, that the mounting debts of the United States are financed by the credit from Japan and Germany, one can see that perhaps the Gulf region and particularly Saudi Arabia is a close second, if not as vital, to the security of the United States as Mexico. [Khalid bin Sayeed, Western Dominance and Political Islam - Oxford University Press, Karachi, p-22]

[17] M. B. Naqvi, Third World and realpolitik - Dawn 29.4.1996

[18] Jochen Hippler, The Next Threat: Western Perceptions of Islam p-123

[19] Ibid. p-122,3

[20] Dr. Ziaul Haq, Islamic Fundamentalism - Dawn 14.2.1992

[21] Oliver Roy, The Failure of Political Islam (1994) - p-18-19

[22] Ibid. p-52

[23] Ibid.

[24] Khalif Bin Sayeed, op. cite., p-1

[25] Dr. Maqbool Ahmad Bhatty - Muslim world and new global order - Dawn 8.4.1994

[26] Dr. R. T. Abed, Islamic Fundamentalism: a new political mythology? Weekly Middle East International - London 4.3.1994

[27] Ibid.

[28] Ibid.

[29] BBC March 24, 2014

[30] The Kuwait Declaration, www.UAEInternet.com

[31] BBC, February 7, 2012

[32] Reuters report of August 15, 2012

[33] War and the "New Middle East": US Coalition Building and the Arab League By Mahdi Darius Nazemroaya Global Research, April 09, 2008

[34] Ibid.

[35] Al-Ahram Weekly, no. 628, March 6-12, 2003.

[36] BBC, March 25, 2003

[37] U.S. Sends Arms to Aid Iraq Fight With Extremists - New York Times, Dec 25, 2013

[38] The Express Tribune, May 27, 2014

[39] Letter from Iraq: What we left behind by Dexter Filkins, The New Yorker, April 28, 2014

[40] The real reasons Bush went to war by John Chapman, a former assistant secretary in the British civil service. The Guardian, July 28, 2004

[41] Ibid.

[42] Ibid.

[43] Iraq: the Biggest Petroleum Heist in History? by Mike Whitney - Counterpunch, May 23, 2014

[44] Cited by Asad Ismi, Iraq Nation Destroyed, Oil Riches Confiscated. Surviving Population Impoverished - Global Research, March 30, 2014

[45] Western Oil Firms Big Winners In Iraq By Sherwood Ross - OpEd News - January 16, 2012

[46] Iraq Nation Destroyed, Oil Riches Confiscated. Surviving Population Impoverished By Asad Ismi - Global Research, March 30, 2014

[47] Financial Times, 2 August 1990, 1; Wall Street Journal, 3 August 1990, A5; Washington Post, 3 August 1990, A27) Washington-based Peterson Institute for International Economics

[48] The author is an eye witness to the Iraqi invasion and occupation of Iraq. He was working at the Kuwait TV English News Department as a senior editor.

[49] CNN Sept 6, 2013

[50] Charge sheet & judgment

[51] Wikipedia

[52] Ibid.

[53] Ibid.

[54] International War Crimes Tribunal

[55] Ibid.

[56] Desert Warrior: A Personal View of the Gulf War by the Joint Forces Commander by Khalid Bin Sultan.

[57] International War Crimes Tribunal - Op cit

[58] *Ron Paul Enters Evidence of Bush War Crimes in Congressional Record by Kurt Nimmo - Infowars.com - February 4, 2011*

[59] The Egyptian-Israeli peace treated followed a meeting between President Sadat of Egypt and Prime Minister Begin of Israel at the presidential retreat of Camp David in the Maryland countryside. They met from September 5 to 17, 1978 at the invitation of President Jimmy Carter, and signed the so-called Camp David peace accord.

[60] In Sept, 2011, Egypt's interim Prime Minister Essam Sharaf said a peace deal with Israel was not "sacred" and could be changed for the benefit of peace or the region. His comments, made in an interview with a Turkish television channel and broadcast on state television, were the strongest yet by the new government which took over after president Hosni Mubarak was overthrown in February. "The Camp David agreement is not a sacred thing and is always open to discussion with what would benefit the region and the case of fair peace ... and we could make a change if needed," he said in the interview. Essam

Sharaf was PM from 3 March 2011 to 21 November 2011. [Egypt PM says peace deal with Israel not sacred Reuters, Sept 15, 2011]

[61] Press TV April 22, 2013

[62] The New York Times reported: The new status will give the Palestinians more tools to challenge Israel in international legal forums for its occupation activities in the West Bank, including settlement-building, and it helped bolster the Palestinian Authority, weakened after eight days of battle between its rival Hamas and Israel.... Still, the General Assembly vote — 138 countries in favor, 9 opposed and 41 abstaining — showed impressive backing for the Palestinians at a difficult time. It was taken on the 65th anniversary of the vote to divide the former British mandate of Palestine into two states, one Jewish and one Arab, a vote Israel considers the international seal of approval for its birth..."We do not recognize Israel, nor the partition of Palestine, and Israel has no right in Palestine," said Salah al-Bardaweel, a spokesman for Hamas in Gaza. "Getting our membership in the U.N. bodies is our natural right, but without giving up any inch of Palestine's soil." [*U.N. Assembly, in Blow to U.S., Elevates Status of Palestine - New York Times, November 29, 2012*]

[63] Army Ousts Egypt's President; Morsi Is Taken Into Military Custody - New York Times, July 3, 2013

[64] Turkey was perhaps the only Muslim country which bluntly linked President Morsi's ouster to Arab-Israeli conflict. On August 20, 2013, Turkish Prime Minister Recep Tayyip Erdogan accused Israel of being behind the ouster of President Morsi. "What is said about Egypt? That democracy is not the ballot box. Who is behind this? Israel is. We have the evidence in our hands," Erdogan said in a televised address to officials from his ruling party. "That's exactly what happened." Erdogan criticized Muslim nations for not denouncing Morsi's ouster, saying: "Today, despite the betrayal of brothers, no one will be able to prevent the Egyptian people from taking over the administration of Egypt." A day earlier, Turkish leaders had strongly criticized the Turkish secretary general of the 57-member Organization of Islamic Cooperation, accusing him of inaction over events in Egypt and suggesting he should resign.

The Turkish leader has drawn parallel between Morsi's ouster and a series of anti-government protests in Turkey in June 2013 that he has blamed on an International conspiracy to topple his democratically elected government through illegal means. - *Huffington Post August 20, 2013*

[65] Egypt judge sentences 683 to death in mass trial, including Muslim Brotherhood leader - The Associated Press - April 28 2014

[66] Ibid.

[67] Egypt judge sentences 683 to death in mass trial, including Muslim Brotherhood leader - The Associated Press - April 28 2014

68. www.al-monitor.com

69. Egyptian kangaroo court confirms 20-year-prison sentence on Morsi by Adus Sattar Ghazali, OpEd October 28, 2016.

70. Mysterious killing of senior Muslim Brotherhood leaders once again highlights brutal policies of Egypt's military govt by Abdus Sattar Ghazali OpEd October 5, 2016.

Chapter I (Continued)
From the "Afghan Jihad" to the Islamic State

- *Brzezinski explains how he started the so-called Afghan Mujahideen*
- *The so-called Islamic State*
- *The Origin of ISIS*
- *Muslim extremism was knowingly fomented as a weapon of foreign policy*

It is said that there is a three-step pattern of US-led Western geopolitical strategy.

Step 1: Build up a dictator or extremist group which can then be used to wage proxy wars against opponents. During this stage any crimes committed by these proxies are swept under the rug. [**Problem**] Examples: Dictators in the Muslim World such as General Ziaul Haq of Pakistan. President of Hosni Mubarak of Egypt. Backing of Afghan militants in 1979.

Step 2: When these nasty characters have outlived their usefulness, that's when it's time to pull out all that dirt from under the rug and start publicizing it 24/7. [**Reaction**] Examples: Hosni Mubarak removed through the so-called Arab Spring demonstrations. Afghan Mujahideen abandoned in 1980s after the withdrawal of the Soviet troops from Afghanistan.

Step 3: Finally, when the public practically begging for the government to do something or anti- government groups seek foreign intervention, a solution is proposed. Usually the solution involves military intervention and the loss of certain liberties. [**Solution**] Example: Rebel groups in Libya were backed by the West in 2011 to topple Gaddafi regime.

Those who know recent history will remember that Zbigniew Brzezinski, President Jimmy Carter's National Security, was directly involved in the funding and arming the militants in Pakistan and Afghanistan in order to weaken the Soviets. By the way Osama bin Laden was one of these anti-Soviet "freedom fighters" the U.S. was funding and arming.

Tellingly, officially the U.S. government's arming and funding of the Mujahideen was a response to the Soviet invasion in December of 1979, however in his memoir entitled "From the Shadows" Robert Gates, director of the CIA under Ronald Reagan and George Bush Senior, and Secretary of Defense under both George W. Bush and Barrack Obama, revealed that the U.S. actually began the covert operation 6 months prior, with the express intention of luring the Soviets into a quagmire.

The strategy worked. The Soviets invaded, and the ten years of war that followed are considered by many historians as being one of the primary causes of the fall of the USSR.

Brzezinski explains how he started the so-called Afghan Mujahideen [1]

In an interview with Jeffrey St. Clair and Alexander Cockburn published by Counter Punch on January 15, 1998, Zbigniew Brzezinski, President Jimmy Carter's National Security Advisor from 1977 to 1981, explained how Jimmy Carter and he started the so-called Afghan Mujahideen.

He said: According to the official version of history, CIA aid to the Mujahadeen began during 1980, that is to say, after the Soviet army invaded Afghanistan, 24 Dec 1979. But the reality, secretly guarded until now, is completely otherwise: Indeed, it was July 3, 1979 that President Carter signed the first directive for secret aid to the opponents of the pro-Soviet regime in Kabul. And that very day, I wrote a note to the president in which I explained to him that in my opinion this aid was going to induce a Soviet military intervention.

He went on to say: That secret operation was an excellent idea. It had the effect of drawing the Russians into the Afghan trap and you want me to regret it? The day that the Soviets officially crossed the border, I wrote to President Carter: We now have the opportunity of giving to the USSR its Vietnam war. Indeed, for almost 10 years, Moscow had to carry on a war unsupportable by the government, a conflict that brought about the demoralization and finally the breakup of the Soviet empire.

In response to another question Brzezinski said: What is most important to the history of the world? The Taliban or the collapse of the Soviet empire? Some stirred-up Moslems or the liberation of Central Europe and the end of the cold war?

The so-called Islamic State

In recent years the US created the so-called Islamic State in Iraq. Juan Cole, history professor at the University of Michigan wrote on November 23, 2015: The Bush administration's patent favoritism toward Shiite religious parties and marginalization of the Sunni Arabs had created a powerful constituency for the Islamic State in Iraq. The U.S. occupation created the conditions under which the group flourished. [2]

Certainly, prominent ISIS leaders were held in US prisons. ISIS leader, Ibrahim al-Badri (aka Abu Bakr al-Baghdadi) is said to have been held for between one and

two years at Camp Bucca in Iraq. In 2006, as al-Baghdadi and others were released, the Bush administration announced its plan for a 'New Middle East', a plan which would employ sectarian violence as part of a process of 'creative destruction' in the region. [3]

With 'major Arab allies' backing ISIS and substantial collaboration between US-armed 'moderate rebels' and ISIS, it is not such a logical stretch to suppose that the US and 'coalition' flights to ISIS areas (supposedly to 'degrade' the extremists) might have become covert supply lines. That is precisely what senior Iraqi sources began saying, in late 2014 and early 2015. [4]

The Origin of ISIS [5]

, founder of Truth in Media, gives an insight into the origins of the so-called Islamic State. On March 12, 2015 he writes:

Angela Keaton, the founder of Antiwar.com, said that ISIS is "entirely a creation of the United States' behavior in Iraq." "That's how we got to where we are, because of war, because of occupation, because of torture," Keaton said. "The United States government completely destabilized and wrecked Iraq. They caused it to fail miserably and that is entirely the fault of the United States government. There is no one else to blame."

The militant group ISIS was formed as a small insurgent group in Iraq in 2006. While they tried to create problems for the U.S. military, they had no money and no real ability to recruit.

It wasn't until 2009 that ISIS shifted its focus from Iraq, where it was largely unsuccessful in developing a foothold, and focused on the civil war in Syria.

It wasn't until June 2014 that ISIS went from being a "no-name group in Syria" to a group that was heavily armed and trained by U.S. and Coalition Special Forces. This revitalized group made a dramatic entrance by crossing back over the Syrian border into Iraq and capturing Mosul and much of the northern part of the country.

One of the most important facts that mainstream media ignores time and time again is that ISIS was able to grow so fast, because of all the U.S. military equipment they were able to seize – equipment that our military left in Iraq. Truckloads of Humvees, tanks and weaponry that instead of taking or destroying, the U.S. government simply decided to leave behind.

However, even when the U.S. government became aware that ISIS fighters were capturing U.S. equipment, it did nothing. Swann attributed the lack of action to the fact that ISIS fighters were taking the equipment back into Syria to continue fighting Assad, which was what the U.S. government wanted.

Daniel McAdams, the executive director of the Ron Paul Institute asks:

"How is it that the United States, with all of its intelligence capabilities, didn't know this threat was coming?" . "How many billions did we spend, maybe a hundred billion on total intelligence community budge over the year? How did they have no idea?"

The answer is simple: "The U.S. did know who ISIS was, but the so-called Islamic State was doing what the Obama administration wanted."

There are three facts:

Fact #1: "Our government armed Osama bin Laden and the Mujahideen in Afghanistan and created al-Qaeda."

Fact #2: "Our government put Saddam Hussein into power – we helped supply and create chemical weapons for him to use against Iran in 1980 – and then we overthrew him in 2003."

Fact #3: "Our government trained rebel fighters in Syria who would become the group today known as ISIS. We have watched them commit every violent atrocity you can imagine to people living in Iraq and Syria, and now we want American taxpayers to fund a 30-year war with them."

In reality the legions of terrorists fighting across the Arab World under the flag of "ISIS" are the same Al Qaeda militants the US, Saudi Arabia and others in an utterly unholy axis have been backing, arming and exploiting in a variety of ways for decades. [6]

The fighters are real. Their atrocities are real. The notion that they've sprung out of the dunes of Syria and Iraq, picked their weapons from local date trees and have managed to wage war regionally against several collective armies is entirely fantasy. Required to maintain ISIS' ranks would be billions in constant support. These are billions ISIS simply cannot account for from hostage ransoms and black market oil alone. The only source that could prop ISIS up for as long as it has allegedly existed and to the extent it allegedly exists, is a state or collection of states intentionally sponsoring the terrorist enterprise. [7]

Muslim extremism was knowingly fomented as a weapon of foreign policy [8]
According to Garikai Chengu, a research scholar at Harvard University, much like Al Qaeda, the Islamic State (ISIS) is made-in-the-USA, an instrument of terror designed to divide and conquer the oil-rich Middle East and to counter Iran's growing influence in the region. The fact that the United States has a long and torrid history of backing terrorist groups will surprise only those who watch the news and ignore history. Chengu says:

"In order to understand why the Islamic State has grown and flourished so quickly, one has to take a look at the organization's American-backed roots. The 2003 American invasion and occupation of Iraq created the pre-conditions for radical Sunni groups, like ISIS, to take root. America, rather unwisely, destroyed Saddam Hussein's secular state machinery and replaced it with a predominantly Shiite administration. The U.S. occupation caused vast unemployment in Sunni areas, by rejecting socialism and closing down factories in the naive hope that the magical hand of the free market would create jobs. Under the new U.S.-backed Shiite regime, working class Sunni's lost hundreds of thousands of jobs. Unlike the white Afrikaners in South Africa, who were allowed to keep their wealth after regime change, upper class Sunni's were systematically dispossessed of their assets and lost their political influence. Rather than promoting religious integration and unity, American policy in Iraq exacerbated sectarian divisions and created a fertile breeding ground for Sunni discontent, from which Al Qaeda in Iraq took root.

"The Islamic State of Iraq and Syria (ISIS) used to have a different name: Al Qaeda in Iraq. After 2010 the group rebranded and refocused its efforts on Syria. ISIS is not merely an instrument of terror used by America to topple the Syrian government; it is also used to put pressure on Iran. America is using ISIS in three ways: to attack its enemies in the Middle East, to serve as a pretext for U.S. military intervention abroad, and at home to foment a manufactured domestic threat, used to justify the unprecedented expansion of invasive domestic surveillance. By rapidly increasing both government secrecy and surveillance, Mr. Obama's government is increasing its power to watch its citizens, while diminishing its citizens' power to watch their government. Terrorism is an excuse to justify mass surveillance, in preparation for mass revolt."

The CIA first aligned itself with extremist Islam during the Cold War era. Back then, America saw the world in rather simple terms: on one side, the Soviet Union and Third World nationalism, which America regarded as a Soviet tool; on the other side, Western nations and militant political Islam, which America considered an ally in the struggle against the Soviet Union, Chengu said adding:

"The director of the National Security Agency under Ronald Reagan, General William Odom recently remarked, "by any measure the U.S. has long used terrorism. In 1978-79 the Senate was trying to pass a law against international terrorism – in every version they produced, the lawyers said the U.S. would be in violation." During the 1970's the CIA used the Muslim Brotherhood in Egypt as a barrier, both to thwart Soviet expansion and prevent the spread of Marxist ideology among the Arab masses. The United States also openly supported Sarekat Islam against Sukarno in Indonesia, and supported the Jamaat-e-Islami terror group against Zulfiqar Ali Bhutto in Pakistan. Last but certainly not least, there is Al Qaeda.

"Lest we forget, the CIA gave birth to Osama Bin Laden and breastfed his organization during the 1980's. Former British Foreign Secretary, Robin Cook, told the House of Commons that Al Qaeda was unquestionably a product of Western intelligence agencies. Mr. Cook explained that Al Qaeda, which literally means an abbreviation of "the database" in Arabic, was originally the computer database of the thousands of Islamist extremists, who were trained by the CIA and funded by the Saudis, in order to defeat the Russians in Afghanistan.

"The Islamic State is its latest weapon that, much like Al Qaeda, is certainly backfiring. ISIS recently rose to international prominence after its thugs began beheading American journalists. Now the terrorist group controls an area the size of the United Kingdom."

"The so-called "War on Terror" should be seen for what it really is: a pretext for maintaining a dangerously oversized U.S. military. The two most powerful groups in the U.S. foreign policy establishment are the Israel lobby, which directs U.S. Middle East policy, and the Military-Industrial-Complex, which profits from the former group's actions. Since George W. Bush declared the "War on Terror" in October 2001, it has cost the American taxpayer approximately 6.6 trillion dollars and thousands of fallen sons and daughters; but, the wars have also raked in billions of dollars for Washington's military elite. Put simply, the War on Terror is terrorism; only, it is conducted on a much larger scale by people with jets and missiles."

References

1. Counter Punch – January 15, 1998.

2. How the United States helped create the Islamic State by Juan Cole, Richard P. Mitchell collegiate professor of history at the University of Michigan, November 23, 2015.

3. The Relationship between Washington and ISIS: The Evidence By Prof. Tim Anderson - Global Research, March 08, 2015.

4. Ibid.

5. Truth in Media: The Origin of ISIS By Ben Swann Truth in Media – March 12, 2015.

6. US War on ISIS a Trojan Horse by Ulson Gunnar July 3, 2015.

7. Ibid.

8. America Created Al-Qaeda and the ISIS Terror Group By Garikai Chengu - Global Research, September 19, 2014

Libya : More than five years after Gaddafi's brutal murder Libya remains in turmoil [1]

More than five years after the Libyan leader Muammar Gaddafi's overthrow and brutal murder (on October 20, 2011), the situation is now far worse than it was five years ago as rival militias fight for control.

Libya has been split between rival parliaments and governments, each backed by a loose array of militias and tribes. Now five years on, Libya is caught between two rival governments, with the western-recognized parliament forced into exile in the eastern city of Tobruk in 2014, following a military uprising from the opponent group known as 'Libyan Dawn', who have since set up parliament in the capital, Tripoli.

While accurate figures are hard to ascertain, estimates suggest tens of thousands have died in Libya as a result of the conflict since 2011.

Libya's conflict has left 1.9 million people with serious health needs in a country that lacks medical professionals, medicines and vaccines, according to the World Health Organization.

CIA-Backed General Khalifa Haftar Seizes Control Of Libyan Oil Fields (The African Globe)[2]

In a dramatic development, 1n September 2016, forces loyal to CIA-backed General Khalifa Haftar took control of two key oil ports. His troops seized Al Sidra, Ras Lanuf and I Zueitina terminals on Libya's Mediterranean coast.

General Haftar has refused to endorse a UN-backed national-unity government in Tripoli and remains loyal to the rival administration based in the east of the country.

His forces took the Ras Lanuf and Al Sidra terminals, together capable of handling 700,000 barrels of oil per day, from a militia loyal to the Government of National Accord (GNA). The majority of Libya's oil exports went through the three terminals before the militia, known as the Petroleum Facilities Guards, seized them more than two years ago.

Following the capture of the oil ports, the House of Representatives has promoted Haftar from general to field marshal.

General Haftar was a military chief under Muammar Gaddafi before turning against him and calling for his overthrow from exile in the United States. In 2011, General Haftar returned to Libya and commanded some of the rebel units that defeated Gaddafi, aided by Nato air power.

According to The New Yorker, as military commander of the Salvation Front, he plotted an invasion of Libya--but Gaddafi outflanked him. The C.I.A. had to airlift Haftar and three hundred and fifty of his men to Zaire and, eventually, to the United States. Haftar was given citizenship, and remained in the U.S. for the next twenty years.

Leaked tapes expose Western support for renegade Libyan general [3]

General Haftar enjoys the support of several Arab nations, including Egypt, the UAE and Jordan, as well as others in the West.

General Haftar's air-force commander, Saqr Geroshi, was quoted as saying by the UAE newspaper The National in July that, along with 20 French personnel, small units of British and American Special Forces were also deployed with the Tobruk army at Benghazi's Benina airport.

A multinational military operation involving British, French and US forces is coordinating air strikes in support of a renegade general battling militia groups from a base near Benghazi in eastern Libya, according to air-traffic recordings obtained by Middle East Eye reveal.

The leaked tapes appear to confirm earlier reports suggesting the existence of an international operations centre that is helping General Khalifa Haftar in his campaign to gain control of eastern Libya from groups he has declared to be "extremists".

The leaked tapes feature pilots and air traffic controllers speaking in Arabic and English. British, American, French and Italian accents can be heard.

The presence of foreign special forces in Libya has been known for several months, but until now they were thought to be working only with the western-recognized GNA. In May, the Pentagon confirmed it had units advising local forces. Pro-GNA militias from Misurata have said British special forces were helping them to capture the extremist group's main base in the town of Sirte. What is new is that western

Special Forces are also on the ground supporting General Haftar.

The French connection [4]

In July last, it was reported that three French special-forces operatives killed in Libya were working with General Khalifa Haftar.

France first admitted that its units were in the country. Hours later president Francois Hollande said three operatives on a "dangerous reconnaissance mission" had been killed in a helicopter crash there previously.

French newspaper Le Monde has reported that the three men were not soldiers but agents from its elite intelligence service, Direction Generale de la Securite Exterieure (DGSE).

The Associated Press reported that France had launched air strikes on the militia that claimed to have shot down the helicopter, the Benghazi Defense Brigades, killing at least 14 fighters. Five years after Muammar Gaddafi's brutal murder the situation is now far worse than it was five years ago. While accurate figures are hard to ascertain, estimates suggest tens of thousands have died in Libya since 2011 as a result of the NATO's intervention to depose Gaddafi.

The militants' attack on the US diplomatic mission in Benghazi, Libya, on September 11, 2012, remains a burning issue among Republicans, who hold the former secretary of state, Hillary Clinton, partially responsible for the deaths of four Americans, including the ambassador John Christopher Stevens.

Libyan strongman met an undignified and horrific end that was deliberate to send a strong message to the western client leaders in the Muslim world that they can meet the same fate as Gaddafi and the Iraqi President Saddam Hussein, who was hanged on the first day of Eid ul-Adha, December 30, 2006.

Muammar Gaddafi was a controversial figure in his lifetime and is sure to be controversial in his death as well. There is so much confusion and so many lies being told about Muammar Gaddafi and the Libya of which he was the leading figure for 42 years. [5]

The treatment meted out to Muammer Gaddafi is reminiscent, only in harsher form, to the way the Yugoslav leader Slobodan Milosevic was treated. Milosevic was taken to a criminal court by the very criminals who waged the war against the Yugoslav people, for the sole purpose of demonizing Milosevic and his government, and, to legitimize NATO's predatory war. Something similar is being done now in the case of Libya. [6]

Normally, if a cat is run over by a driver in a London street, there are days and days of news coverage about how the cat died – was it really taken care of? – was it taken to the right vet? And all the rest of it – if not why not? The people in charge should be called to account. [7]

In the case of Libya and Colonel Gaddafi, as with all opponents of imperialism, the organs of bourgeois propaganda have been showing their concern for life by gloating over Colonel Gaddafi's murder at the hands of Nato's mercenaries. Here is a small bouquet of headlines carried by the British press on Friday 21 October (the day after the murder of Colonel Gaddafi) to express their sordid delight: "*No mercy for a merciless tyrant*" (*Daily Telegraph*); "*End of a Tyrant*" (*Independent*); "*Gaddafi gunned down in a sewer - murdering rat gets his deserts*" (shrieked the *Express*); "*Death of a dictator*" (thus spake the 'humanitarian' *Guardian*); "*A ruthless dictator who impoverished and oppressed his people*" (wrote the 'truth-loving' chief organ of British finance capital, the *Financial Times*). [8]

God alone knows how the *Financial Times* managed to say that Gaddafi "*impoverished his people*"! The truth is that the standard of living in Libya was the highest anywhere in the whole of the African continent. Their per capita GDP was $16,500 a year; the literacy rate stands at 95 per cent; life expectancy is over 70 years. Every Libyan had free access to education and health; every Libyan received free accommodation. And every Libyan was, at the time of getting married, given $50,000 to start life. Every Libyan had $5,000 put in his account every year out of the oil money. These are just a few of the statistics indicative of the prosperity and quality of life of the Libyan people during the time that Gaddafi was at the helm. [9]

References

1. Libya: Five years after Gaddafi's brutal murder by Abdus Sattar Ghazali – OpEd News October 19, 2016.

2. Ibid.

3. Ibid.

4. Ibid.

5. Tribute to Colonel Muammar Gaddafi: A great Arab and African leader murdered by imperialism by Harpal Brar http://www.lalkar.org/issues/contents/nov2011/gaddafi.html

6. Ibid.

7. Ibid.

8. Ibid.

9. Ibid

Chapter II

Clash of Civilization or Clash of Interests?

- Western civilization
- West's self interest
- Western domination
- The greatest peacetime transfer of wealth
- Mechanism of western domination of the global economy
- The clash of civilizations?

Western civilization

There is a tendency in the West to consider its own tradition alone as rational and scientific and denigrate other traditions as mere propaganda, religious obscurantism or superstition. Cultural development is often measured by comparison with Western culture. Consequently, modernity is not considered a characteristic of Islamic societies. Instead, it is seen as an integral part of a universal process of becoming civilized. According to this scheme, the West is progressive, rational, enlightened and secular. Islam is backward, fanatical, irrational and fundamentalist. What is interesting is that it is not Islam and Christianity that are contrasted, or the West and the East, but Islam and the West, a religion and a geographical area. Even in the Age of Enlightenment the European attitude to Islam remained unenlightened. In the writings of illustrious European poets and playwrights - from Dante and Shakespeare to Byron and Shelly - there were pejorative references to the Quran and the Prophet, to Moors and Saracens. They became part of the regular intellectual diet of many a European student right down to the present. Voltaire himself wrote a play entitled Fanaticism, or the Prophet Mohammed.

As Jochen Hipplier has said: By caricaturing different cultures, by arbitrarily and willfully misrepresenting Islamic societies we grant ourselves absolution. Others are fanatical, we are not. Other are irrational, we are not. [1] Furthermore, it is clearly very important for us in the West to feel superior and to see Western culture as the 'best' and 'most progressive. [2]

The term civilization is usually used in the singular to mean Western civilization which since the eighteenth century has been in the West as the civilization that has set about to destroy and obliterate systematically all other civilizations including the a universal mission of redemption, is in many respects the same. Whereas it was earlier deemed necessary to 'win the world for Christ,' now 'modernization' - that is, adherence to the model of the West - is exported and preached with almost evangelical fervor as a sure means of redemption.

However, the concept of Western modernization is highly political. As Reinhard Schulze asserts convincingly, it allows all attributes of modernity to be defined as European, and Europe or the West to be described as the creator of modernity. The non-European, particularly the Islamic, world is simply cast in the role of the sufferer who was infected by the West's modernity, and can now no longer come to terms with it.[3] ....This conviction is also represented in the new western literature of Islamic studies and the social sciences.[4]

It goes without saying that many people in the West no longer feel connected to Christianity as a religion, but rather as a cultural influence. Their culture is directly or indirectly shaped by it and they do not feel there is anything unusual in this. But, Islam is hardly ever seen as a cultural category, but as a religion, one which is threatening. [5] The West concentrates on Islam as a religion which is made out to be responsible for countless political, cultural and social phenomena in Islamic countries. And it is clearly Islam as a religion that generates such fear in Western culture, a fear of religion that the West thought it had banished from its enlightened societies. As Reinhard Schulze said:

"The West appears to re-enact, indeed to prove its own Enlightenment and its own independence from the power of religion by comparison with the Orient. This is surely also because doubts have arisen about the victory of the world over religion, or of reason over irrationality in the West itself." [6]

Hippler got to the heart of the matter when he said: the perception of the Islamic threat has virtually nothing to do with the Middle East or Islam, but everything to do with the establishment of an inter-Western identity. It is about reassuring ourselves, about reassuring each other of how rational, enlightened and sensible we Westerners are. The need for this has of course arisen from the regrettable fact that standards of civilization in Europe are not high, and are constantly being dragged down by explosive set-backs. Fascism, Stalinism and other archaic phenomena such as the wars in Balkans, the civil war in Northern Ireland, or racism in the USA which exceeds even what is prevalent in Europe - to mention but a few examples -- should urge us to be careful in our estimation of Western civilization. [7]

West's self interest

Over the past two centuries the Islamic world, like the other Third World or developing countries, has come to be penetrated and shaped by the West, and much more so than ever the West was affected by influences from its neighbor. Western power has dictated the boundaries of Muslim countries and fashioned the modern states. Western power, too, has integrated Muslim economies into the new western-dominated world economy.

The Western policies towards the Islamic world are primarily determined by the analysis of economic and power interests, not by the evaluation of a religion. These policies are single-mindedly pursued by Western self-interest, at times brutally, with little regard for the lives of people there. It is a question of power politics, of control. The problem is the growing military power of many states in the so-called Third World, who could escape Western dominance. The problem is that a widening circle of states reserve the right to use their power as they fit. This is a dreadful nightmare for the West. The countries in question should, hence, behave in a manner that the Western countries 'see fit' and not as they themselves 'see fit.' Therefore, if any country's policies are found contrary to the Western interest, it is dubbed as against the international law and world peace.

Western domination

The existing world order, in which the West has retained its privileged economic position despite the end of the colonial system that contributed to its prosperity, perpetuates the inequalities and protects the vested interests derived from that system. The international system functions now on a single criterion -- the interests of the major developed powers. All else is irrelevant, and will remain so unless the premises of unipolar absolutism are challenged by those countries whose interests and sovereignty are most at stake.

The realpolitik of the rich and successful states in the West necessarily involves manipulation of the 160 or more Third World states (which include all the Muslim countries) in order to keep them divided. It is actually a function of their power that has necessarily to work for obtaining commercial and economic advantages in the international marketplace. The precise mechanism of international trade and economic relationships are certainly characterized by the exploitation by the rich of the many poor through two simple mechanisms: terms of trade and keeping the many poor nations at one another's throat. This is why the poor states cannot take any united action. Terms of trade mean that the poor commodity producers have to sell cheap and are forced to buy dearer industrial products, including technology. It has to be conceded that such economic exploitation is an integral and unavoidable part of the system. According to Robert Keohane, the author of After Hegemony, "The theory of hegemony, as applied to the world political economy, defines hegemony as preponderance of material resources. Four sets of resources are especially important. Hegemonic powers must have control over raw materials, control over sources of capital, control over markets, and competitive advantages in the production of highly valued goods." [8]

As German economist, Andre Gunder Frank said, the development of the industrialized countries from the fifteenth century was a direct result of their economic, and later political, dominance of today's underdeveloped countries, a huge majority of which were colonies. The process sucked them into a long-term structurally disadvantageous relationship which resulted in the development of some countries and the current underdevelopment of Latin America and by extension other Third World regions. This is the foundation of Frank's argument: that the development of the industrialized states was only made possible (and continues to be) by the underdevelopment of the Third World. [9]

The greatest peacetime transfer of wealth:

The last half of the 20th-Century saw the greatest peacetime transfer of wealth in history from the already-impoverished to the already-wealthy according to By J.W. Smith, the author of WHY? The Deeper History Behind the September 11th Terrorist Attack on America. Smith adds: "Enormous wealth and power is dependent upon maintaining a system of unequal trades and this inequality needs protection to continue. The secrets of plunder-by-trade, well hidden from mainstream history, are still operational today. Protecting the rights and freedoms of you and I are not the issue at all, they never really were. The issue is, as it has been throughout history, the protection of wealth and power—the struggle for control of resources and the wealth-producing-process..... Western society went from plunder-by-raids to plunder-by-trades centuries ago and today's plunder-by-trade is the unspoken reason for world violence today—just as plunder of another society's wealth has been the cause of wars for centuries.... Today's wars are protecting a monopolized wealth-producing-process just as aristocracy fought to retain the monopolization of nature's wealth, the source of their wealth and power." [10]

It is obvious from complicated web of open diplomacy, and the covert moves being planned and executed by the powers of the day, that the West would like the Islamic world to remain weak, disunited and incapable of achieving its dues status as well as its share of the world's resources. According to Dr. Haider Mehdi, "the West wants to grab all the benefits of all the resources of the word, to attain the highest living standard for its own peoples, and impose its political will and cultural dominance, at whatever cost to the rest of humanity." [11]

The west only acts in its self-interest, or what it sees as its interest, irrespective of country or creed. The capitalists of the West are afraid of the rapid development of the Third World. This would mean that they would lose their money, their affluent lifestyle and their way of life. These are the permanent interests of the West and it is threat to them that they oppose through every means moral, amoral or downright immoral. The west is selfish and ruthless in its interests. Some western experts, like British Prof. John Barrett Kelly in Arabia, the Gulf and the West (1980), demanded outright invasion of Muslim countries, like those in the Gulf, in order to capture their wealth, their oil wells and ports, to make them safe for the West.

The Islamic states are part of the so-called Third World that is dominated by the West. The Western dominance is of a multi-dimensional nature, not just military or political hegemony. Economic and intellectual forces are also important components of the dominant power that the West wields. The dominant country or countries of the West have not only penetrated the Third World, particularly, the Islamic or Arab countries in economic and political terms but also in very significant cultural areas.

As W. J. Smith pointed out "World trade was monopolized at the start of the industrial revolution under the philosophy of mercantilism and the wealthy and powerful simply never abandoned monopolization, rhetoric and the teachings in universities notwithstanding. Every attempt to establish a more equitable system was suppressed by massive military power backed by an equally massive propaganda system....Utilizing labor and capital, all wealth is processed from scarce natural resources most of which are in the impoverished world, and powerful nations must control those resources and the wealth-producing-process. The resulting appropriation of the wealth of others is the secret of their wealth and power and the cause of poverty in weak nations. Through economic warfare, financial warfare, covert warfare, and overt war, powerful nations throughout history have obtained weaker nations' resources for a fraction of their true value. The simple cause of world terrorism is that the wealth of powerful nations was stolen, and is still being stolen, from weak nations." [12]

The dominant Western systems were created to enforce the rules of an international economic order the main purpose of which was to promote the interests of the respective dominant power. The international economic system is heavily tilted in favor of the industrialized West. This imposes severe restraints on the modernization and development processes in the developing countries. In economic terms, growth and modernization are key concerns of the so-called liberal philosophy. But it is more concerned with increasing the size of the cake than distributing it fairly and equitably.

Mechanism of western domination of the global economy

Professor Michel Chossudovsky provides an insight to the mechanism of western domination of the global economy. In his book " The Globalization of Poverty and the New World Order," Prof. Chossudovsky [13] says:

"War and the "free market" go hand in hand... War physically destroys what has not been dismantled through deregulation, privatization and the imposition of "free market" reforms. (p10) The New World Order is based on the "false consensus" of Washington and Wall Street, which ordains the "free market system" as the only possible choice on the fated road to a "global prosperity". All political parties including Greens, Social Democrats and former Communists now share this consensus. The Western military and security apparatus endorses and supports dominant economic and financial interests - i.e. the build-up, as well as the exercise, of military might enforces "free trade... NATO coordinates its military operations with the World Bank and the IMF's policy interventions, and vice versa. Consistently, the security and defense bodies of the Western military alliance, together with the various civilian governmental and intergovernmental bureaucracies (e.g. IMF, World Bank, WTO) share a common understanding, ideological consensus and commitment to the New World Order. (p11) The global media fabricates the news and overtly distorts the course of events. This false consciousness" which pervades our societies, prevents critical debate and masks the truth. The only promise of the "free market" is a world of landless farmers, shuttered factories, jobless workers and gutted social programs with "bitter economic medicine" under the WTO and the IMF constituting the only prescription. (p12)

Under IMF jurisdiction, the same "menu" of budgetary austerity, devaluation, trade liberalization and privatization is applied simultaneously in more than 150 indebted countries... A "parallel government", which bypasses civil society, is established by the international financial institutions (IFIs). Countries which do not conform to the IMF's "performance targets" are blacklisted. ... the structural adjustment program requires the strengthening of the internal security apparatus and the military intelligence apparatus: political repression - with the collusion of the Third World elites - supports a parallel process of "economic repression." ... Structural adjustment promotes bogus institutions and a fake parliamentary democracy which, in turn, supports the process of economic restructuring. Structural adjustment programs affect directly the livelihood of more than four billion people. The application of the structural adjustment program in a large number of individual debtor countries favors the internationalization of macroeconomic policy under the direct control of the IMF and the World Bank acting on behalf of powerful financial and political interests (e.g. the Paris and London Clubs, the G7). The Washington-based international bureaucracy has been entrusted by international creditors and multinational corporations with the execution of a global economic design, which affects the livelihood of more than 80 percent of the world's population. (p20)

The clash of civilization?
The concept of a clash of civilizations, suggested by the Harvard Professor Samuel Huntington, is based on the notion of the Western domination of the world. In an article entitled "The Clash of Civilizations?"

Huntington [14] predicts that future world politics will be determined by conflicts between different civilizations/cultures. He envisaged that future competition and conflict would be based not on national perceptions and goals but on larger cultural groupings "civilizations", of which he identified eight civilizations: the Western, Confucian, Japanese, Islamic, Hindu, Slavic-Orthodox, Latin American and possibly African. He took note of the fact that the failure of western ideas of nationalism and socialism had produced a return to the roots phenomenon among non-western civilizations, such as Asianisation in Japan, Hinduisation in India, "re-Islamization" in the Middle East, and Russianisation in Russia. He further concluded that the most potent challenge to the West would arise from the anti-western cooperation between Islamic and Confucian states. He obviously had in mind the cordiality between China and such Islamic countries as Pakistan and Iran.

Let us discuss briefly the salient features of Huntingon's thesis. The four basic assumptions, around which the whole argument is built, are: (1) The centuries old military interaction between the West and Islam could become more virulent and that Islam has bloody borders (2) Differences between China and the US are unlikely to moderate. (3) A Confucian-Islamic military connection has come into being, designed to promote acquisition by its members of weapons and weapons technologies needed to counter the military power of the West. (4) The cultural division of Europe between Western Christianity, on one hand, and Orthodox, on the other, has re-emerged after the end of the cold war. These assumptions have been used by Huntington to build up his thesis and to conclude that there would be clash of civilizations and there is need, therefore, for the West to impose its will on the rest of the world.

He also notes with satisfaction that through IMF and other international economic institutions the West promotes its economic interests and imposes on other nations the economic policies it thinks appropriate. "In any poll of non-Western peoples, the IMF undoubtedly would win the support of finance ministers and a few others, but get an overwhelmingly unfavorable rating from just about everyone else, who would agree with Georgy Arbatov's charaterization of IMF officials as "neo Bolsheviks who love expropriating other people's money, imposing undemocratic and alien rules of economic and political conduct and stifling economic freedom."

Huntington, who is hostile to the Muslims and the Chinese, suspicious of the Slav-Orthodox and indifferent to the Africans and South Americans, is convinced that the West is all powerful and can impose its will on the rest of the world. "The West is now at an extraordinary peak of power in relation to other civilizations. Its superpower opponent has disappeared from the map. Military conflict among Western states is unthinkable, and Western military power is unrivaled. Apart from Japan, the West faces no economic challenge. It dominates international political and security institutions and with Japan international economic institutions."

Huntington provides a graphic description of how the West manipulates the world political and economic order. "Global political and security issues are effectively settled by a directorate of the United States, Britain and France, world economic issues by a directorate of the United States, Germany and Japan, all of which maintain extraordinarily close relations with each other to the exclusion of lesser and largely non-Western countries. Decisions made at the UN Security Council or in the International Monetary Fund that reflect the interests of the West are presented to the world as reflecting the desires of the world community. The very phrase "the world community" has become the euphemistic collective noun (replacing "the Free World") to give global legitimacy to actions reflecting the interests of the United States and other Western powers.

He says: "Western domination of the UN Security Council and its decisions, tempered only by occasional abstention by China, produced UN legitimation of the West's use of force to drive Iraq out of Kuwait and its elimination of Iraq's sophisticated weapons and capacity to produce such weapons. It also produced the quite unprecedented action by the United States, Britain and France in getting the Security Council to demand that Libya hand over the Pan Am 103 bombing suspects and then to impose sanctions when Libya refused. After defeating the largest Arab army, the West did not hesitate to through its weight around in the Arab world."

Huntington also points out that the West has redefined the concept of arms control. "During the Cold War the primary purpose of arms control was to establish a stable military balance between the United States and its allies and the Soviet Union and its allies. In the post-Cold War world the primary objective of arms control is to prevent the development by non-Western societies of military capabilities that could threaten Western interests. The West attempts to do this through international agreements, economic pressure and controls on the transfer of arms and weapons technologies."

The conclusion which Huntington draws from his analysis is that "the West in effect is using international institutions, military power and economic resources to run the world in ways that will maintain Western predominance, protect Western interests and promote Western political and economic values. That at least is the way in which non Westerners see the new world, and there is a significant element of truth in their view". Huntington argues that: "A West (now) at the peak of its power confronts non-West that increasingly have the desire, the will and the resources to shape the world in non-Western ways." The conflicts of the future will be between "the West and the rest," the West and the Muslims, the West and an Islamic-Confucian alliance, or the West and a collection of other civilizations, including Hindu, Japanese, Latin American and Slav-Orthodox.

After explaining his argument, Huntington prescribes short and long term measures to promote the Western interests:

"In the short term it is clearly in the interests of the West to promote greater cooperation and unity within its own civilization, particularly between its European and North American components; to incorporate into the West societies in Eastern Europe and Latin America whose cultures are close to those of the West; to promote and maintain cooperative relations with Russia and Japan; to prevent escalation of local inter-civilization conflicts into major inter-civilization wars; to limit the expansion of the military strength of Confucian and Islamic states; to moderate the reduction of Western military capabilities and maintain military superiority in East and Southwest Asia; to exploit differences and conflicts among Confucian and Islamic states; to support in other civilizations group sympathetic to Western values and interests; to strengthen international institutions that reflect and legitimate Western interests and values and to promote the involvement of non-Western states in those institutions.

"In the long term other measures could be called for. Western civilization is both Western and modern.

"Non-Western civilizations have attempted to become modern without becoming Western. To date only Japan has fully succeeded in this quest. Non-Western civilizations will continue to attempt to acquire the wealth, technology, skills, machines and weapons that are part of being modern. They will also attempt to reconcile this modernity with their traditional culture and values. Their economic and military strength relative to the West will increase. Hence the West will increasingly have to accommodate these non-Western modern civilizations whose power approaches that of the West but whose values and interests differ significantly from those of the west. This will require the West to maintain the economic and military power necessary to protect its interests in relation to these civilizations."

Huntington's entire argument about Islam and civilizations is full of contradictions and superficialities. But this is of little consequence, since it is only meant as a politically motivated sales pitch to secure Western superiority in all areas. That is why Islam must be dangerous and irreconcilable, and that is why the West cannot afford to disarm itself excessively in the wake of the Cold War. It must arm itself against the threat. This is the essence of Huntington's thesis, and everything else, including the laws of Aristotelian logic, are consistently subordinated to it. What is significant, however, is that the rationales of his perceived threat is not based on an analysis of the interests or policies of countries or political powers in the Middle East, but on his contradictory formulation of 'civilizing' basic categories. According to Huntington, it is not the clash of interests that leads to conflict; the simple fact is that differences between cultures engender war. To borrow from Hippler: In a certain sense you could call his argument 'culturally racist'. The Muslims (or Chinese) are different from us and therefore dangerous. Unlike in classic racism, this difference is not generically but culturally based. There is such a gulf between their values and ways of thinking and ours that understanding or cross-pollination is almost unthinkable. Only military solutions can promise result. [15]

Hippler further elaborates this point very convincingly: Huntington's image of Islam (or of other Asian cultures) is hardly original. It follows the current stereotypes and clichés of popular literature and some of the media. Yet he manages brilliantly to embellish these repeated fears pseudo-scientifically and elevate them ideologically. His success is in making the old clichés acceptable in foreign policy debate. For Huntington, Islam is ideologically hostile and anti-Western. It is also a military threat in itself due to Chinese (Confucian) arms supplies. Islam is bloody, with a long warring tradition against the West. (The fact that Muslims have often been the victims rather than the perpetrators of violence from Bosnia to India hardly troubles him.) [16]

According to Stephen M. Walt, The Clash of Civilizations is also strangely silent about Israel, which has been a central concern for U.S. foreign policy since its founding in 1948. During the Cold War, U.S. support for Israel could be justified on both ideological and strategic grounds. From a cultural perspective, however, the basis for close ties between Israel and the "West" is unclear. Israel is not a member of the West (at least not by Huntington's criteria) and is probably becoming less "Western" as religious fundamentalism becomes more salient and as the Sephardic population becomes more influential. A "civilizational" approach to U.S. foreign policy can justify close ties with Europeans (as the common descendants of Western Christendom) but not Israelis. Moreover, given that Huntington wants to avoid unnecessary clashes with rival civilizations and given that U.S. support for Israel is a source of tension with the Islamic world, his civilizational paradigm would seem to prescribe a sharp reduction in Western support for the Jewish state. I do not know whether Huntington favors such a step, but that is where the logic of his argument leads. His silence on this issue may reflect an awareness that making this conclusion explicit would not enhance the appeal of the book, or Israel may simply be an anomaly that lies outside of his framework. In either case, however, the issue reveals a further limitation of the civilizational paradigm. *[Building Up New Bogeyman by Stephen M. Walt- Foreign Policy, Spring 1997]*

What Edward Saeed has to say is illuminating as well: Huntington is an intellectual serving the interests of the last superpower (he is actually quite frank about this) whose pre-eminence as a world power he is set on serving and maintaining. The real subject of his work therefore is not how to reduce the conflict of cultures, but how to turn them to American advantage, as a way of conceding to the United States the right to lead the whole world. Yet none of his grandiose rhetoric can conceal the fact that this style of thought derives from the same polluted source to be found in all cultures, the notion that my way of life, my traditions, my way of thinking, my religion or civilization can neither be shared with anyone nor understood by anyone who does not have the same religion, color of skin, etc. India, Pakistan, Bosnia, Ireland, South Africa, Lebanon and of course Israel-Palestine bear the ravages of such a logic, which in the end leads to more, not less narrowness, misunderstanding, violence. [17]

Huntington and his associates are apparently trying to demoralize the followers of the cultures of the East, especially the Islamic culture. Their policy seems to be to demoralize and dominate! They have the strength of their systems of trade, industry, science, technology, education and democracy. They built these systems through evolutionary process spreading over a period of many centuries.

For Huntington, cultural difference is not one possible factor among others which might contribute to conflicts: it is the potential conflict. However, the major conflicts of the 20th century contradict Huntington's assertion. Walter C . Clemens [18] enumerates major conflicts of the century to refute Huntington's "exaggeration":

"Cultural influences may distort our perception and aggravate our feuds, but no major conflict of this century resulted from a clash of civilizations. In 1914, Protestant Berlin aligned with Catholic Vienna and Muslim Istanbul. Orthodox Russia allied with Catholic France and largely Protestant Britain. Orthodox Serbia opposed Catholic Austria but fought Orthodox Bulgaria. The aggressors in World War Two (Italy, Germany, Japan, the USSR) cooperated despite divergent heritages. Later, when Hitler attacked the USSR, Churchill did not ask whether Stalin was Orthodox or even communist. London immediately proposed to Moscow to combine against a common foe.

"The subsequent cold war had little to do with rival cultures. It was a struggle for hegemony - Soviet Russian imperialism against the West. Moscow's camp at times included China and other non-Orthodox countries, While Washington's partners included many non-Western societies. Most wars since 1945 have been waged by rivals from the same civilization - Korea, Vietnam, Cambodia, Somalia, Iraq and Kuwait.

"All this means that there is still hope for enlightened self-interest. Rifts between civilizations play second or third fiddle to other factors in world affairs -- individual vision and myopia, bureaucratic rhythms and ruts, generosity and greed, resource bounty and scarcity, United Nations clout and frailty. Now, as before, states cooperate or clash based on perceived interest. Increasingly, interdependence and technology make it possible and useful to cooperate across cultural boundaries, even though individuals and groups may not see these realities."

Jean Kirkpatrick [19] corroborates Clemens' views by saying: "It is not clear that over the centuries differences between civilizations have led to the longest and most violent conflicts. At least in the twentieth century, the most violence conflicts have occurred within civilizations: Stalin's purges, Pol Pot's genocide, the Nazi holocaust and World War Two. It could be argued that the war between the United States and Japan involved a clash of civilizations, but those differences had little role in that war. The Allied and Axis sides included both Asian and European members. The liberation of Kuwait was no more a clash between civilizations than World War II or the Korean or Vietnamese wars. Like Korea and Vietnam, the Persian Gulf war pitted one non-Western Muslim government against another. Once aggression had occurred, the United States and other Western governments became involved for geo-political reasons that transcended cultural differences.

Kirkpatrick also points out that "Huntington knows that the great question for non-Western societies is whether they can be modern without being Western. He believes Japan has succeeded. He is probably right that most societies will simultaneously seek the benefits of modernization and of traditional relations. To the extent that they and we are, successful in preserving our traditions while accepting the endless changes of modernization, our differences from one another will be preserved, and the need for not just a pluralistic society but a pluralistic world will grow ever more acute."

In order to illustrate the point further, it would be worth our while to glance at what Akio Kawato [20], has to say on the issue of values: Perhaps the debate regarding value differences reflects the on-going redistribution of political and economic interests in the post-Cold War world, rather than the fact that values continue to differ. However, it would be an inverted argument to say that unless the current Western paradigm is used, economic expansion could not occur, and that people should therefore switch immediately to the Western model.

It is a matter of elementary truth that the opportunities that allowed Western Europe to become what it is today, especially through the proliferation of individualism, stem from the economic development that occurred beginning in the 16th Century. Even though the economic development of Western Europe since the 16th Century can be said to be largely self-made, it cannot be denied that the coincidental development of the gun and the sacrifices of the colonies played a large role. Furthermore, Western civilization has developed to its present heights while continuing a pattern of bloodshed through revolution and war.

Industrialized nations should realize how unwise their practice is of pushing developing countries into rapidly adopting new policies, how unwise it is to imply that to advance economically they must adopt modern values and new social systems before they embark on economic development. In Western Europe, it took more than 300 years between the dawn of economic expansion in the 17th Century to the granting of universal suffrage. In the United States, civil rights issues were the cause of much debate until very recently. A sudden change in values and social systems can increase tensions within a society.

Reverting to Huntington's clash of cultures, what Kishore Madhubani [21] has to say is illuminating: "It is Ironic that the West should increasingly fear Islam when daily the Muslims are reminded of their weakness. "Islam has bloody borders," Huntington says. But in all conflicts between Muslims and pro-Western forces, the Muslims are losing and losing badly, whether they be Azeris, Palestinians, Iraqis, Iranians or Bosnian Muslims. With so much disunity, the Islamic world is not about to coalesce into a single force.

"The West protests the reversal democracy in Manamar, Peru or Nigeria, but not in Algeria. These double standards hurt. Bosnia has wreaked incalculable damage. The dramatic passivity of powerful European nations as genocide is committed on their doorsteps has torn away the thin veil of moral authority that the West had spun around itself as a legacy of its recent benign era. Few can believe that the West would have remained equally passive if Muslim artillery shell had been raining down on Christian populations in Sarajevo or Srebrenica. Arms sales to Saudi Arabia do not suggest a natural Christian-Islamic connection. Neither should Chinese arms sales to Iran. Both are opportunistic moves, based not on natural empathy or civilizational alliances.

"The failure to develop a viable strategy to deal with Islam or China reveals a fatal flaw in the West: an inability to come to terms with the shifts in relative weights of civilizations that Huntington well documents. Two key sentences in Huntington's essay, when put side by side, illustrate the nature of the problem: first, "In the politics of civilizations, the peoples and governments of non-Western civilization no longer remain the objects of history as targets of Western colonization but join the West as movers and shapers of history," and second "The West in effect is using international institutions, military power and economic resources to run the world in ways that will maintain Western predominance, protect Western interests and promote Western political and economic values." This combination is a prescription for disaster.

"Simple arithmetic demonstrates Western folly: The West has 800 million people; the rest make up almost 4.7 billion. In the national arena, no Western society would accept a situation where 15 per cent of its population legislated for the remaining

85 percent. But this is what the West is trying to do globally," Madhubani concludes.

Huntington's image of other cultures is not new and he is resurrecting an old controversy. In his assessment of his thesis Albert Weeks [22] explains: "Sameul P. Huntington has resurrected an old controversy in the study of international affairs: the relationship between "microcosmic" and "macrocosmic" processes. Partisans of the former single out the nation state as the basic unit, or determining factor, in the yin and yang of world politics. The "macros," on the other hand, view world affairs on the lofty level of the civilizations to which nation states belong and by which their behaviour is allegedly largely determined.

"His methodology is not new. In arguing the macro case in the 1940s, Arnold Toynbee distinguished what he called primary, secondary and tertiary civilizations by the time of their appearance in history, contending that their attributes continued to influence contemporary events. Quincy Wright, likewise applying a historical method, classified civilizations as "bellicose" (including Syrian, Japanese and Mexican), "moderate bellicose" (Germanic, Western, Russian, Scandinavian, etc.) and "most peaceful" (such as Irish, Indian and Chinese). Like Toynbee and now Huntington, he attributed contemporary significance to these factors. Huntington's classification, while different in several respects from those of his illustrious predecessors, also identifies determinants on a grand scale by "civilizations."

"His endeavor, however, has its own fault lines. The lines are the borders encompassing each distinct nation state and mercilessly chopping the alleged civilizations into pieces. With the cultural and religious glue of these "civilizations" thin and cracked, with the nation states' political regime providing the principal bonds, crisscross fracturing and cancellation of Huntington's own macro-scale, somewhat anachronistic fault lines are inevitable.

The world remains fractured along political and possibly geopolitical lines while cultural and historical determinants are a great deal less vital and virulent. As Albert Weeks [23] astutely points out: Politics, regimes and ideologies are culturally, historically and "civilizationally" determined to an extent. But it is willful, day-to-day, crisis-to-crisis, war-to-war political decision-making by nation-state units that remains the single most identifiable determinant of events in the international arena. How else can we explain repeated nation-state "defection" from their collective "civilizations" As Huntington himself points out, in the Persian

Gulf war "one Arab state invaded another and then fought a coalition of Arab, Western and other states."

One may agree with Akito that in key Western capitals there is a deep sense of unease about the future. The confidence that the West would remain a dominant force in the 21st century, as it has for the past four or five centuries, is giving way to a sense of foreboding that forces like the emergence of fundamentalist Islam, the rise of East Asia and the collapse of Russia and Eastern Europe could pose real threats to the West. A siege mentality is developing. Within these troubled walls, Samuel P. Huntington's essay "The Clash of Civilizations?" is bound to resonate.

References

1. Jochen Hippler, The Next Threat: Western Perception of Islam, p-147

2. Ibid. p-20,21

3. Ibid. p-57

4. Ibid. p-67

5. Ibid. p-11

6. Schulze, lecture in Colone, September 1991

7. Hippler op. cit. p-146

8. Cited by Khalid Bin Sayeed, Western Dominance and Political Islam, p-17

9. Jeff Haynes, Religion in the Third World Politics, p-24

10. J.W. Smith, Introduction to WHY? The Deeper History Behind the September 11th Terrorist Attack on

11. Dr. Haider Mehdi, Behind the facts - Dawn 9.7.1993

12. J.W. Smith op. cit.

13. Michel Chossudovsky, The Globalization of Poverty and the New World Order, Global Research, 2003, paperback [first edition 1997]

14. The article was first published in the Foreign Affairs (Summer 1993) was later expanded and published as a book titled "The Clash of Civilization and the Remaking of World Order" in 1996.

15. Hippler, op. cit. p-149

16. Ibid. p-148-49

17. Edward Saeed, The uses of Culture, Dawn 24.2.1997

18. Walter C. Clemens Jr. - Interests clash but civilizations can cooperate, Dawn - 8.1.1997

19. Jean J. Kirkpatrick (Leavey Professor of Government at Georgetown University, Tradition and Change, Foreign Affairs, Sept./Oct. 1993

20. Akio Kawato, Former Deputy Director-General, Cultural Affairs Department, Ministry of Foreign Affairs of Japan, Beyond the Myth of "Asian Values"

21. Kishore Mahbuba ni (Deputy Secretary of Foreign Affairs and Dean of the Civil Service College, Singapore), The Dangers of Decadence, ForeignAffairs Sept./Oct.1993

22. Albert L. Weeks (Professor Emeritus of Internationa Relations at New York University), Do Civlizations Hold? Foreign Affairs, Sept./Oct. 1993

23. Albert L. Weeks (Professor Emeritus of Internationa Relations at New York University) Do Civlizations Hold? Foreign Affairs, Sept./Oct. 1993

Chapter III

Islam and the West

- The west's search for a new bogyman
- Islam and communism / Arab nationalism
- The Afghan connection
- Islamic Republic of Pakistan
- Historical antagonism with the west
- West's double standard
- Bosnia-Herzigovina
- The revival concerned only the Islamic world
- Who violates the international law?

The west's search for a new bogyman

The demise of the Cold War involving the USA and the Soviet Union at the beginning of the 1990s left military strategists in the West searching for a new bogyman. To borrow Richard Conder, author of the Munchurian Candidate: "Now that the communists have been put to sleep, we are going to have to invent another terrible threat." Former US Secretary of Defense, McNamara, in his 1989 testimony before the Senate Budget Committee, stated that defense spending could safely be cut in half over five years. For the Pentagon it was a simple choice: either find new enemies or cut defense spending. Topping the list of potential bogeymen were the Yellow Peril, the alleged threat to US economic security emanating from the East Asia, and the so-called Green Peril (green representing Islam). The Pentagon selected "Islamic fundamentalism" and "rogue states" as the new bogeymen.

According to Jochen Hippler: the West no longer has the Soviet Union or communism to serve as enemies justifying expensive and extensive military apparatuses. Now, given the loss of the old military opponent, instead of reducing the military apparatus in the West to a symbolic vestige or getting rid of it altogether and thinking about 'security' completely afresh, new threats are being invented to serve the old purpose. This is our main problem, not an Islamic fundamentalist threat which, in any case, could only be dealt with by political and economic means. [1] It was in the mid-1980s at the very latest that the search began for new enemies to justify arms budgets and offensive military policies, at first as part of the communist threat and then in its place. First the 'War on Drugs', the somewhat absurd and naturally failed attempt to solve New York's drug problem by naval exercise off the coast of South America and military operations in Bolivia, then 'Terrorism', a term applied to real terrorists as well as to various unpleasant freedom movements in the Third World which (of course) demanded military responses, were two such attempts during the 1980s. [2]

And as with the 'Islamic (or fundamentalist) threat' today, then too there were enough good reasons to be against drug dealers and terrorists. Neither of these social evils was ever fought seriously at its roots. Instead, they were exploited for other purposes. At that time the aim was to legitimize the newly development doctrine of low-intensity warfare; today it is to justify high military expenditure when the traditional enemy has disappeared and we are objectively no longer threatened by conventional war. Fundamentalism, then, has not been invented by Western politicians but is being used by them. [3]

What is new, following the end of the Cold War, is the tendency in the West to build up Islam as the dangerous ideological successor to Marxism-Leninism. In an article the New York Times Magazine, Judith Miller points out with characteristic accuracy: "The west tends to regard the growing political popularity of Islam as dangerous, monolithic and novel ... The rise of militant Islam has triggered a fierce debate about what, if anything, the West can or should do about it. Some American officials and commentators have already designated militant Islam as the west's new enemy, to be 'contained' much the way communism was during the cold war." [4] John Esposito summaries this perception of Islam as a threat: "According to many Western commentators, Islam and the West are on a collision course. Islam is a triple threat: political, demographic, and socio-religious ... Much as observers in the past retreated to polemics and stereotypes of Arabs, Turks or Muslims rather than addressing the specific causes of conflict and confrontation, today we are witnessing the perpetuation or creation of a new myth. The impending confrontation between Islam and the West is presented as part of a historical pattern of Muslim belligerency and aggression." [5]

In short, having lost their chief enemy, the seasonal practitioners of cold war have decided that the new global enemy is Islam. They came up with the 'fundamentalist Muslims' of North Africa and the Middle East; a contemporary version of the Crusades pitting Christian knights against Muslim warriors in the new international conflict. Director of the U.S. Foreign Policy Research Institute, Daniel Pipes, in his article "Muslims are Coming," published in the National Review (Nov. 19, 1990), writes "and so it is that American, and Europeans as well, are turning in increasing number to a very traditional bogeymen.: The Muslims. The weekly Time published a cover story, "Who is afraid of Islam?" On the cover it showed a Kalashinkov being raised higher than a minaret of a mosque. In France, Jean Marie Le Pen, depicts Islam as a "religion of intolerance: and fears, an "invasion of Europe by a Muslim immigration." The Republicans in Germany share Le Pen's outlook and program.

While covering Islam and Muslims, the western media applies most negative images and characterization for Muslims. For example, at the level of mass media coverage of Islam land Muslims, on practically any day the alert reader or viewer can satiate her or himself with images and characterizations of the most negative and hurtful kind applied to Muslims.

For example, "Islamic terrorists" or "fundamentalists" did this or that; "Shi'ite extremists" shout "Death to America"; the "militant Muslim cleric" Shaykh Omar Abdel Rahman; "I like belonging to Islamic Jihad because it is violent" (Boulder Daily Camera, July 16,1993);"Terrorism bas become Sheik" (caption for Jim Hoagland column published in Daily Times Call, Longmont, Colorado July 16, 1993); "950 million Muslims occupy a world that seems, in the eyes of the West, alien and frightening" (Life, July 1993); "Violence, the Islamic Curse", title of an article in the Chicago Tribune, 1981); "The D ark Side of Islam" (title of Joseph Kraft syndicated column about Mohmet Ali Agca, serving a prison sentence for shooting the Pope; The Washington Post, May I9,1981; "Sudan Becoming a Way Station for Islamic Militants" (San Francisco Chronicle, July 19, 1993), and so forth.

"Bombs in the name of Allah," "The dark side of Islam," "Global network provides financing and havens," "A new strain of terrorism" etc. These and the like are titles of articles flooding in the western print media focusing on shallow and obsessive references to Islam and slandering "Islamists" as well as the Muslim political activists throughout Islamic world. In a map showing, "base support" of the

"International Islamic terrorism," carried out by the Washington Post, in its August 3, 1993 edition, a reference was made to Pakistan, among other Islamic countries, in these words "Evidence points to links between activities here and Manhattan bombing plotters." Terrorism is dealt with, in these articles, as an exclusively Islamic phenomenon. Subversive activities, no matter wherever they are launched, are abruptly linked with Islamic activists.

The US Vice President Dan Quayle at a 1990 conference in Washington listed Islam with Nazism and Communism as the challenges the Western civilization must undertake to meet collectively. Even more ominously, the NATO Secretary General, at a meeting with the Patriarch of the Russian Orthodox Church on February 24, 1992, voiced concern at the possibility of Islamic fundamentalism engulfing the Muslim republics of Central Asia now that the Soviet Union was gone. National interests draped in the mantle of religion became a foreign policy concern. This interpretation of the post-Cold War period is given credence by the results of a Gallop Poll survey in Britain at the end of 1989 (i.e. before the Gulf War), which found that 37 per cent of those questioned thought an international conflict between Christians and Muslims (i.e. between the North Atlantic region and the Middle East) to be 'likely' in the 1990s. [6]

The image of Muslim societies in the West is presented as that of an evil-looking, bearded figures in black robes. Edward Said, a professor of comparative literature at Columbia University, argues that the West cannot know the Orient (for him mainly the Muslim Orient) except as irrational, depraved and infantile.

This perception is rooted in the power relationship between a dominating West and a subjugated Orient. It is in the interest of the West, therefore, to depict the Orient in negative stereotypes. The western attacks on Muslim extremists -- the fundamentalists of the popular press -- easily convert and carry over to an attack on the entire body of Muslims. Stereotyping Islam as aggressive fundamentalism "is part of the West's ideology of domination and control," says Dr. Chanra Muzaffar, director of Just World Trust, a non-government organization based in Penang, Malaysia.

The historical antagonism to Islam is now being exploited by those who seek to demonize Islam in order to justify repression of Muslim reformers and militants by failed governments allied to the West.

Islam and communism / Arab nationalism

It goes without saying that the West has used Islam as a weapon against communism. Islam was often considered a conservative ideology that could be used to resist revolutionary communist ideologies or even Arab nationalism. [7] In the 1970s and 1980s, the perception of Islam or Islamism as hostile was softened by the joint opposition of the West and some Islamic countries towards the Soviet Union and communism. Islamism was either a 'lesser evil' or actually very useful. This has changed completely since the end of the Cold War. Our perception of Islam can no longer be moderated by the existence of an even worse ideological opponent. Neither communism nor Arab nationalism poses a serious threat to Western interests today. As a result, Is lam or Islamism is moving into the filing line, and in fact often replacing the old enemy. In conversation, a German lieutenant Colonel casually put it like this: 'Islam is the new communism. [8] As Hippler has said: In Washington and London and to a lesser extent in Paris, they have repeatedly tried to use Islam and even Islamic fundamentalism for their own purposes, usually against the Soviet Union and communism. If you wanted to fight Marixst-Leninist ideology, it was practical to oppose it with another all-encompassing ideology. Just as Protestant sects were used in the fight against Marxism and liberation theology in Central America, wherever possible Islam has been used to fight secular Arab nationalism/socialism and communism. [9]

From the 1970s till well into the 1980s the Israeli government fostered the Muslim Muslim Brotherhood (and its offshoot, Hamas) in the occupied territories -- the same group that was later considered to be especially dangerous. The American Magazine Newsweek expalined it thus: For years the Arab fundamentalists seemed like dependable pawns in a series of high-states poxy battles. They bitterly opposed the West's main enemies - communism and its regional allies, left-wing Arab nationalists. Hostile to the Palestine Liberation Organization, they seemed perfect for an Israeli divide-and-conquer strategy. And they were theologically in tune with the West's key Arab ally and oil supplier, Saudi Arabia ... In the 1970s, [Israel] began building up the Brotherhood as a counterbalance to the PLO - and continued even after Israeli troops began battling Shiite radical in Lebanon. [10]

The Afghan connection:
During the cold war religion was seen as a bulwark against communism.
Ecumenical movements to bring together the followers of Christianity, Islam and

Judaism were launched, as part of the strategy to resist the ideological onslaught of Marxism. The most recent such example is Afghanistan, where various groups of Islamic-oriented Mujahideen put up the stoutest resistance to the Soviet occupation, and received generous support, mainly in the forms of arms and ammunition. No objections were raised when representatives of militant Islamic groups from other countries joined the Afghan resistance groups in what was perceived as their heroic resistance to the Soviet occupation forces.

At the end of 1979, shortly after the Soviet army rolled into Afghanistan, President Jimmy Carter and his advisers decided on a working alliance with Muslim activists. Secret directives, later amplified and expanded by the Reagan and Bush administrations and a US Congress which in the 1980s appropriated a war chest of billions of dollars, covered the recruiting, training and arming of one of the largest mercenary armies in American military history. The bulk of the recruits, including many Arab-Americans and some Muslim afro-Americans, were devout if not fanatical Muslims. Some were in for gain or adventure, but most utterly committed to the Jihad, or holy war, against communism and Russians.

With the help and money from a mostly coalition of Muslim and Arab states, such as Saudi Arabia and then President Anwar Sadat's enthusiastically pro-Western Egyptian government (an enthusiasm which contributed to Mr. Sadat's murder by Egyptian "Afghanis"), the CIA acted as manager. The Carter, Reagan and Bush administrations all delegated to Pakistan's powerful military intelligence agency, Inter-Services Intelligence, crucial controls over the anti-Soviet jihad. These included which fighting groups would get the cash, arms and preferred training.

The Mujahidin received approximately $3.5 billion in arms and other aid from the CIA, regardless of their political orientation or Islamist zeal. In this way, the most radical Islamic group - Gulbuddin Hekmatyar's party -- received two thirds of American aid over two years. Yet for a long time, it did not seem to worry the CIA that Hematyar's party was openly not only anti-Soviet but also anti-American, and that it was responsible for massacres, torture and just about every conceivable human rights abuse, quite apart from the fact that Hekmatyar was also trafficking in heroin on the side. If there is such a thing as the classic fundamentalist leader, straight out of Western stories, then it is Hekmatyar. Despite this Washington had no reservations, but only arms and money to offer. After all, the enemy of my enemy is my friend. of all the Afghan Mujahidin groups, his was the best organized and militarily most powerful -- the natural partner for an anti-Soviet campaign. It was only some time after the USSR had withdrawn from Afghanistan, in fact only when the USA and the Soviet Union cooperated closely in the run-up to the Gulf War of 1990-1 that the USA distanced itself from Hekmatyar's party. [11]

Once the Soviet forces had withdrawn from Afghanistan, the traditional Western attitude of suspicion and hostility towards Islam reasserted itself. Indeed, a perception arose of Islam as being the successor to communism as the principal threat to the Western world.

At the end of the 1980s, when the Russian had withdrawn from Afghanistan amid the crack-up of the Soviet Union, the volunteer holy warriors did not go home to open bakeries of flower shops. Determined to destroy their own governments and Western-corrupted societies, as they saw them, they decided to attack and destabilize these institutions. There were estimated 5,000 trained Saudis, 3,000 Yemenis, 2,800 Algerians, 2,000 Egyptians and perhaps 2,000 Palestinians, Jordanians, Lebanese, Iranians and others. This gives credence to the argument that much of today's Islamic fundamentalist activity is the work of groups funded for years not by Iran but by the united States, which kept a number of Islamic groups going throughout the Cold War era.

Islamic Republic of Pakistan

Western policies towards Pakistan were similar. From 1977 to 1988 Pakistan was ruled by Ziaul Haq, an 'Islamist' general who had come to power through a military coup. In the 1980s the USA gave massive support and arms to this military ruler - they needed his country as a base from which to support the Mujahidin against the Soviet Union in the war in Afghanistan. The building of a Pakistani atom bomb, the involvement of his dictatorship in heroin smuggling to Europe and other activities were looked upon as mere peccadilloes and generously ignored - to say nothing of the repression of the Pakistani people and widespread human rights abuse. On Zia's death the secular members of the Washington government surpassed themselves in their eulogies. Reagan, in a written statement issued from his ranch near Santa Barbara, recalled his meetings with Zia, saying they had 'worked together for peace and stability' ... The Pakistani leader, the statement said, 'also believed in freedom for Afghanistan'... Vice President Bush ... told reporters that

'Pakistan and the United States have a very special relationship, and the loss of General Zia is a great tragedy. [12] The fact that dictator had followed an "Islamist fundamentalist" program in order to widen his political base, and had fostered Islamist parties on a massive scale, presented no problem. The reason: the USA needed Pakistan as a base of operations for the war in Afghanistan. [13]

Historical antagonism with the West

The Islamic confrontation with the West is distinct from that between the West and secular nationalists, Bhuddist, Hindus or Animists because there has been intermittent conflict between the West and Islam for 1,200 years. This conflict has left in the minds of most Westerners a psychological residue of fear, hatred and antagonism towards Islam. Hence, the intellectual legacy of the West in its attitude towards Islam bears the imprint of the Crusades. These were originally a series of conflicts between Christian and Muslim forces for the control of Jerusalem, and from the 11th and 13th centuries, hardly any decade passed without Kings and Barons leading expeditions from various parts of Europe in order either to maintain or recover possession of the Holy Land. Many names have come down through literature and legend, notably those of King Richard or the "Lion Heart" and Saladin (Salahuddin Ayyubi). After the 13th century, as the Ottoman Turks conquered parts of Europe, the anti-Islam struggle assumed a defensive character.

According to Akbar S. Ahmad, the ongoing and complex confrontation between Islam and the West is marked by three historical encounters. The first began with the rise of Islam, the conquest of Spain and the appearance of Islamic armies in France and Sicily. It reached its dramatic climax with the Crusades, and ended in the seventeenth century when the Ottomans were halted at Vienna. When the French general in 1920, preparing to partition Arab lands, knocked on Salhuddin's tomb in Damascus and said, "Awake Saladin, we have returned," he expressed the continuity of the first encounter. The second encounter was brief but ferocious. During it the entire Muslim world was in the grip of European colonial imperialism. When this encounter concluded, after the Second World War, it was assumed that a period of harmony and friendship based on equality between Islamic and western nations would follow. This was not to be. The hoped for symmetry was destroyed as western civilization, driven by the USA and UK, began to dominate the world, a process sharpened by the collapse of Communism in the late 1980s. The present third encounter is, perhaps, the most complex of all. The weapons used in this encounter by the West are culture and media propaganda. TV and the VCR penetrate most Muslim homes. If for Muslims the second encounter, European colonialism, was a siege, the present encounter is a blitzkrieg. Unlike the earlier encounters, it is neither primarily religious, nor colonial nor racist -- but at certain points reflect all three. It is marked by a bewildering fusion of media images, scholarly opinions and atavistic cultural responses. Muslims appear threatened and unable to cope with the cultural onslaught of the West. Their response to the Satanic Verses sump up this encounter; Muslim fury met western incomprehension reflecting the complete lack of communication, the great cultural gap. The study of Islam (by orientalists) and perception of Muslim society are embedded in the socio-political context of these encounters. [14]

West's double standard

Muslims do not have any inherent animus against the west and yet the mutual alienation is growing. One of the main cause of this widening gulf is the perception among many in the Islamic world that the West follows a double standard when it comes to Muslims. Western governments that condemn repression and violations of human rights elsewhere are seen as mute in the face of similar practices by pro-western Muslim governments. "Saddam Hussein is justifiably condemned but none of his neighbors, some of them no less dictatorial, is so systematically scrutinized," according to Ghassan Salame, Middle East expert at the Institute of Political Studies in Paris. Many Muslims also were angered that the United States bombed Iraq for not complying with the UN resolutions that ended the Gulf War, but it fails to take strong action against Israel when that country ignores UN resolutions to leave Lebanon or take back Palestinian Islamic activists it forcibly expelled. [15]

One example of pro-US or anti-Arab stance is the US bid to cover up, down-play or condone by not condemning the brutal Israeli massacre of Arab refugees in a UN compound in Qana in southern Lebanon in April, 1996. There has been no forth right US condemnation of the Israeli aggression. On the contrary, far from objecting to the Israeli occupation of southern Lebanon, in flagrant violation of the UN charter, Washington has been justifying the Israeli military presence on foreign soil on grounds of Israeli compulsions of self-defense. This enunciates a dangerous principle in that it permits stronger states to occupy part of their neighbor's territory on the plea of self-defense, breaching the smaller state's sovereignty and territorial integrity.

Israeli occupation of Arab lands, Israeli atrocities committed on unarmed Arab men, women and even teenagers are normally ignored by the West. Israeli defiance of the Security Council resolutions have never been condemned. But in the case of Kuwait, how is it that the world reaction was so quick and firm? Iraq invaded Kuwait on 2nd August, and by 25 Aug., the Security Council had passed five resolutions against Iraq -- on 3, 6, 9, 18 and 25 August. This was not the end. During September another four -- on 10, 16, 24 and 25 Sept. -- resolutions were adopted. October saw only one, followed by two in November on the 28th and 29th. Thus the total of twelve resolutions were passed with the last one on 29th Nov. "giving Iraq the last opportunity, until 15th Jan, 1991, to comply with all previous resolutions, otherwise "nations allied with Kuwait" were authorized to use all necessary means to force Iraq to withdraw and honor all resolutions." What about other UN resolutions. For example the resolution on plebiscite in Kashmir. Death of hundreds of Kashmiris has not so far echoed in the Security Council.

The United States government prepared vigorously to punish Iraq. It shaped at the United Nations resolutions, their enforcement, and member countries' support of them. Barring the one occasion in 1950 when the Security Council acting in the absence of the Soviet delegate, approved US intervention in Korea, the UN had not issued so open-ended a license to wage what Rudyard Kipling might well have described as a "savage war of peace." Two hours after the war began President Bush spoke from the Oval office, vastly broadening the objectives of the war. They were, he said, "to drive Saddam from Kuwait by force," "knock out Saddam's nuclear bomb potential," "destroy his chemical weapons facilities" and "much of Saddam's artillery and tanks." "And Iraq will eventually comply with all relevant United Nations resolutions..." The last requirement provides the framework for continued US military presence in the Gulf, for the maintenance of harsh sanctions against Iraq, and for intrusive UN inspections of its nuclear and military facilities.

With the end of the cold war the American President George Bush came out in early 1990 with a fresh call for a new world order. Iraq's disastrous attack on Kuwait and the American-led Gulf war were used as the harbingers of the alleged new order. It was claimed that "no aggressor would in the future be allowed to go unpunished," that "occupation by force would not be tolerated," that "international boundaries would not be allowed to be changed arbitrarily," that "human rights would have to be respected by all," that "it would be ensured that any violation of human rights is brought to an end," without constraint of national boundaries, and that "the United Nations would play a new role as the peace-keeper of the world." With the establishment of these principles, it was suggested, the mankind is bound to enter into a new era of democracy and security. Sadly, but not unexpectedly, to those who had never thought there would be any other outcome, the chosen instrument of enforcing the proposed New World Order, the UN Security Council, under American leadership, revealed with indecent haste, that selectivity in reacting to causes and threats of instability and tension were still wholly subservient to its considerations of where the remaining superpower deemed its national interests to lie.

No one can believe that the American objective in unleashing a war of attrition against Iraq was to make Kuwait safe for democracy or safeguard the right of self-determination of its people, just as it was not the concern of its Camp David diplomacy to arrive at a peace settlement on the basis of recognition of Arab sovereignties in the Middle East. What was transparently clear in the conference diplomacy in 1979, and the military adventure a decade later, was to provide a protective cover to Israel to grab Arab lands without fear of retaliation. With the Soviet veto hanging over its heads, the Camp David Accord was concluded outside the United Nations, and now that the veto has been neutralized, and instrumentality of the Security Council has been freely used to give American foreign policy a semblance of international respectability. What America proposes the Council cannot dispose. Never before in its history had the United Nations been reduced to such imbecility and impotence. The role of the United Nations under the NWO is restructured by the western powers, particularly the US. The Security Council dominated by the western NATO powers has turned into an instrument of new colonialism under high sounding objectives. The UN, which has in large served the interests of major powers, once again will be used as a tool by these powers against the integrity of small states.

Israel is above nuclear non-proliferation. Its nuclear program has not been subject to scrutiny by the US Congress or pressure by the US government. The US anti-proliferation laws have not been invoked against it. The U.S. Congress has passed country-specific legislation such as the Pressler and Solarz amendments which do not apply to Israel. The full extent of its nuclear capability is not known. What we do know is that Israel broke with impunity many laws to acquire American technology, designs, and material for its nuclear program. It's awesome nuclear arsenal now includes at least 300 high density nuclear devices, and a delivery system which parallels in many areas those of the US, Russia and NATO. This delivery system is provided largely by the United States. Israel is also immune from the seven-power Missile Technology Control Regime of 1987, which embargoes missiles technology, including space launchers, to any nation that has missiles of over 300-km range and more than 500-kg payload. Both Jericho and Shevit II as well as Ofeq I fall under this category, but the West has no problem with them. And as if it was not enough, Israel is developing the Arrow anti-missile missile, under American-Israeli Strategic Cooperation, funded mainly by the U.S. from its Star War program.

Washington's determination to prevent any other country in the region from becoming Israel's atomic equal is comprehensible as a continuation of old policy. The only difference is that in the 1970s, the US perceived and armed Israel as one of two or more polar stars in its Middle Eastern constellation of clients. Now, it seeks to assure Israel the status of the sole regional power. Israel is now a publicly acclaimed "strategic ally." ; This alliance enjoys consensus in America; and it is assured the permanent support of a powerful lobby. What it lacks still is legitimacy and formal acceptance by countries in the region. Those Muslims and Arabs who subscribe to a conspiracy theory of international affairs would argue that the establishment of Israel in 1948 was deliberately designed by the West so that the state might serve as the outpost of Western hegemony. [16] In the eyes of Muslim and Arab countries, the United States, ever since the formation of the state of Israel has followed a consistent policy of excessive cordiality and favoritism toward Israel. They would argue that Arab oil has contributed heavily toward the enrichment and growth of the Western economy, but that oil has been used to help Israel in such a way that the legitimate interests of the Arab and Muslim states have not only been disregarded but adversely affected. [17]

Bosnia-Herzigovina

What happened in Bosnia-Harzegovina is another glaring example of western policy of double standard in implementing the UN resolutions. Western powers failed to convey an effective message that aggression is to be punished. They gave the Serbian aggressors, a free hand to perpetuate whatever atrocities they wanted to inflict on the Muslims; aggrandize as much land as they wanted; kill as many people they choose to massacre; 'cleanse' as many areas they want to 'cleanse'. Those who stand for international law, peace and security were not prepared to meet force by force. They waited for the moment when the aggressor had finished its job and then they used their influence to get an agreement between the aggressor and the victim to legitimize what had been acquired by force.

The UN had passed several resolutions condemning aggression and genocide in Bosnia, a member state. These resolutions, and the sanctions imposed on Serbia, were notably mild and indulgent by comparison with the Iraq sanctions. And for an entire year the UN had not taken effective measures to enforce them. Bosnian Foreign Minister was murdered under UN escort. Women and children were massacred in its custody. In October 1992, the UN declared a No Fly Zone in Bosnia but, in contrast with the practice in Iraq, it did not enforce the ban until late in spring of 1993. By December 15, UN observers had reported 225 aerial infringements by the Serbian air force which included bombing of Muslim villages and towns. Serbs had repeatedly broken cease-fires and safe-passage agreements.

The great powers had denied to Bosnians the means of their own defense. By May 1992, 'ethnic cleansing' had emerged as a systematic Serb goal. As Bosnians lost ground Serbia's rival Croatia also began to grab Bosnian territories. Its extreme vulnerability was exposing Bosnia to assault from both its neighbors. Yet, the Western powers insisted on maintaining the arms embargo on Bosnia. Technically, the embargo applied equally to Serbia, Croatia and Bosnia. But it hurt only the Bosnians. Serbia had inherited the bulk of former Yugoslav army and its impressive arsenal. Croatia got much of the remainder. Both have coastlines, neutral or friendly frontiers, and plenty of suppliers. When the aggrieved sought for arms and support to defend themselves, UN embargo came in the way. If by any chance some sympathizers were able to cross these 'civilized' barriers they were called fanatics and fundamentalists.

Neither the Muslims in Bosnia were "fundamentalists" nor did they wanted to establish an "authoritarian theocratic regime." They made it clear that they wanted to establish a secular "civic" state. Despite all of that they were subjected to the harshest crimes and atrocities history has ever witnessed. Everyone saw what had been done to them because they were looked upon as a Muslim nation, and as such, were perceived to be a potential threat to Western interest in Christian Europe. To the West, nationalism, in the case of Muslims, is a synonym to Islamism. The case of Bosnian Muslims is sufficient proof for West's total refusal to accept Muslims, even if nominal, in the post-cold war era. One thing which needs to be considered as well settled is that there isn't any difference between the so-called liberals, the moderates and the fundamentalists among Muslims as far as the West is concerned. The "zealots," the "extremists," the "fundamentalists," " moderates" and the "liberals" all fall in the same category. The Islam other than the one approved by the West was described as Islamic fundamentalism, extremism and radicalism.

Facts as opposed to fantasies, reveal the indulgence in double-standards always present in the conduct of international affairs, throughout the centuries, and this became the way of political life on both sides of the Iron Curtain between the Soviet Union and the West, during the near half-century of the Cold war, arising largely from a need, at all costs, to avert a nuclear conflict. Under these circumstances over, and over again, truth, reason and justice had to be subordinated to expediency as interpreted by each contestant superpower in order, (in seeking to prevent either side from extending its own spheres of influence at the expense of the other,) to do so without starting a third global conflict. Hence, when the Soviet Union collapsed, and the danger of nuclear war had been correspondingly reduced, we all surely had a right to believe that there would be comparable reductions in our common addiction to double standards, and a greater sense of faith, in practice as well as theory, in the pursuit of justice in the settlement of international disputes. Certainly there was a fleeting, probably never to be repeated opportunity to abandon selectivity in making political decisions in the field of international affairs, in favor of objectivity and fair-mindedness.

The revival concerned only the Islamic world

Today the Islamic states may present a rhetorical threat to the West, and may engage in individual acts of pressure, military or economic, against it: but the strategic situation is quite different. They are incapable of mounting a concerted challenge, let alone a redrawing boundaries. [18] Muslims do not constitute a threat to the West. There is no indication or even a remote possibility of any Muslim armed incursion into any Western country or even a threat of sabotage of their political system. The irony, however, is that this very Muslin world which has suffered at the hands of the West in the past and which remains even today weak materially, economically, technologically and militarily, is now being projected as a threat to the West. According to Fred Halliday, the contemporary challenge of "Islam" is demagogy on both sides apart, not about inter-state relations at all, but about how these Islamic societies and states will organize themselves and what the implications of such an organization for their relations with the outside world will be. The more recent rise of Islamic politics in the states and popular movements of the Muslim world poses little threat to the non-Muslim world without; it is primarily a response to the perceived weakness and subjugation of the Islamic world, and is concerned with an internal regeneration. That this process is accompanied by much denunciation of the outside world and the occasional act of violence against it should not obscure the fact that the Islamic revival concerns above all the Muslim world itself. [19]

The urge for self-assurance has increased manifold with Muslims being at the receiving end, thanks to the Western uni-polar system. Now a majority of the Muslims believe that if a strong Islamic revival does not take place immediately, Muslim identity would be crushed, particularly when there exists a trend in the West, especially in the United States, which views Islam as a potential threat to higher US national interests. For instance, Daniel Pipes, Director of the Foreign Policy Research Institute, proclaimed that "Islamic fundamentalists are a danger to their own people and to the United States. The United States should block the progress of this movement." However, majority of US scholars disagree with Pipes and his assessment of what he calls "Islamic fundamentalism." For example, S, Nayang of Howard University, stressed, "Fundamentalists are not going to disappear. No one can wish them away. They must be dealt with." According to Michael Hudson of Georgetown university, "Islamic fundamentalism has some anti-Western characteristics, but the movement is not inherently anti-American." Hudson called on the West and Muslim world "to work for a greater understanding of each other. Both societies should reject negative stereotyping and underscore shared religious values." [20]

Who violates the international law?

Recent instances -- in the Middle East, the Balkans, and South Asia -- suggests that as during the century before the World War I, perceived Western interests rather than the larger considerations of peace and the so-called international security will be the chief determinants of which aggrocoion ohall be punished, who will violate international law, and who will not. For the last many years, almost total control of protecting human rights all over the world has been taken over by the west. The Western media has converted the concept of human rights into an ideology which parallels any religion. From this, the west has assumed the privilege to interfere in the internal affairs of any country. On top of it, America can declare any state a terrorist leading to punishment -- all in the name of human rights. In which country human rights are being violated, this decision also lies with America. So if America kills hundreds of innocent citizens with aerial bombardment, it is considered a rightful action with reference to human rights. On the other hand, thousands of Muslims have been killed by the Serbs in Bosnia without disturbing the American conscience because Bosnia happens to be a Muslim country. Likewise, if Pakistan extends moral help to Kashmir it is threatened with dire consequences. But if India kills thousands of Muslims, it is conveniently ignored.

Again, given the double standards applied by the west, one has to ask what is terrorism and what exactly is the definition of a terrorist state? In 1993 Pakistan, was persistently warned by the US administration that, if it did not stop supporting the "Militants" in Indian controlled Kashmir, the US would be obliged to declare it a "terrorist state." Supporting Kashmiri freedom fighters, in their just struggle for self-determination, against the Indian authorities is terrorism, while the atrocities being committed by the Indian authorities are something negligible. The UN Security Council resolutions on the issue are no more of a substantial value. Why? Because it is not in the interest of the West and the US that the Muslim majority state of Kashmir accede to Pakistan or become independent. Pakistan's support to Afghan mujahideen was laudable not because the mujahideen were fighting a holy war -- a jihad -- against an atheist occupation power but because they were efficiently contributing to the containment of communism -- the most vital interest of the West in the cold war era -- and finally to the collapse of the Soviet led Eastern bloc. In explicable, Israel's continued unlawful occupation of Arab lands and its oppression and persecution of Palestinian people does not come under the purview of terrorism! Permitting Serbs and Croats, in Bosnia, to go ahead unhindered with their "ethnic cleansing" and genocide of defenseless Bosnian Muslims is also not terrorism! On the contrary any attempt to supply the armless victims of aggression -- the Muslims -- in Bosnia with weaponry to enable them to defend themselves would fall under the definition of terrorism because such attempts would entail gross violation of UN Security Council resolutions.

What Happler has said on the phenomenon of terrorism in the Middle East is relevant here: It would be completely absurd to believe that this terrorism had arisen from ideological or even religious sources, as the German expert on terrorism Tophoven would have us believe. It is far more plausible that it arose because sections of society and civil movements (in Lebanon, for example) saw no other possible way of exerting political influence. Without the Israeli invasion of Lebanon and the long occupation of South Lebanon, without Israel's undisputed military and political dominance there, it would not have been possible for Shiite terrorism to emerge in the form it did. This fact does not justify terrorist crimes, but helps us to understand connections. Without the West's support of Israeli policy and without the Western intervention in Lebanon in 1982-84 (with American, French, British and Italian troops) so many Western citizens would hardly have become victims of kidnapping and hostage taking. The Lebanese Shiites had nothing else with which they could, politically and in a narrower sense militarily, seriously oppose the occupying Israelis, the Western troops or the power structure of their own country. They would not have had a ghost of a chance in 'open battle'. Using guerrilla tactics, raids, kidnappings and assassination attempts they were able to deal very painful blows to their enemies despite their own weakness. In fact using these methods they were able to drive the American and West European troops from their country in a relatively short space of time. The attacks on the American, French and Israeli headquarters in Lebanon resulted in hundreds dead and buildings completely destroyed - military attacks would not have been possible using conventional means. Essentially, such strategies have nothing to do with 'fanaticism', plainly something to do with violent, unscrupulous, but ultimately achieve the maximum effect using the limited means at one's disposal. This is precisely what was achieved: the Western powers abandoned Lebanon in a virtual panic, and Israel too had to withdraw. What other tactics would had such a result? [21]

The West is not only selective in its choice of enemies but also in the UN resolutions it wishes to be implemented. The only principle that the West strictly adheres to is "crusade for morality stops where interest starts." Hence, there isn't any abstract principle for declaring a group, a country or a regime as a terrorist. Rather it is only one's position on Western interest which identify his character. Hence the US voices its concern about "terrorism" -- but tends to pay little heed to the root-cause of terrorism, the elimination of which alone can resolve conflicts. Apparently, terrorism is used as a pretext to further dominate the world by the use of force. And all this is done in the name of justice. To this end, the West makes clever use of mass media, applying subtle methods of persuasion -- the same principles as used in advertisements and marketing. For instance, the holocaust suffered by the Jews is kept alive by the media, to draw sympathy and legitimize the existence of Israel; but significantly, not the holocaust suffered by the citizens of Hiroshima and Nagasaki, and not the holocaust suffered by the Vietnamese in the American B-52 'milk-runs,' to state just two examples.

References

1. Jochen Hippler, The Next Threat: Western Perception of Islam, p-4

2. Ibid. p-4

3. Ibid. p-4

4. The New York Times Magazine, 31 May 1992

5. John Esposito, The Islamic Threat - Myth or Reality? New York and Oxford: Oxford University Press, 1992, p-175,

6. Jeff Hynes, Religion in Third World Politics - p-3

7. Hippler, op. cite. p-127

8. Ibid. p-131

9. Ibid. p-130,31

10. Newsweek, 15-2-1993, cited by Hippler

11. Hippler, op. cite, p-128,29

12. USIS 17.8.1988 cited by Hippler

13. Hippler, op. cite. p-130

14. Akbar S. Ahmed, Studying the roots of misperception - Orient vs Occident - Dawn 26.2.1993

15. Ibid.

16. Khalid Bin Sayeed, Western Dominance and Political Islam - p-7,8

17. Ibid. p-23

18. Fed Halliday, A Challenge to the West? - Dawn 11.6.1995

19. Ibid.

20. Dr. Jassim Taqui, Americans debate 'fundamentalism' - The Muslim 8-9-92

21. Hippler, op. cite., p-143-44

Chapter IV

Islam & Muslims in the Post-9/11 Era

- Bush calls his war on terror a crusade
- Crusade 2.0
- Teaching hatred against Islam to American soldiers
- Revamping of Islam
- Neo-Orientalism in USA
- The Neo-Orientalists of the Rand Corporation
- Practical guide to create a defanged version of Islam:
- Exploit Sunni, Shiite and Arab, non-Arab divides to promote the US policy objectives in the Muslim world
- Rand Corporation's new recipe to handle the Muslim World
- Islamophobia is systematically promoted in America
- Islamophobia – now in American Children's books
- Coloring book demonizes Muslims and Islam
- Anti-Islam film sparks anti-US demonstrations in the Muslim World
- Violent anti-US demonstrations
- Hidden causes of the Muslim protests
- The fallacy of free speech
- French blasphemous cartoons fuel the Muslim anger over the anti-Islam film
- The Libyan episode
- Anti-Islam and anti-Muslim rhetoric in US elections
- Negative image of Islam in the USA

The US, since the end of the cold war, has been reluctant to press secular authoritarian and military regimes that it supported as agents in the fight against communist forces to open their political systems to include 'Islamic' actors. Instead of pressing for political reforms, the US is essentially offering to continue to prop up repressive authoritarian regimes in return for assistance in fighting in the 'Islamic radicals.' In fact, in cases where democratic elections have taken place, the US has proved reluctant to endorse the results if Islamic political parties emerge victorious. The problem with this approach was first clearly demonstrated in the Algerian case. In 1991, an election was held, in which the Islamic Salvation Front (FIS) soundly defeated the governing party in the first round of parliamentary elections. Rather than allow the Islamic party to form a government, the military removed President Chadli Benjedid in January, 1992, and cancelled elections that would have given the FIS control of parliament. The US and other Western powers failed to put pressure on the generals to respect the results of the election.

Pointing to contradictions in US definitions of democracy, experts of Islamic politics say that the West is seeking to lay down one set of standards for those it sees as friends and those regarded as adversaries. Ironically, the United States becomes a champion of Muslim values when it supports Saudi King Fahad's argument that Western democratic norms are incompatible with Islam. The king, in 1992, announced the formation of a Majlis (consultative council) for the first time. US Assistant Undersecretary of State for the Near East, Edward Djerejian, in a speech in July 1992 accepted the manner and pace in which the sheikhdoms of the Persian Gulf are seeking to open their feudal political systems: "The United States is not trying to impose an American model on others. Each country must work out, in accordance with its own tradition, history and circumstances how and at what pace to broaden political participation." But no such tolerance is shown towards Muslim democracies like Algeria, where the Islamic Salvation Front was denied its election victory by a military junta. Djerejian's argument against Islamic revivalists seeking to win elections is that they were using the democratic process to come to power only to destroy the system in order to retain power. "While we believe in the principle of one-person-one-vote, we do not support one-person-one-vote-one-time," he argued. [18] 18. The News, Rawalpindi 17.7.1992

For many in the Muslim world, this smacks of certifying brands of democracy on the basis of whether elections are conducted by "good Muslims or bad Muslims." Besides Iran and Algeria, the double standards become apparent in Afghanistan where a fragile guerrilla coalition announced elections in the war-ravaged nation. The United States has made clear through its "moderate" friend in the guerrilla coalition, Sibghatullah Mojaddedi, that it does not favor polls, arguing that the country is not yet ready. Interestingly, it is the 'radical' Islamic group of guerrilla chieftain Gulbuddin Hekmatyar and pro-Iranian Hizbe Wahdat that wanted elections. The Wahdat even favored giving women the right to vote. According to western analysts, free elections -- as Algeria was well on its way to proving -- do not necessarily produce open governments, human rights or economic prosperity. In Asia, too, the pattern seems to be prosperity first, democracy later. South Korea, Taiwan, Hong Kong and Singapore all built up their booming economies under regimes that tolerated little opposition. Gerald Segal, a London-based Asia scholar, concludes that "democracy, as conceived of in Western Europe and North America, is not necessarily applicable to the rest of the world." [Kenneth Auchincloss, The Limits of Democracy - Newsweek 27.1.1992]

Bush calls his war on terror a crusade

Just five days after the September 11, 2001 terrorist attacks on the Word Trade Center in New York and Pentagon, President George W. Bush called his war on terror a "crusade," for which he later apologized as a verbal slip. However, as his later policies proved it was not a verbal slip, but - in the words of Prof. Sam Hamod [1] - a Freudian slip. Dr. Gary Leupp, Professor of History at Tufts University, and Adjunct Professor of Comparative Religion says that as a Yale history major, he ought to have known what the medieval Crusades were all about: Christians against Muslims, mostly for control of Palestine, fought with all the viciousness and duplicity reflected in the film "The Kingdom of Heaven." [2]

The explosive term was guaranteed to incite Muslim ire and alarm, and protests from everywhere (including the State Department, I'd imagine) caused Bush to drop it from his fevered rhetoric, Prof Leupp said adding: "But yes, ladies and gentlemen, this is indeed a Crusade, an anti-Muslim project conducted from a Judeo-Christian command center of a particularly unholy type. No matter how much administration officials profess their respect for Islam, denying any religious character to the war, and however they express wide-eyed amazement that Muslims might misunderstand the "war on terrorism" as an anti-Muslim war, it really is a crusading "holy war"---for the following reasons."

Here are more excerpts from Professor Leupp's insightful article [3]:

"After 9-11 President Bush found an opportunity to attack Iraq, which as the books by Richard Clarke and Paul O'Neill attest, he had hoped and planned to do in any event. There was no connection between 9-11 and Iraq, and no Iraqi weapons of mass destruction found.....

"In defiance of reason, the Bush administration insisted that an attack on weak, sanctions-bled Iraq would help prevent hate-filled Muslim minds in Baghdad from executing another 9-11 against America, whose overwhelmingly Christian people Bush said he knew were "good people." How he pandered to the self-righteousness of those who believe they're "saved"! Good versus evil. "You are either with us or against us," he warned a startled world in November 2001. Bush echoed the words of Christ in Matthew 12:30: "He who is not with me is against me, and he who does not gather with me scatters." Thus did the preacher-man gather his own flock, which loudly bayed "amen" to his planned Crusade....

"This is a faith-based war, with all the irrationality of the medieval Crusades, or the wars of religion that accompanied the Reformation. The fundamentalists are big on the Reformation of course, but downright hostile to the Enlightenment that succeeded it. Not just hostile to Diderot and Voltaire and Kant but to Thomas Jefferson who heretically declared, "Question even the existence of God, for if there be one, He will more likely pay homage to Reason than to blind faith."

"Hostile too to the norms of international relations prevailing in recent centuries. One can look at the Treaty of Westphalia (1648) as the midpoint between the wars of religion launched by the Reformation, and the dawn of reason in the Enlightenment. That treaty posited the sovereign state as the basic unit in world politics and promoted non-intervention in order to maintain peace. All very rational. But the Christian right, some of whose members want to chuck the constitution and impose their holy "dominion" over your life, are happy to chuck hundreds of years of international law to irrationally assault the world. All in the name of God! Their hero George Bush specifically said of his illegal invasion in 2003, "God told me to smite [Saddam Hussein], and I smote him."

"It's a Crusade that brilliantly exploits ethnic and religious prejudices in the U.S. It mixes the holier-than-thou triumphalism of the End Times believers with both Jewish and Christian Zionist dreams of a Middle East transformed by U.S. power. The "for us or against us" formulation borrowing from New Testament language pits the Judeo-Christian "us" against everybody else (including Cuba, North Korea, and leftist movements) but particularly at present against the Muslim world. Those vague categories "terrorism" and the religious-sounding "evil" were deftly used to morph bid Laden into Saddam; they may be used to conflate these with the Iranian mullahs. The war on all the evil in the cosmos begins with Muslim targets but at a certain point the religious attack can be diverted back to Godless communism too.....

"Throughout the world, not merely the Muslim world, the reputation of the U.S. plummets. But especially in the Muslim countries, with 20% of the world's population. The hateful behavior of the U.S. towards Muslims in Afghanistan, Iraq, and Guantanamo inevitably provokes hatred among Muslims with worldviews as diverse as you will find among Christians. One needn't embrace an "ideology of hatred" to oppose the unprovoked attack on a sovereign state, the deliberate public humiliation of its toppled leader, the Abu Ghraib tortures and humiliations......."

"There were seven Crusades between 1096 and 1254. The Crusaders lost, the Muslims won, in the end graciously according Christians the right to trade and to visit as pilgrims while Christian Europe went about its religious inquisitions and pogroms," Prof. Leupp pointed out and said:

"The current Crusade of Bush tells Muslims they can't go about their own business---because Christ through Bush commands that they change so as not to frighten American children. While the U.S. military disdains to count civilian dead in Afghanistan or Iraq, Lt. Gen. William G. Boykin, a deputy Undersecretary of Defense says, "We're a Christian nation" and "the enemy is a guy called Satan." Bush's religious mentor Franklin Graham calls Islam a "wicked, evil religion." The Graham father and son are well known for their televangelizing extravaganzas, which they call---what else?---"crusades." Born-again boys from believing communities march off to the Muslim world to respond to 9-11, as their Christian predecessors (peasants, children, knights) set forth from Europe a century ago, waywardly, many to their doom. Onward, Christian soldiers, "with the cross of Jesus going on before"

Crusade 2.0

John Feffer, [3a] in his most recent book - " Crusade 2.0: The West's Resurgent War against Islam" - also calls the so-called war on terrorism as a new crusade. He writes:

"Crusade 1.0 was not a simple "clash of civilizations" between cross and crescent. Although religion certainly played a motivating factor, the Crusades were also about the more mundane objectives associated with war: power, territory, economic gain. These grubbier motives prompted Crusaders sometimes to attack other Christians and sometimes even to ally with Muslims for tactical reasons. But the image of the Crusade that comes down to us today is that of a concerted effort to save civilization from the infidel.

"Our current crusade—Crusade 2.0—is similarly complicated. The United States has gone to war in defense of a different professed faith, not Christianity but rather liberal democracy. But this professed faith also conceals less no¬ble designs. Like the original Crusaders, the United States and its European partners have been concerned with geopolitical advantage in a strategically important area of the world. For the Crusaders, Jerusalem and its environs were an important pilgrimage site but also a vital trade route. Today's Crusaders have been more concerned about energy sources, whether the oil of Iraq or the natural gas pipelines that pass through Central Asia. To realize these more mundane goals, the West has made certain tactical alliances with actors in the Muslim world—the Northern Alliance in Afghanistan, Sunni fighters in Iraq, and the illiberal governments of Saudi Arabia, Bahrain, and Yemen. These Pentagon counterinsurgency efforts to partner with Muslim governments and Muslims on the ground often put the U.S. military at cross-purposes with Islamophobes. As New York Times columnist Frank Rich puts it, "How do you win Muslim hearts and minds in Kandahar when you are calling Muslims every filthy name in the book in New York?" [Crusade 2.0, p20]

But few soldiers enlisted to fight in Afghanistan or Iraq to win Muslim hearts and minds or even to preserve Western access to oil and gas. To justify a war and to mobilize young people to fight, Western governments needed a flesh-and-blood enemy. Citizens would only tolerate a more paranoid national security state at home if it was arrayed against a major enemy in the neighborhood. The grander the war and the more intrusive the national security state, the more epic the enemy needed to be. Osama bin Laden was not big enough. But bin Laden plus the Taliban plus Saddam Hussein plus Iran and Syria and Hamas and Hezbollah and radical imams in London, New York, and Hamburg raised the stakes considerably. To more closely approximate the world-historical enemies of the twentieth century—fascism and communism—the enemy had to pose a threat not just to territory but to civilization itself.

Like its medieval precursor, then, Crusade 2.0 has its paradoxes and complexities. But the image of Crusade 2.0—that of a liberal West battling unreasoning religious fanatics—has proven to be as enduring an ideological frame as the original "clash of civilizations" of the eleventh century. [Crusade 2.0, p21]

The current conflicts between the United States and its allies on the one hand and so-called radical Islam on the other are not an inevitable outgrowth of earlier history. After all, with the decline of the Ottoman Empire, the larger narrative of Islam versus the West largely disappeared in the nineteenth century. During the Cold War the United States and Israel actually sided with radical Islam against Arab nationalism. Perhaps more importantly, the religion of the parties arrayed against the United States is incidental, not essential. "The Iraqis have negative attitudes toward the United States because we are occupying their freaking land," Iraqi-born blogger Raed Jarrar told me, "not because they are majority Muslim and we are majority Christian." [Crusade 2.0, p21]

In other words, we are experiencing a clash of civilizations not on the ground but only in the violent jihadist visions of warriors in the wild East and wild West. Islamophobes and the al-Qaeda leadership, like gunslingers in a terrorized town, share an apocalyptic vision and a preference for illegal violence that keeps Crusade 2.0 alive. "No negotiations, no conferences and no dialogues"—this slogan of Abdullah al-Azzam, Osama bin Laden's mentor, could apply equally to both sides. [Crusade 2.0, p22]

Earlier in 2003, in the Introduction of "Power Trip: U.S. Unilateralism and Global Strategy After September 11," John Feffer wrote: "The war on terrorism, like the war on Communism before it, serves as an organizing principle, combining with a zeal for military preeminence and a drive to secure more foreign oil to form a threefold path to global dominance." [Crusade 2.0, p18]

Teaching hatred against Islam to American soldiers

While a "crusade" is launched against the Muslim countries, the American soldiers were taught hate against Islam as a enemy. Noah Shachtman and Spencer Ackerman of the Danger Room [4] reported on May 11, 2012 that the US military has been offering a course which teaches that its enemy is Islam in general, suggesting a Hiroshima-type massacre to obliterate the Islamic holy cities of Mecca and Medina.

The course, titled "Perspectives on Islam and Islamic Radicalism," was offered five times a year since 2004, with about 20 students each time, meaning roughly 800 students have taken the course over the years before it was removed in April 2012 after protests.

The course suggests: Islam is enemy. Islam is an ideology not a religion. The barbaric (Islam) ideology will no long be tolerated. There is no such thing as "Moderate Islam." Islam must change or we will facilitate its self destruction. Total war against all Muslims would be necessary. The well documented ongoing aggression of Islam is observed for over 1300 years and only gaining momentum. The course also suggests that the US is infiltrated by Muslim Brotherhood and Hamas. Major American Muslim groups like CAIR have links with Hamas. [4a]

"They [Muslims] hate everything you [Americans] stand for and will never coexist with you, unless you submit," the instructor, Lieutenant Colonel Matthew Dooley, said in a presentation in July 2011 for the course at Joint Forces Staff College in Norfolk, Virginia, the Associated Press reported. The college, for professional military members, teaches mid-level officers and government civilians on subjects related to planning and executing war. [5]

Dooley also presumed, for the purposes of his theoretical war plan, that the Geneva Conventions that set standards of armed conflict are "no longer relevant." "This would leave open the option once again of taking war to a civilian population wherever necessary (the historical precedents of Dresden, Tokyo, Hiroshima, Nagasaki being applicable...)," Dooley said. His war plan suggests possible outcomes such as "Saudi Arabia threatened with starvation, Islam reduced to cult status," and the Muslim holy cities of Mecca and Medina in Saudi Arabia "destroyed." In his July 2011 presentation on a "counter-jihad," Dooley asserted that the rise of what he called a "military Islam/Muslim resurgence" compels the United States to consider extreme measures, "unconstrained by fears of political incorrectness." [6]

Revamping of Islam

At the same time the US policy makers are embarked to change the face of Islam. According to a 2005 research report by U. S. News & World Report [7]: "The White House has approved a classified new strategy, dubbed Muslim World Outreach, that for the first time states that the United States has a national security interest in influencing what happens within Islam. Because America is, as one official put it, "radioactive" in the Islamic world, the plan calls for working through third parties-- moderate Muslim nations, foundations, and reform groups--to promote shared values of "democracy, women's rights, and tolerance."

In at least two dozen countries, Washington has quietly funded Islamic radio and TV shows, coursework in Muslim schools, Muslim think tanks, political workshops, or other programs that promote moderate Islam, the report said adding:

"At the peak of the Cold War, the U.S. government fielded a worldwide network of propagandists, publicists, and payoff artists. The United States Information Agency (USIA) ran hundreds of information specialists abroad and produced enough films to rival Hollywood's top studios, all to sell the world on the goodness of America-- and the evils of communism. There were USIA-run cultural centers and libraries in foreign capitals, Fulbright Scholarships and other exchange programs from the State Department, plus the broadcasts of Radio Free Europe and Radio Liberty. The CIA's covert payoffs, for better or worse, bought the allegiance of entire political parties in Italy and Japan. Other funds went secretly to sympathetic journalists, scholars, and labor leaders.

Approved by President Bush, the Muslim World Outreach strategy is now being implemented across the government. "You do it quietly," says Zeyno Baran, a terrorism analyst at the Nixon Center who advised on the strategy. "You provide money and help create the political space for moderate Muslims to organize, publish, broadcast, and translate their work." Baran, an expert on Islam in central Asia, says the dilemma for Americans is that the ideological challenge of our day comes in the form of a religion--militant Islam, replete with its political manifestos, edicts, and armies. "Religion is just not an issue American policymakers are comfortable discussing," she says. "But we're talking about a fascist ideology." [8]

In crafting their strategy, U.S. officials are taking pages from the Cold War playbook of divide and conquer. One of the era's great successes was how Washington helped break off moderate socialists from hard-core Communists overseas. "That's how we're thinking   It's something we talk about all the time," says Peter Rodman, a longtime aide to Henry Kissinger and now the Pentagon's assistant secretary of defense for international security affairs. "In those days, it was covert. Now, it's more open." Officials credit publicly funded programs like the National Endowment for Democracy, which have poured millions into Ukraine and other democratizing nations. [9]

Times have certainly changed. The nation's highest officials now seem convinced that America's greatest ideological foe is a highly politicized form of radical Islam and that Washington and its allies cannot afford to stand by. More proof that the administration is finally engaged in waging a war of ideas came last month, when the president tapped his longtime communications adviser, Karen Hughes, to be the State Department's new head of public diplomacy. [10]

In a bold move to influence the direction of Islam, Washington since 9/11 has quietly funded a variety of projects to boost Muslim religious moderates and generate goodwill in at least 24 countries where programs range from training Islamic-school teachers in civics to funding think tanks that promote moderate interpretations of the Quran, the report concluded.

Neo-Orientalism in USA

It will not be too much to say that for centuries European Orientalists have been working to defame and ridicule Islam through their 'scholarly' enterprises and the Neo-Orientalists in Europe and America are now following their footsteps. Alarmingly, such semi-official US think tanks as the Rand Corporation, in their "scholarly" enterprises, are demeaning Islam and Muslims while suggesting to exploit Sunni, Shiite and Arab, non-Arab divides to promote the US policy objectives in the Muslim world. Not astonishingly, the American neo-Orientalists are asking for the subordination of Islamic/Middle Eastern study in universities to American foreign policy interests.

According to Mucahit Bilici of the University of Michigan, in the aftermath of the 9/11 the decades old media habit of association of Islam with terrorism found its eternal justification in the attacks of 9/11. Islam is perceived to be an inherently violent religion and approached to within the reductionist framework of security. [10A]

"Groups and individuals who have a vested interest in the demonization of Islam and Muslims in the United States have also seized the opportunity to attack Musims and Islam. A phenomenon reminiscent of anti-semitism is emerging and Islamophobia finds expression in the multitudes of ways without being subjected to anti-discriminatory measures.

"One theoretical aftershock of 9/11 has been the return of orientalism as a veteran body of perspectives on Islam and Muslims. Advocates of orientalist framework such as Martin Kramer took the opportunity to popularize their critique of not only postcolonial theory but also the entire discipline of Middle Eastern Studies in America. Neo-orientalism has a large spectrum of participants from academia to the media. The neo-orientalists fighting back are asking for the subordination of Middle Eastern scholarship to American foreign policy interests and certain brands of American patriotism. Even veteran orientalist scholars such as Bernard Lewis made a return to the popular corners of American public sphere where he explained "the crisis of Islam" or answered "what went wrong" with the Muslims. According to Danny Fostel of *The Chronicle of Higher Education* return of orientalism have already found some echo in new generation academics.

"Return of orientalism is currently taking place more in popular literature than in academic works. The shock and impact of 9/11 has created a fertile ground for the proliferation of what can be called an alarmist literature. This growing body of popular literature on Islam simply demonizes Islam and Muslims. A representative sample of titles would include the following: *The Crisis of Islam, What Went Wrong, American Jihad: The Terrorists Living Among Us, Militant Islam Reaches America, Islam Unveiled: Disturbing Questions about the World's Fastest Growing Religion, Sword of the Prophet, The Terrorist Hunter.* Among the known alarmist writers and, in some cases, Islamophobes are journalist Steven Emerson, the author of *American Jihad: The Terrorists Living Among Us,* and the Middle East analyst Daniel Pipes, author of *Militant Islam Reaches America.* There has been a vicious war of images between such ideologically motivated critics of Muslims and the Muslim advocacy groups in the United States.

The Neo-Orientalists of the Rand Corporation

Not astonishingly, in the post-9/11 era, a long series of policy papers were written by the "embedded intellectuals" dedicated to further the military and economic objectives of the West as well as cultural onslaught on the Muslims.

The former US Deputy Defense Secretary, Paul Wolfowitz, a leading newcon, said on the eve of the U.S. invasion of Iraq in March 2003: "We need an Islamic reformation and I think there is real hope for one. A year later in March 2004, the semi-official think tank, the Rand Corporation issued its first study for global revamping of Islam. [11]

Author of the study, Cheryl Benard, arguing that Islam is not necessarily a very "accessible" religion, arbitrarily compartmentalizes the 1.5 billion Muslims into four categories depending on their degree of affinity for Western values and concepts:

1. Fundamentalists, who reject democratic values and contemporary Western culture.
2. Traditionalists, who want a conservative society. They are suspicious of modernity, innovation, and change.
3. Modernists, who want the Islamic world to become part of global modernity. They want to modernize and reform Islam to bring it into line with the age.
4. Secularists, who want the Islamic world to accept a division of church and state in the manner of Western industrial democracies, with religion relegated to the private sphere.

Although Benard arbitrarily divides all Muslims into four categories – fundamentalists, traditionalists, modernists and secularists – but pay attention to what's there, but not spelt out. For her objectives all Muslims, except modernists, are virtually the same.

Benard says that though the secularists should be our most natural allies in the Muslim world because Western democracies are premised on the separation of church and state but the problem has been, and continues to be, that many important secularists in the Islamic world are unfriendly or even extremely hostile to us on other grounds. "Leftist ideologies, anti-Americanism, aggressive nationalism, and authoritarian structures with only quasi-democratic trappings have been some of the manifestations of Islamic secularism to date."

Therefore, Benard suggests that Moderanists are our allies in the Muslim world. This group is most congenial to the values and the spirit of modern democratic society.

With the goal of selectively ignoring or rejecting elements of the original religious doctrine of Islam she also defines parameters for Muslim modernists:

- Modernists believe that Islam is responsible for the underdevelopment of the Muslims because prosperity and progress depends on modernity and democracy.

- Modernists believe in the historicity of Islam, i.e., that Islam as it was practiced in the days of the Prophet reflected eternal truths as well as historical circumstances that were appropriate to that time but are no longer valid.

- Modernists do not regard the original Islamic community or the early years of Islam as something that one would necessarily wish to reproduce today.

- Modernists believe that some verses (suras) may have been falsely or inaccurately recorded in the Quran.

- Modernists believe that the Quran is legend.

Benard questions the authenticity of the Qu'ran itself.

In the chapter on "The Hadith Wars" she says that two verses were lost in the process of recording of the Quran after the death of the Prophet. To authenticate her argument, she quotes from chapter 11 of an eminent scholar of Islam, Allama Ghulam Ahmed Parwez's book entitled: *The Status of Hadith . . . The Actual Status of Hadith - Holy Quran According to Our Traditions.* Ironically, this chapter is written to refute the premise that the Quran was recorded after the death of the Prophet. The references of Hadith in this chapter were given for argument's sake which Benard misquoted to prove her argument. Allama Parwez points out that the Quran was recorded in its present shape during the lifetime of the Prophet. He questions the authenticity of collections of Hadith which were collected by the Persian scholars more than 200 years after the death of the prophet.

Benard's "research" on Quran is the latest attack on the authenticity of the holy book of Islam. In July 2003, Newsweek launched a similar attack with an article entitled "Challenging the Qur'an." The punch of the article was that in the West, questioning the literal veracity of the Bible was a crucial step in breaking the church's grip on power—and in developing a modern, secular society and the Muslims should follow this. The Newsweek article referred to the "research" of a pseudonymous German scholar Christoph Luxenberg who claims that the original language of the Qur'an was not Arabic but something closer to Aramaic.

Practical guide to create a defanged version of Islam: A close reading of Benard's work indicates that the main thrust of the study is to create a defanged version of Islam - to develop a Western Islam, a German Islam, a U.S. Islam, etc.

Now how to achieve this objective?

The daunting and complex task of religion-building (or revamping Islam in America's image) will include the necessity to depart from, modify, and selectively ignore elements of the original religious doctrine of Islam, Benard argues.

After establishing her case against Islamic tenets as practiced or accepted today by almost all the Muslims Benard provides a Machiavellian formula to achieve the goal of creating a defanged version of Islam acceptable to America and the West:

Support the modernists first, support the traditionalists against the fundamentalists, confront and oppose the fundamentalists and selectively support secularists.

The focus will be on education and youth, since "committed adult adherents of radical Islamic movements are unlikely to be easily influenced into changing their views. The next generation, however, can conceivably be influenced if the message of democratic Islam can be inserted into school curricula and public media in the pertinent countries."

It may not be out of place to mention that efforts are already underway to eliminate Quranic verses from school text books in Muslim countries. In Pakistan, Musharraf government is trying to eliminate Quranic verses from school text books amid mounting opposition from religious and non-religious political parties. In 1990s Kuwaiti Education Minister, Dr. Rubai, was forced to resign when he ordered deletion of the Quranic verses from the school text books. To many Muslims deletion of verses from the school text books is an endeavor to open a window for editing the Quran that survived 1400 years of distortion attempts.

Benard advocates another strategy, that will be promoting Sufism - which she includes in modernism - in the Muslim world. "Sufi influence over school curricula, norms, and cultural life should be strongly encouraged in countries that have a Sufi tradition, such as Afghanistan or Iraq. Through its poetry, music, and philosophy, Sufism has a strong bridge role outside of religious affiliations.....Encourage countries with strong Sufi traditions to focus on that part of their history and to include it in their school curricula. Pay more attention to Sufi Islam."

Apparently, she is suggesting to use Sufism now to counter Wahabi doctrine as Americans used Wahabism in 1980s to launch "Jihad" against the Soviet troops in Afghanistan and also to counter Shiism after the Iranian revolution of 1979.

The fact of the matter is that historically Islamic fundamentalism or the so called "Militant Islam" has not posed a threat to Western interests (corporate, oil, and geopolitical interests) but rather been exploited to serve those interests. Remember Lawrence of Arabia? What was his objective other than to forge a British alliance with the Hashemites during World War I? Later, the British boosted the Saudi royal family, patrons of the Wahhabi school of thought, into power. The U.S. inherited Saudi Arabia as a client state after World War II, and we all know how well U.S. oil companies have done there ever since. Aramco alone, prior to its nationalization in the mid-1980s, yielded some $ 3 trillion from the Arabian reserves. (Challenging Ignorance on Islam: a Ten-Point Primer for Americans by Gary Leupp, an Associate professor, Department of History, Tufts University and coordinator, Asian Studies Program. (August 2002)

The U.S. helped create, recruit, and finance the fundamentalist Mujahideen, including some 30,000 young volunteers who came from throughout the Muslim world to fight "godless Communism" in Afghanistan in the 1980s. The U.S. encouraged them to view their war as a jihad "Holy War," and put many in contact with young Osama bin Laden, then a US ally. The Reagan administration was in love with fundamentalist Islam, so long as it served its purposes. On June 16, 1986, President Reagan told four Afghan Mujahideen who were invited to the White House: "I feel I am in the company of the founding fathers of this country."

The California-based company Unocal was cordially negotiating right up to Sept. 11 with Afghanistan's Taliban for an oil pipeline through Afghan territory, State Department official Zalmay Khalilzad, now US ambassador to Afghanistan, was arguing up through 1998 that the Taliban were friendly, potential business partners who did "not practice the anti-U.S. style of fundamentalism practiced in Iran.

Benard's study completely ignores that cause of anti-American and anti-West attitude and violence in the Muslim world. She holds Islam and Muslims responsible for this. While ignoring the root cause she made a passing remark on this critical issue: "a number of authors believe that fundamentalist hostility to the United States and to the West primarily reflects anger over some aspects of our foreign policy or discomfort over the more-liberal aspects of Western culture. It is important to be aware that, while such concerns play a part, fundamentalism represents a basic and total rejection of democracy and of the core values of modern civil society."

What she suggests is that Islam and Muslims are against democracy and civil society norms.

The release of the Rand study coincided with the formation of "Islamic Progress Institute" (IPI) by Daniel Pipes, an anti-Muslim and anti-Islam scholar, to articulate a moderate, modern and pro-American viewpoint on Islam. Pipe says: Islam in America must be American Islam or it will not be integrated (read accepted). The Rand Corp. study provides an ideological ground for creating an American version of Islam while IPI hopes to serve as a vehicle to implement that agenda in America.

Within the United States, "all Muslims, unfortunately, are suspect", Pipes wrote in a recent book, which called for the authorities to be especially vigilant towards Muslims with jobs in the military, law enforcement, or diplomacy. Last year, he cited as evidence of this insight the arrest on suspicion of espionage of Muslim chaplain Captain James Yee at the Guantanamo Bay detention facility that houses hundreds of prisoners from Bush's war on terrorism. The Army later withdrew charges against Captain Yee. In his grant proposal, Pipes writes that he is working on launching the IPI with "a group of anti-Islamist Muslims", whom he does not identify. [12]

Exploit Sunni, Shiite and Arab, non-Arab divides to promote the US policy objectives in the Muslim world

In December 2004 the Rand Corporation issued another study which suggested that Sunni, Shiite and Arab, non-Arab divides should be exploited to promote the US policy objectives in the Muslim world.

The new Rand study - titled "The Muslim World After 9/11" – was conducted on behalf of the US Air Force. One of the primary objective of the study was to "identify the key cleavages and fault lines among sectarian, ethnic, regional, and national lines and to assess how these cleavages generate challenges and opportunities for the United States." [13]

"The majority of the world's Muslims are Sunni, but a significant minority, about 15 percent of the global Muslim population, are Shi'ites..... The expectations of Iraqi Shi'ites for a greater say in the governance of their country presents an opportunity for the United States to align its policy with Shi'ite aspirations for greater freedom of religious and political expression, in Iraq and elsewhere," the study said.

The study pointed out that with the moves toward rapprochement between Tehran and Riyadh, there are reports that Saudi Arabia's Shi'ites are now turning from Iran and placing their hopes on the United States. "Their expectation is that any move toward democracy in Iraq would give the Shi'ite majority a greater say in the politics of that country and increase their ability to help their brethren in Saudi Arabia. Such expectations could present an opportunity for the United States to align its policy with Shi'ite aspirations for greater freedom of religious and political expression and a say in their own affairs in countries controlled by others."

On the division between the Arab and the non-Arab worlds, the Rand Study pointed out: "Arabs constitute only about 20 percent of the world's Muslims, yet interpretations of Islam, political and otherwise, are often filtered through an Arab lens. A great deal of the discourse on Muslim issues and grievances is actually discourse on Arab issues and grievances. For reasons that have more to do with historical and cultural development than religion, the Arab world exhibits a higher incidence of economic, social, and political disorders than other regions of the so-called developing world."

"By contrast, the non-Arab parts of the Muslim world are politically more inclusive, boast the majority of the democratic or partially democratic governments, and are more secular in outlook. Although the Arab Middle East has long been regarded (and certainly views itself) as the core of the Muslim world, the most innovative and sophisticated contemporary work in Islam is being done on the "periphery"—in countries such as Indonesia and in Muslim communities in the West, leading some scholars to ask whether Islam's center of gravity is now shifting to more dynamic regions of the Muslim world."

The Rand Report holds the post independence political and economic failures responsible for the current political environment of the Muslim world in general and the Arab world in particular. "Many of the ills and pathologies that afflict many countries in this part of the world and that generate much of the extremism we are concerned about derive from—and contribute to—economic and political failure."

This situation, the study argued, leads to the concept of structural anti-Westernism (or anti-Americanism). "This concept holds that that Muslim anger has deep roots in the political and social structures of some Muslim countries and that opposition to certain U.S. policies merely provides the content and opportunity for the expression of this anger."

According to the Rand study, "outside the Arab Middle East, Islamization has involved the importation of Arab-origin ideology and religious and social practices— a phenomenon that we refer to as *Arabization."*

The Rand study said that a number of critical or catalytic events have altered the political environment in the Muslim world in fundamental ways. "Catalytic events include the Iranian revolution, the Afghan war, the Gulf War of 1991, the global war on terrorism that followed the September 11 terrorist attacks, and the Iraq war of 2003."

The Palestinian-Israeli conflict and the Kashmir conflict, the study said, are not catalytic events per se but rather chronic conditions that have shaped political discourse in the Middle East and South Asia for over half a century, the study said.

The Palestinian-Israeli conflict and the Kashmir have retarded the political maturation of the Arab world and Pakistan by diverting scarce material, political, and psychic resources from pressing internal problems, the study added.

The Rand study called for madrassa and mosques reforms in the Muslim world and suggested that US should "support the efforts of governments and moderate Muslim organizations to ensure that mosques, and the social services affiliated with them, serve their communities and do not serve as platforms for the spread of radical ideologies." In chapter on Islam & Politics in Pakistan, the Rand Study even suggested that there should be government appointed and paid professional imams in all mosques to promote "civil Islam".

"While only Muslims themselves can effectively challenge the message of radical Islam, there is much the United States and like-minded countries can do to empower Muslim moderates in this ideological struggle," said Angel Rabas, RAND senior policy analyst and lead author of the report. "The struggle in the Muslim world is essentially a war of ideas, the outcome of which will determine the future direction of the Muslim world and profoundly affect vital U.S. security interests," he added.

The Rand Study also calls on the United States and its allies to support efforts in Muslim nations to:

- Create a strong and vocal network to unite the fractured voices of moderate Muslims. This can provide moderates with a platform for their message and provide alternatives to extremist movements. An external catalyst may be needed to give life to this goal.

- Support Muslim civil society groups that advocate moderation and modernity. The United States may have to assist in the development of civil society institutions where they do not currently exist.

- Disrupt radical networks. Engage Islamists to participate in the political process, and strengthen relations with the military in Muslim nations. In the war against terror, the U.S. should demonstrate that its efforts are meant to promote democratic change.

- Reform Islamic schools. Educational systems have long been a vital component of radical Islamic indoctrination and recruitment. The best way to counter this is to help Islamic schools ensure they are providing modern education and marketable skills for future generations.

- Create economic opportunities in Muslim nations, particularly for young people. Economic assistance programs will not guarantee an end to extremism or terrorism, but could reduce the perception that the U.S. relies solely on military instruments. Creating jobs and social services would also give young people an alternative to radical Islamic organizations.

Rand Corporation's new recipe to handle the Muslim World

IN March 2007, the semi-official U.S. think tank, Rand Corporation, issued another study suggesting creation of networks of the so-called moderate Muslims to promote US policy objectives in the Muslim World. In its new report, titled "Building Moderate Muslim Networks" the Rand Corp advocates that the building of moderate Muslim networks needs to become an explicit goal of the U.S. government policy, with an international database of partners and a well-designed plan.

Just as it fought the spread of Communism during the Cold War, the United States must do more to develop and support networks of moderate Muslims who are too often silenced by violent radical Islamists, according to the report. [14]

Lead writer of the report Angel Rabasa says that the United States has a critical role to play in aiding moderate Muslims, and can learn much from the way it addressed the spread of Communism during the Cold War. "The efforts of the United States and its allies to build free and democratic networks and institutions provided an organizational and ideological counter force to Communist groups seeking to come to power through political groups, labor unions, youth and student organizations and other groups."

The report defines a moderate as a Muslim who supports democracy, gender equality, freedom of worship and opposition to terrorism. This looks an amplification on its two previous reports - "Civil Democratic Islam: Partners, Resources, and Strategies" (March 2004) and "US strategy in the Muslim World after 9/11" (December 2004) - which also suggested supporting moderate Muslims and exploitation of inter-Muslim religious differences.

In the December 2004 study Rabasa had suggested to exploit Sunni, Shiite and Arab, non-Arab divides to promote the US policy objectives in the Muslim world. Echoing this theme, the latest report recommends reaching out to Muslim activists, leaders and intellectuals in non-Arab countries such as Turkey as well as in Southeast Asia and Europe. The report recommends targeting five groups as potential building blocks for networks: liberal and secular Muslim academics and intellectuals; young moderate religious scholars; community activists; women's groups engaged in gender equality campaigns; and moderate journalists and scholars.

The report warned that moderate groups can lose credibility – and therefore, effectiveness – if U.S. support is too obvious. Effective tactics that worked during the Cold War include having the groups led by credible individuals and having the United States maintain some distance from the organizations it supports. "This was done by not micro-managing the groups, but by giving them enough autonomy," Rabasa said. "As long as certain guidelines were met, they were free to pursue their own activities."

To help start this initiative, the report recommends working toward an international conference modeled in the Cold War-era Congress of

Cultural Freedom, and then developing a standing organization to combat what it called radical Islamism.

Not astonishingly, the three Rand Reports are silent on the reasons of discontentment in the Muslim world. The report does not address any of the core issues that are central in developing the perceptions of the Muslim world like; Palestine, Kashmir and Chechnya issues and the exploitative political systems supported by the American or European elites. No reference is made to the West's support for totalitarian secular Muslim regimes, Israel 's endless pogroms against the Palestinians and ethnic cleansing perpetrated against Muslims in Eastern Europe and Chechnya.

Now a word about the Washington-based semi-official think tank – the RAND Corporation. Among other government departments, the Rand Corp conducts studies for the Office of the Secretary of Defense, the Joint Staff, the Unified Commands, the defense agencies, the Department of the Navy and the U.S. intelligence community. Obviously, writers of the three under discussion reports on Islam may be considered as neo-Orientalists with clear intention to belittle Islam.

When the European nations began their long campaign to colonize and conquer the rest of the world for their own benefit, they brought their academic and missionary resources to help them with their task. Orientalists and missionaries, whose ranks often overlapped, were the servants of an imperialist government who was using their services as a way to subdue or weaken an enemy. The academic study of the *Oriental East by the Occidental West* was often motivated and often co-operated hand-in-hand with the imperialistic aims of the European colonial powers. The foundations of Orientalism were in the maxim "Know thy enemy". This equally applies to the modern day Orientalists of such semi-official think tanks as the Rand Corporation.

We are experiencing the re-emergence of Orientalism of the 19th century. This neo-Orientalism is coming in the shape of such research documents as the Rand Reports which question the authenticity of Islam's holy scripture, the Quran. Even a fake version of Quran is now available in print. It was distributed in a private school in Kuwait in 2004.

Islamophobia is systematically promoted in America

Islamophobia is systematically promoted and financially supported in the United States. An in-depth investigation into Islamophobia carried out by the Center for American Progress in the United States dubbed as 'Fear, Inc. The Roots of the Islamophobia Network in America', sheds light on the collective efforts of the Zionist groups funded by the United States in pedaling a hatred for and a fear of Islam in the form of books, reports, websites, blogs, and carefully crafted talking points.

According to the report, these wealthy donors and foundations also provide direct funding to anti-Islam grassroots groups. The project of Islamophobia which has cost more than $40 million over the past ten years has been funded by seven foundations in the United States: 1. Richard Mellon Scaife Foundation; 2. Lynde and Harry Bradley Foundation; 3. Newton and Rochelle Becker; 4. Foundation and Newton and Rochelle Becker Charitable Trust; 5. Russell Berrie Foundation, Anchorage Charitable Fund and William Rosenwald; 6. Family Fund; 7. Fairbrook Foundation.

Not surprisingly, the self-proclaimed Islamic expert Steven Emerson has collected 3.39 million dollars for his for-profit company in 2008 for researching alleged ties between American Muslims and overseas terrorism. In an investigative report titled "Anti-Muslim crusaders make millions spreading fear," Bob Smietana of The Tennessean pointed out that Emerson is a leading member of a multimillion-dollar industry of self-proclaimed experts who spread hate toward Muslims in books and movies, on websites and through speaking appearances. He went on to say: "Leaders of the so-called "anti-jihad" movement portray themselves as patriots, defending America against radical Islam. [15]

Islamophobia – now in American Children's books

As if the adult media's vitriol wasn't enough, the American Muslims are now being faced by the alarming publication of a series of 'children's books', containing misleading and inflammatory rhetoric about the Islamic faith. The 10-book series – entitled the "World of Islam," – is published by Mason Crest Publishing in collaboration with the Philadelphia-based pro-Israel and pro-war Foreign Policy Research Institute.[16]

Anti-Islamic sentiment pervades the entire series, portraying Muslims as inherently violent and deserving suspicion. It encourages young readers to believe Muslims are terrorists, who seek to undermine US society. For example:

The book "Muslims in America", says that "some Muslims began immigrating to the United States in order to transform American society, sometimes through the use of terrorism." The cover of Radical Islam features a machine gun and a Muslim head scarf, with what looks like bloodstains underneath the scarf and the title word Radical. The book is rife with incorrect information and fear mongering and ultimately seeks to paint a picture that Muslims in America are to be treated with suspicion and that they all have links to terrorism.

The text titled ISLAM, LAW AND HUMAN RIGHTS begins and ends with the same thing, that Muslim majority nations are the only ones that violate human rights laws set forth by the United Nations – for some reason China and North Korea are exceptions to that rule.

THE HISTORY OF ISLAM offers only a stunted glimpse of Islamic History and focuses primarily on extremism and contains an outrageous quote: "Today, the great majority of Muslims accept the idea that jihad means a struggle against non-Muslims to increase the area under the rule of Islam."

Another book shows an image of two 7-year-old girls wearing head scarves under the heading "Security Threats."

The books cited a well-known Islamophobe, Daniel Pipes, who received the "Guardian of Zion" award, in May 2006. The award is given annually to a prominent supporter of the state of Israel, from the Rennert Center for Jerusalem Studies at Bar-Ilan University in Israel. Not surprisingly, Pipes circulated his own e-mail to defend the controversial series. The books also cite anti-Islam activists such as Ayaan Hirsi Ali, a fan of Geert Wilders, an infamous Dutch lawmaker, renowned for being a rabid Islamophobe.

In the post-9/11 America, the Mason Crest FPRI controversial Series on Islam are the latest episode in the reinforcement of Islamophobia which may be defined as "alienation, discrimination, harassment and violence rooted in misinformed and stereotyped representations of Islam and its adherents." No doubt the new series on Islam reinforce Islamophobia through misleading and inflammatory rhetoric about the Islamic faith.

Americans' attitudes about Islam and Muslims are fuelled mainly by political statements and media reports that focus almost solely on the negative image of Islam and Muslims. The vilification of Islam and Muslims has been relentless among segments of the media and political classes since 9/11. Politicians, authors and media commentators are busy in demonizing Islam, Muslims and the Muslim world. In the post 9/11 America attacking Islam and Muslims became the fashionable sport for the radio, television and print media. While print and electronic media continues unabated campaign to smear Islam, radio talk show hosts are busy in spewing out venoms against Islam and Muslims. Surprisingly, even a higher court rules that a letter calling for killing Muslims is protected by the freedom of speech.

Coloring book demonizes Muslims and Islam

Another attempt to demonize Muslims and Islam came in the shape of a children coloring book titled "We Shall Never Forget 9/11: The Kids' Book of Freedom." The 36-page "graphic novel coloring book" published recently by St. Louis, Mo. Publisher Wayne Bell virtually characterizes all Muslims as linked to extremism, terrorism and radicalism, which may lead children reading the book to believe that all Muslims are responsible for the tragedy of 9/11. It could give a message to children that followers of the Islamic faith are their enemies.

As ABC 7 reports, the book contains the phrase "radical Islamic Muslim extremists" at least 10 times. The publisher writes in the book that, "'they' also will never forget. Yes, they know of whom "they" are. Given the chance, 'they' would do it again" and in another passage, the books reads, "Some Muslim people believe the attacks were a conspiracy caused by Jews."

The book could give a message to children that followers of the Islamic faith are their enemies since another section reads: "These attacks will change the way America deals with and views the Islamic and Muslim people around the world…"

Near the end of the narrative is an image of Osama bin Laden, hiding behind a woman as he's confronted and killed by US Navy SEALs. Text under this picture reads: "Children, the truth is, these terrorist acts were done by freedom-hating radical Islamic Muslim extremists. These crazy people hate the American way of life because we are free and our society is free."

A comment posted on ABC Chicago website exposes the real intention of the publisher: "It doesn't take a genius to see the mask the publisher, Bell, is hiding behind. I am not Muslim, but a Christian, and I feel this coloring book is totally inappropriate for children, period! There is no need to depict a tragic incident such as 9/11 in a coloring book for kids. What other tragic events do you know of that are made into coloring books? Think about it." [17]

Anti-Islam film sparks anti-US demonstrations in the Muslim World

In September 2012, massive violent anti-US demonstrations were triggered in the Muslim world and elsewhere by an anti-Islam film produced in the United States. The film that sparked the violence depicts the Prophet Mohammed as a child molester, womanizer and ruthless killer.

The anti-Islam movie known as "Innocence of Muslims" was written, produced and directed by Nakoula Basseley Nakoula, a convicted drug manufacturer and scam artist, who has told authorities he actually wrote the script in federal prison and began production two months after his June 2011 release from custody. Nakoula, a Coptic Christian from Egypt, was arrested was on September 27, 2012 for violating terms of his probation in a 2010 bank fraud case. Nakoula served about a year of a 21-month prison term for orchestrating a check-kiting scheme against Wells Fargo Bank, according to court records. As part of his sentence, Nakoula was ordered to pay restitution of $794,700.

The film was promoted by Terry Jones, a once little-known Florida pastor who gained international notoriety for burning the Quran despite a plea by the then US defense secretary Robert Gates that the act would put the lives of US troops in danger. Alex Kane of AlterNet said that as the more information came out, the more it became clear that the origins of the film lie in an alliance between members of the Egyptian Coptic Christian community, right-wing Christians and the well-funded network of Islamophobes in the U.S.

Apparently, the makers of the film had deliberately set out to goad Muslims into just such violent and irrational reactions as were seen in Egypt, Pakistan and elsewhere. The objective was to show Muslims as irrational, violent, intolerant and barbaric, all of which are attributes profoundly inscribed into the racist anti-Muslim discourse in the West.

The United States condemned the content of the video while defending the right to free speech, and took a similar line on the French cartoons. "We know that these images will be deeply offensive to many and have the potential to be inflammatory. But we've spoken repeatedly about the importance of upholding the freedom of expression that is enshrined in our constitution," White House spokesman Jay Carney told reporters. "In other words, we don't question the right of something like this to be published, we just question the judgment behind the decision to publish it."

The anti-Islam film was widely condemned globally.

The U.N. Secretary-General Ban Ki-moon said the maker of an anti-Islam film abused his right to freedom of expression by making the movie, which he called a "disgraceful and shameful act." "Freedoms of expression should be and must be guaranteed and protected, when they are used for common justice, common purpose," Ban told a news conference. "When some people use this freedom of expression to provoke or humiliate some others' values and beliefs, then this cannot be protected in such a way." "My position is that freedom of expression, while it is a fundamental right and privilege, should not be abused by such people, by such a disgraceful and shameful act," he said. [18]

On September 30, 2012, the foreign ministers of Islamic countries, meeting at the sidelines of the UN General Assembly session in New York, unanimously adopted a resolution against the anti-Islam film posted on the internet and the blasphemous caricatures published in a French magazine that desecrates the Prophet Mohammad. Ministers from the 57-nation Organization of Islamic Cooperation (OIC) said that freedom of expression had to be used with "responsibility." The declaration called the moves as "sheer acts of incitement to hatred, discrimination and hostility towards Muslims, their peaceful religion Islam and the Holy Prophet." The OIC ministers condemned "intolerance, discrimination, profiling, negative stereotyping, stigmatization, religious hatred and violence against Muslims, as well as denigration of their religion" caused by the release of the film and cartoons of Islam's Prophet Mohammad. "These Islamophobic acts stand in violation of the freedom of religion and belief, guaranteed by international human rights instruments, and have deeply offended" Muslims around the world, the statement added. [19]

The speaker of the European parliament strongly condemned the anti-Islam film. "I condemn strongly not only the content but also the distribution of such a movie, which is humiliating the feelings of a lot of people all over the world," said a press statement issued yesterday by Martin Schulz, the speaker of the European parliament, in reaction to the anti-Islam film. [20]

On October 29, 2012, a Moscow court banned as "extremist" thr US-made anti-Islamic film. Moscow's Tverskoi District judge sided with prosecution arguments presented in court that the low-budget "Innocence of Muslims" production "promoted the rise of religious intolerance in Russia". Tverskoi court's ruling follows a similar decision on October 26 taken by a court in Grozny, the provincial capital of Russia's Muslim-dominated province of Chechnya. Russia's communications minister had warned that authorities would bar access to YouTube if its owner, Google Inc., failed to abide by a court order to block access to the U.S.-produced film. [21]

As many countries faced public protests over the anti-Islam 'Innocence of Muslims" video, the Russian Lower House denounced the film and took the first move to outlaw insults to religions. The State Duma approved a special address 'On protection of the religious feelings of the citizens of Russia,' which was submitted jointly by all four parliamentary parties. MP Yaroslav Nilov of the Liberal Democratic Party, the head of the Lower House's Legislative Committee, presented the document, citing a number of "sacrilegious, outrageous, obscurantist situations and events" that took place in 2012, including the assassination of two Muslim clerics in Russia's internal republics of Tatarstan and Dagestan. He argued that Russia was facing a campaign aimed at destabilizing the country, and called for the Lower House to take urgent measures to curb the growing problem. Deputy Chair of the State Duma, MP Sergey Zheleznyak, said that it was necessary to institute specific punishments for insulting believers on the Internet, especially on blogs and social networks. The profile committee of the Lower House suggested administrative offenses for insulting believers' feelings, punishable by fines of 100,000 to 200,000 rubles ($3,000 to $6,000). [22]

Violent anti-US demonstrations

I he anti-Islam film sparked protest demonstrations throughout the Muslim World. Muslims in Iran, Turkey, Sudan, Egypt, Yemen, Tunisia, Bangladesh, Malaysia,

Indonesia, Pakistan, Afghanistan, India, Iraq, Morocco, Syria, Lebanon, Kuwait, Nigeria, Kenya, Mali, Nigeria, Australia, Britain, the United States, France, Belgium, and several other countries held many demonstrations to condemn the movie. Protests were also held in Kashmir and the Gaza Strip.

As the protests sparked by the online anti-Islam film entered a second week the CNN said on September 18, the protests raised questions about whether the furor is isolated or a sign of broader anti-American sentiment in the Muslim world.

This incident has exposed the deep vein of anger against the United States that runs through the Muslim world, wrote Lawrence Davidson. "This anger is nothing new and we continue to ignore it at our peril. The Muslim world continues to be a tinder box that someone resident in the West, someone like Nakoula Bassely Nakoula, can throw a match into and spark something akin to another 9/11." [23]

Hidden causes of the Muslim protests

What are the sources of simmering hostility toward America that helped fuel these protests? Robert Wright, a senior editor of The Atlantic, posed the question and then enumerated three major reasons:

[1] DRONE STRIKES. Obviously, President Obama doesn't want to say anything bad about the gobs of strikes he's authorized. Neither does Mitt Romney; if you're going to spend your whole campaign calling Obama a hyper-apologetic girly boy, you can't turn around and complain that he kills too many people! But American drone strikes--which seem to always target Muslim countries, and sometimes kill civilians--are famously unpopular in the Muslim world. Note which countries tend to cluster toward the bottom of this graph from the Pew Global Attitudes Project. And watch the one-minute-clip below of my conversation on BhTV with Robert Becker, an American who lives in Cairo, taped after the protests had started. I asked him to list the most common Egyptian complaints about America, and here's what he said:

[2] Israel-Palestine. That's the second issue Becker mentions in the video clip, and it is also cited in a recent Atlantic piece by Middle East expert Steven Cook of the Council on Foreign Relations. Again, don't expect to hear about this from Romney or Obama. During an election campaign, especially, neither man wants to dwell on the downside of America's essentially unconditional support of Israel even as Israel pursues policies that violate both international law and basic principles of justice,

such as the expansion of settlements in the West Bank. But rest assured that the Israeli-American relationship gets plenty of airtime in Muslim, and especially Arab, nations. And, while some of this assumes the form of wild conspiracy theories, the core fact that American support helps sustain highly objectionable Israeli policies is not a figment of anyone's imagination. Neither is the fact that when President Obama did try to get Israel to freeze settlement expansion, he encountered so much blowback in Israel and America that he had to give up.

[3] American troops in Muslim countries. Though American soldiers have left Iraq, they remain in Afghanistan. Noting the downside of this fact doesn't fit into either Obama's or Romney's game plan as they try to out-hawk each other. But, while they stay silent, there are people who are happy to talk about American troops in Afghanistan: Jihadi recruiters. And the reason is that they know this subject strikes a chord among young Muslim men who for various reasons (including local ones such as unemployment) are unhappy campers to begin with. This demographic played an important role in many of the protests.

Robert Wright argues that the three grievances he has listed (and there are others) aren't wholly unrelated to that horrible YouTube video. "They're interpreted by some Muslims as evidence of American contempt for the Muslim world, and the video was taken as yet more confirmation." [24]

Similarly, Arlen Grossman argued that Americans were being attacked and shot at in the Middle East for more than just bad movies. "A long history of war and interference in this region is the main reason we are disliked in the many of these countries. The United States and other Western powers have been attacking, occupying, and otherwise interfering with oil-rich countries in this region for decades now, most recently with our unprovoked war in Iraq and our eleven-year ongoing occupation in Afghanistan. It would be strange if most of the people in the Middle East weren't sick of us. But it wouldn't be strange to assume that every military strike causing civilian deaths is creating future enemies for the United States." [25]

The fallacy of free speech

The Associated Press reported on September 21, 2012, that at least 47 people have been killed in violence linked to the protests over the film, which has also renewed debate over freedom of expression in the U.S. and in Europe.

Tellingly, when Google was asked to remove the highly inflammatory video, it immediately cited its long established policy of supporting freedom of speech. The Google told the New York Times, that the "Innocence of Muslims" video does not violate terms of service for YouTube regarding hate speech because it is focused on the Muslim religion and not the people who practice it.

However on August 1, 2012 Google had no problem removing 1,710 videos and closing their affiliated accounts because "a substantial number of those videos concerned Holocaust denial and defense of Holocaust deniers." Google "closed the user's account within 24 hours" of receiving the complaint by a group that monitors anti-Semitism in Australia, as Esam Al-Amin wrote in OpEd News on Sept 15, 2012 quoting Jewish Press. [26]

People in the U.S. may not be aware of these incidents where hate or disfavored speech was taken down, Al-Amin says adding: "But many people in the Muslim world are aware of such interventions that run contrary to stated principles. Plausibly, they wonder, if foreigners such as the Attorney General of Israel or an Australian monitoring group can get Google or Facebook to shut down videos or close accounts, how can one argue that the President or the Secretary of State cannot make similar requests? They also recall that in 2009 Secretary Clinton intervened and prevailed over the executives of Facebook and Twitter on behalf of the activists of the so-called Green movement in Iran. This is not an argument to advocate closing down accounts or removing videos but simply to illustrate the hypocrisy and double standard practiced by public officials and business conglomerates when dealing with Muslim concerns." [27]

Writing in the Guardian on September 16, 2012, Glenn Greenwald recall the so-called "request" in December 2010 from Joe Lieberman, made in his capacity as chairman of the Senate Homeland Security Committee, that private corporations such as Amazon, Visa, MasterCard and others cut off all services to WikiLeaks, including hosting its website and allowing payments to the group. Those corporations instantly complied – how many American companies will continue with behavior which a leading senator announces is harming US national security? – and few Democrats had trouble understanding why such a "request" was so odious. It should be equally easy to see why this is the case with the Obama White House's request to Google. [28]

French journalist Thierry Meyssan argues that Western European states have passed "historical memory" laws which have transformed a historical event—the Nazi destruction of European Jews—into a religious occurrence: the "Shoa" in Jewish terminology, or the "Holocaust" as expressed in Christian evangelical parlance. "Nazi crimes are thereby elevated to the level of a unique event at the expense of the victims of other massacres, including other victims of the Nazis. Questioning the dogma, i.e. this religious interpretation of historical facts, subjects one to criminal penalties, just as blasphemy was punished in the past." [29]

Many European countries enacted laws in the past three decades that criminalize any speech or writings that question the official accounts of the Holocaust. In 1996 French philosopher Roger Garaudy published his book, The Founding Myths of Modern Israel. Critics charged that his book contained Holocaust denial and consequently the French government indicted him, and shortly thereafter, the courts banned any further publication of the book. In 1998 Garaudy was convicted, sentenced to a suspended jail sentence of several years, and fined forty thousand dollars.

In 2005, English writer David Irving was apprehended in Austria on a 1989 arrest warrant of being a Holocaust denier. He was subsequently convicted of "trivializing, grossly playing down, and denying the Holocaust," and sentenced to three years imprisonment.

As Soraya Sepahpour-Ulrich recalls, there is a precedent in the US to curbing free speech when deemed harmful. [30] In a landmark Supreme Court hearing — Schenck v. United States, 249 U.S. 47 (1919) , the actions of Schenck, an anti-war individual who had printed and distributed leaflets in order to discourage enlisting servicemen, was not afforded protection under the First Amendment. The issue before the court was whether Schenck's actions (words, expression) were protected by the free speech clause of the First Amendment. The Court ruled:

"The most stringent protection of free speech would not protect a man in falsely shouting fire in a theatre and causing panic." Holmes argued that "the question in every case is whether the words used are used in such circumstances and are of such nature as to create a clear and present danger that they will bring about the substantive evils that congress has a right to prevent."

On the fallacy of free-speech Soraya Sepahpour-Ulrich also recalls: On October 16, 2004, President George W. Bush signed the Israel Lobby's bill, the Global Anti-Semitism Review Act which requires the US Department of State to monitor anti-Semitism worldwide. (It is noteworthy that 4 years later, Republican candidates ran on a platform of promoting hatred of Islam). In line with policies of selective "free speech", in August 2012, California State Assembly passed a resolution (House Resolution 35) against criticism of Israel.

The House Resolution 35, in part said: "....the Assembly recognizes recent actions by officials of public postsecondary educational institutions in California and calls upon those institutions to increase their efforts to swiftly and unequivocally condemn acts of anti-Semitism on their campuses and to utilize existing resources, such as the European Union Agency for Fundamental Rights' working definition of anti-Semitism to help guide campus discussion about, and promote, as appropriate, educational programs for combating anti-Semitism on their campuses...."

To borrow Glenn Greenwald "those who apply free speech values inconsistently are not merely being hypocritical; worse, they are attempting to exploit free speech precepts to protect and legitimize the views of themselves and their own side while suppressing those views they dislike and which are advocated by the other side." Indeed, it's often the very people who insist that "advocacy of violence" should not be permitted who, in the next breath, justify the wars and bombings and drone-attacks of their government, Greenwald concludes. [31]

French blasphemous cartoons fuel the Muslim anger over the anti-Islam film

After a week of deadly international protests against the anti-Islam film, the French weekly Charlie Hebdo fanned its own flames by publishing blasphemous caricatures of the Prophet Muhammed on September 19, 2012.

Editor in chief Gerard Biard claimed he did it to satirize the anti-Muslim video. He called its violent reaction absurd. Editorial director Stephane Charbonnier said "We have the right to express ourselves." Charbonnier added the Charlie Hebdo is "a newspaper against religions as soon as they enter into the political and public realm." He claims Muslim religious leaders manipulate French followers for political reasons. "You're not meant to identify yourself through a religion, in any case not in a secular state," he claims.

Charlie Hebdo is no stranger to controversy. Its Paris offices were firebombed November 2011 after it published a mocking caricature of Mohammad, and Charbonnier has been under police guard ever since.

White House spokesman Jay Carney stopped short of denouncing Charlie Hebdo editors, saying: "We don't question the right of something like this to be published. We just question the judgment behind the decision to publish it." Stephen Lendman called it a back door endorsement. [32]

French officials also backed their hate speech rights but banned street protest demonstrations against the cartoons. Interior Minister Manuel Valls said prefects throughout the country had orders to prohibit any protest over the issue and to crack down if the ban was challenged. "There will be strictly no exceptions. Demonstrations will be banned and broken up," he told a news conference. [33]

To borrow Thierry Meyssan, "at home, the French government presented itself as the guarantor of the freedom of expression. Accordingly, it defends the right of the enemies of Islam to indulge in blasphemous caricatures. But then, openly contradicting itself, the same government announced a prohibition of any demonstration hostile to the film or the magazine, thus denying freedom of expression to the defenders of Islam." [34]

On the hypocritical Western stance on the freedom of expression, Stephen Lendman points out: "Try denouncing the holocaust in France and see what happens. Try wearing a hijab, other head covering, or head to toe burqah and find out. Try denouncing Israeli crimes on US television or in mainstream publications, and see how long you keep your job. Try supporting right over wrong and fair no better." [35]

Arab League Secretary-General Nabil Elaraby called the drawings outrageous but said those who were offended by them should "use peaceful means to express their firm rejection". Tunisia's ruling Islamist party, Ennahda, condemned them as an act of "aggression" against Mohammad but urged Muslims not to fall into a trap intended to "derail the Arab Spring and turn it into a conflict with the West".

The Libyan episode

Initially it was announced by the US officials that the US ambassador in Libya J Christopher Stevens and three other diplomats were killed as anti-US protestors attacked the US Consulate in Ben Ghazi on September 11, 2012 but later it was affirmed that it was a premeditated attack by the Libyan militants that burnt the consulate building. It was a mere coincidence that the Benghazi attack happened on the eleventh anniversary of 9/11 and there were anti-US demonstrations on that day against the anti-Islam film. Administration officials ultimately declared the Benghazi incident to be a "deliberate and organized terrorist attack" carried out by "extremists" affiliated with or sympathetic to al Qaeda. The Benghazi attack had turned into election-year fodder, with Republicans charging that the Democratic Obama administration was caught unprepared for the assault, and Democrats claiming that Republicans were trying to exploit tragic events for political gain.

Anti-Islam and anti-Muslim rhetoric in US elections [36]

In the post-9/11 America, anti-Islam and anti-Muslim rhetoric and hate has become commonplace and increasingly acceptable in political and civic discourse. Anti-Islam and anti-Muslim rhetoric or Islamophobia is no longer questioned, even by our elected representatives. During 2004, 2006, 2008 and 2010 elections many Religious Right leaders and opportunist politicians asserted repeatedly that Islam is not a religion at all but a political cult, that Muslims cannot be good Americans and that mosques are fronts for extremist 'jihadis.' There was a substantial increase in the number of political candidates using Islamophobic tactics in an effort to leverage votes, and use such tactics as a platform to enhance their political visibility.

During 2011 there was phenomenal rise in anti-Islam and anti-Muslim rhetoric particularly by the Republican Party politicians. As the 2012 election nears, some Republican presidential hopefuls and congressional candidates have clearly opted to try to win votes by denigrating Islam and disparaging Muslims.

To borrow Wilfredo Amr Ruiz of Huffington Post, taking the lead in the anti-Muslim frenzy is Herman Cain, who has consistently held a hostile discourse on Islam, belittling almost anything or anyone resonating Muslim. Among many instances we may take as example Cain's opposition to the construction of an Islamic Center in Murfreesboro, Tenn., unreasonably arguing that it's not religious discrimination for a community to ban a mosque. On this same line, Cain has also affirmed that he wouldn't appoint Muslims to his cabinet and even suggested to impose a loyalty test on any Muslim before allowing him to serve in his administration. His anti-Muslim rhetoric returned recently when he expressed that more than half of American Muslims are extremists based on a "trusted adviser" who informed him so. Herman Cain abandoned his White House ambitions in December after a string of accusations of sexual misconduct.

Rick Santorum, another presidential hopeful, has joined the Islam-bashing team, expressing misleading comments on the question of Sharia taking over the U.S. court system. In a recent debate Santorum was even more assertive on his opinion on Muslims. When asked if he would support ethnic and religious profiling he replied: "The folks who are most likely to be committing these crimes ... obviously Muslims would be someone you'd look at, absolutely."

Rep. Michele Bachmann, another presidential aspirant said: "not all cultures are equal, not all values are equal, letting it be known that she thought that people of the Muslim faith had an inferior culture to that of the United States and the West."

To the dismay of seven-million strong American Muslim community, another Republican Presidential candidate, Mitt Romney, appointed Dr. Walid Phares, the author of "Future Jihad: Terrorist Strategies Against America," foreign policy adviser to his team. To his credentials, Phares also worked as an official in the Lebanese Forces, a Christian militia, and other militias that reportedly took part in various massacres of Muslims.

Not surprisingly, the stance on issues related to Islam and American Muslims of another presidential contender and former house speaker, Newt Gingrich, has also been scornful. Falling victim to the Muslim hysteria on the debate on the Park51 project, popularly known as Ground Zero Mosque, in August 2010, Gingrich compared the Islamic Community Center project to building a Nazi monument outside the Holocaust Museum. He also said: "America is experiencing an Islamist cultural-political offensive designed to undermine and destroy our civilization."

Gingrich once suggested that the right of Muslims to build mosques should be infringed upon by the U.S. government until Christians are permitted to build churches in Saudi Arabia, a straightforward suggestion that we violate the Constitution in order to mimic authoritarians. He favors a federal law that would preempt sharia—although not the religious law of any other faith—from being used in American courts, which would be the solution to a total non-problem.

Continuing his tirade against Muslims, Gingrich told a town hall gathering in South Carolina on Jan.17, 2012 that he would only support a Muslim for the presidency if that person would "commit in public to give up Sharia." At the town hall meeting in

West Columbia, S.C., a man asked: "Would you endorse…a Muslim-American, [who] could possibly be running for president, given that we had a woman running for president in Hillary Clinton, and we had a Jewish-American, in Joe Lieberman, running for vice president?" A truly modern person who happened to worship Allah would not be a threat, Gingrich replied but added: "A person who belonged to any kind of belief in Sharia, any kind of effort to impose that on the rest of us, would be a mortal threat." According to Huffington Post, in the past, Gingrich has repeatedly decried Sharia, a legal code derived from Islam, and called for a federal law to pre-emptively bar its use in any U.S. courts. He didn't soften his position on Jan 17, saying his support would be contingent on a candidate's willingness to denounce Sharia.

Negative image of Islam in the USA

Not surprisingly, the anti-Islam and anti-Muslim rhetoric resulted in a negative image of Muslims and their faith among the American masses. According to a Gallup Poll of January 2010, 53 % of Americans have unfavorable views of Islam, more than any other religion, and 43% admit to feeling "at least a little prejudice" toward Muslims. *[Gallup Poll – January 21, 2010]* At least 4 in 10 in every major religious group in the U.S. say Americans are prejudiced toward Muslim Americans, with Jews (66%) saying this, according to the August 2011 Gallup (Middle East) poll. Shockingly, ten years after 9/11, 80 percent of Jews, 59 percent of Catholics, 56 percent of Protestants and 56 percent of Mormons believe that American Muslims are not loyal to their country, the Gallup (Middle East) poll finds. *[Gallup (Middle East) August 2, 2011]* A Newsweek poll of July 2007 indicated that thirty-two percent Americans believe that their fellow citizen Muslims are less loyal to the U.S. Although forty percent of those surveyed believe Muslims in the United States are as loyal to the U.S. as they are to Islam but 46 percent of Americans said the U.S. allows too many immigrants to come here from Muslim countries.

Anti-Islam & anti-Muslim rhetoric in 2016 election campaign

The 2016 election campaign season has brought an unprecedented level of anti-Islam and anti-Muslim rhetoric into presidential politics. Like the previous election cycles, the Republican leaders' anti-Islam bigotry was **extremely disturbing**.

Donald Trump has called for a ban on Muslims from entering into this country. Not surprisingly, on January 27, 2017 President Trump issued an Executive Order banning Muslim immigrants and refugees. *[Read: Trump orders Muslim Ban]*

Trump has advocated for the creation of a database for American Muslims, and has proposed shutting down mosques. Donald Trump has also brought up vivid imagery about killing Muslims with bullets dipped in pig's blood and has claimed that "Islam hates us."

A presidential hopeful, Ben Carson says that a Muslim should not be in charge of running this country. He also claimed that after studying Islam: "…you won't call it a religion, you'll call it a life organization system." Carson said Islam is not consistent with the U.S. Constitution.

Senator Rand Paul stated that he would support restricting immigration into the United States from Muslim countries. Senator Ted Cruze calls for empowering the law enforcement to patrol and secure Muslim neighborhoods before they become "radicalized."

Former Pennsylvania Senator Santorum claimed that the U.S. Constitution does not equally protect the religious liberties of Islam as it does Christianity.

The anti-Islam and anti-Muslim rhetoric was so intensive that on January 17, 2017 about 90 civil advocacy groups organizations issued an open letter denounced the rhetoric and said as anti-Muslim rhetoric became more prevalent during the presidential campaign, the rate of crimes against Muslims also increased. "Establishing anti-Muslim policies, such as forcing Muslims to register on a national scale, goes directly against the American principles of freedom of religious belief and of expression."

Donald Trump: In December 2015, Trump called for a "total and complete shutdown" of Muslims entering the United States. In the press release release accompanying the policy proposal, Trump cited a biased and unscientific poll conducted by Islamophobe Frank Gaffney's Center for Security Policy.

Trump later altered the Muslim ban saying, "We must immediately suspend immigration from any nation that has been compromised by terrorism until such time it's proven that vetting mechanisms have been put in place."

In an interview on Fox News, Trump said if elected he might consider former New York City Mayor Rudolph Giuliani to lead a commission that would "take a very serious look" at "radical Islam" and study his proposed ban on Muslims entering the U.S.

Donald Trump and advisors close to him have publicly said that the Trump administration would revive and expand the federal registry that once targeted visitors mostly from Muslim-majority countries. When asked by a reporter on November 19, 2015 about implementing a Muslim database to combat terrorism, Trump said, "There should be a lot of systems, beyond databases," and emphasized the need for building a wall. When the reporter followed up, he didn't back away from the idea and said, "I would certainly implement that, absolutely."

Trump said he would "shut down" mosques he deemed "extreme" if he is elected president.

Believes "Islam hates us" and American Muslims have a "level of hatred." Trump told CNN's Anderson Cooper: "I think Islam hates us. I think Islam hates us. There is something there, a tremendous hatred," and "and we can't allow people coming into this country who have this hatred of the United States." Responding to a follow-up question by Cooper on whether or not he was talking about violent extremist or Islam itself, Trump said: "It's radical but it's very hard to define, it's very hard to separate because you don't know who's who."

Uses debunked story about killing Muslims with pork-covered bullets. During a campaign rally in South Carolina Trump referenced the long-debunked anecdote that General John Pershing shot Muslims with bullets dipped in pig's blood as part of a counterinsurgency campaign during the Philippine-American War of 1899-1902. Trump told the crowd: "They were having terrorism problems, just like we do." At a California campaign stop Trump again repeated the long-debunked story.

Rick Santorum: In December, 2015, Former Pennsylvania Senator Santorum claimed on Des Moines television station KCCI's "Close Up" program that the U.S. Constitution does not equally protect the religious liberties of Islam as it does Christianity. Santorum also said that he would restore the NSA's illegal metadata spying program to target American Muslims.

Bobi Jindal: Speaking on the Family Research Council's podcast, WASHINGTON WATCH, in January 2015, Bobi Jindal, Republican Governor of Louisiana, reiterated his belief in the existence of Muslim "no-go zones" and said this about Muslim immigrants: "They want to use our freedoms to undermine that freedom in the first place. This is a place where you have freedom of self-determination, freedom of religious liberty, freedom of speech. This is an amazing place and we're a majority Christian country. We're a Judeo-Christian heritage, but we don't discriminate against those that have no beliefs and or have different beliefs."

Ben Carson: Former presidential candidate Ben Carson has claimed that a Muslim should not be in charge of running this country. In a January 2016 debate, Ben Carson spoke about a Muslim plan of "civilization jihad" on America. In an exchange with MEET THE PRESS host Chuck Todd on, September 20, 2015, Ben Carson said: "I would not advocate that we put a Muslim in charge of this nation. I absolutely would not agree with that."

In an interview with American radio show host Hugh Hewitt on October 1, 2015, Carson said that he would be willing to appoint a Muslim to the Supreme Court if they rejected "the lifestyle … which incorporates Sharia." He added that the Senate hearings for a hypothetical nominee would probe the degree to which they support Islamic law, which he described as "more than just a relationship — it's a political aspect and a whole style of living."

On the Mark Levin show, Carson repeated the discredited conspiracy theory about "civilizational jihad," a fantastical plan about a Muslim plot to take over America. Carson declared that after studying Islam: "…you won't call it a religion, you'll call it a life organization system."

Speaking on Meet the Press, Carson said Islam is not consistent with the U.S. Constitution. He also said he would not vote for a Muslim for President. Even after it was pointed out that Article VI of the Constitution prohibits such religious tests for public office, Carson refused to alter his stand and later added that the next president should "be sworn in on a stack of Bibles, not a Qur'an." Asked about his Meet the Press remarks during a CNN interview, Carson added, "I would have problems with somebody who embraced all the doctrines associated with Islam. If they are not willing to reject sharia and all the portions of it that are talked about in the Quran"

Senator Rand Paul: In an interview, Senator Rand Paul stated that he would support restricting immigration into the United States from Muslim countries. "I'm for increasing scrutiny on people who come on student visas from the 25 countries that have significant jihadism. Also, any kind of permanent visas or green cards, we need to be very careful. I don't think we're being careful enough with who we let in." In addition, Paul stated his interest in re-instating the NSEERS (National Security Entry Exit Registration System) Program. "There was a program in place that Bush had put in place—it stood for entry-exit program from about 25 different countries with a lot of Islamic radicals, frankly."

NSEERS was established in 2002 by the Department of Justice and resulted in a wide scale registration program targeting male visitors from countries with Muslim-majority populations. Portions of the discriminatory program were suspended in 2011 and in 2012 the Department of Homeland Security Office of Inspector General called for a full termination of NSEERS as the "database that supports this program is obsolete" and it "does not provide any increase in security."

In December 2016, President Barrack Obama permanently dismantled the regulatory framework behind the National Security Exit-Entry Registration System (NSEERS) also called "Special Registration." CNN quoted Neema Hakim, a DHS spokesman, as saying: "The Department of Homeland Security is removing outdated regulations pertaining to the National Security Entry-Exit Registration Systems (NSEERS) program, with an immediate effective date." By 2011, nearly a decade after the program was enacted, NSEERS had not resulted in a single terrorism conviction. The Department of Homeland Security determined in 2011 that the program was "redundant and did not provide any increase in security," said Hakim.

The Arab American Anti-Discrimination Committee (ADC) led an effort on behalf of over 200 organizations, calling on the Obama administration to end the program. The letter, which was delivered in November 2016, was followed by vigorous advocacy efforts by a large coalition of community organizations, including allies from the Arab, Muslim, and South Asian communities. Resources were leveraged to build a strong diverse coalition to exert pressure that ultimately led to the dismantling of the NSEERS framework. More than 50 members of Congress had called on President Obama to eliminate the NSEERS regulatory framework, referring to it as "a waste of resources, costing American taxpayers more than $10 million annually."

Senator Ted Cruz: In late March 2015, Senator Ted Cruz appeared at the New England Freedom Conference with anti-Muslim hate group leader, Robert Spencer, a blogger whose work was cited approvingly by the Norway terrorist Anders Breivik. Spencer's organization, the American Freedom Defense Initiative (AFDI), is the group behind controversial and provocative anti-Islam metro and bus ads.

In early February 2015, Cruz was the featured speaker at the "Defeat Jihad Summit," an event organized by Frank Gaffney of the Center for Security Policy in Washington, D.C. Gaffney is largely responsible for spinning the myth of the Muslim Brotherhood's alleged infiltration of the United States, and was the source of Representative Michele Bachmann's claim that then-Secretary of State Hillary Clinton's aide, Huma Abedin, was linked to the group. Gaffney is also on the board of the anti-Muslim hate group, the American Freedom Defense Initiative (AFDI), and, along with David Yerushalmi, claims that Sharia law poses a threat to the United States.

Cruz appointed designated hate group leader Frank Gaffney Jr. and other Islamophobes as foreign policy advisers. Gaffney's organization, the Center for Security Policy (CSP), has been designated as a hate group by the Southern Poverty Law Center (SPLC). Cruz's list of foreign policy advisers also included two people who work for CSP - Fred Fleitz and Clare Lopez.

Cruz also appointed Andrew McCarthy, who has echoed Gaffney's view that Muslims seek to impose Islamic law in America. Another appointee was retired Lieutenant General William G. "Jerry" Boykin, who has stated that "[Islam] should not be protected under the First Amendment," that there should be "no mosques in America" and that there can be no interfaith dialogue or cooperation between Muslims and Christians.

Following a terror attack in Brussels, Belguim, Cruz issued a campaign statement calling for the United States to "empower law enforcement to patrol and secure Muslim neighborhoods before they become radicalized." New York Police Department Commissioner William J. Bratton criticized the proposal as "out of line," an assessment that New York City Mayor Bill de Blasio agreed with.

In an op-ed for the New York Daily News, Cruz invoked the discredited claim that Muslims in Europe have set up so-called no-go zones. Titled, "Ted Cruz replies to Bill Bratton on NYPD's demographics unit and the fight against Jihadist terrorism," the op-ed was written in part to defend Cruz's unconstitutional call for law-enforcement to patrol "Muslim neighborhoods."

Cruz national security advisor Jerry Boykin made the false claim that there were "Sharia courts" in Texas and Michigan on the Sandy Rios in the Morning radio show. Citing false claims made by the Family Research Council, where Boykin serves as executive vice president, he said in part: "it is reported that you have a Sharia court in Texas, for example, and Michigan, and you're going to see more of that if people don't wake up and take a stand against this and recognize the nature of the threat." The statement was not rebuked by the Cruz campaign.

Ted Cruze introduces anti-Muslim Brotherhood bill

On January 10, 2017, Senator Ted Cruz introduced a bill to ask the Secretary of State to designate the Muslim Brotherhood as a foreign terrorist organization. The bill is titled the The Muslim Brotherhood Terrorist Designation Act. The bill states that the group has met the criteria of a terrorist group, and thus should be designated as such. A similar bill was introduced in the House by Representative Mario Diaz Balart (R-FL).

Senator Cruz stated, "The U.S. has officially listed individual members, branches, and charities of the Muslim Brotherhood as terrorists, such as Hamas, al Qaeda, and the Palestinian Islamic Jihad, but has not designated the organization as a whole."

Both Senator Cruz and Rep. Diaz Balart introduced similar bills in the 114th Session. The House version was passed by the Judiciary Committee but neither made it to a floor vote.

Not surprisingly the Washington Post and the Huffington Post were quick to point out the real motives behind the bills related to the Muslim Brotherhood.

The Washington Post said it is also likely to have a far-reaching impact on American Muslims at a time when Muslim community leaders say the religious minority is facing the worst harassment it has seen since the aftermath of 9/11.

The Huffington Post pointed out that American Muslim advocates contend that the real intent of Cruz's bill has little to do with foreign policy rather the legislation would enable the U.S. government to target domestic Muslim groups that Cruz and others earnestly believe are part of a massive, covert conspiracy to destroy the U.S. from within.

"Proponents of the measure, including members of Trump's incoming administration, have long used the Muslim Brotherhood label as shorthand for Muslim organizations, politicians and government officials with whom they disagree, and civil rights advocates fear those allegations could be used as pretext to investigate and alienate those who challenge the government's treatment of Muslims" the Washington Post said adding:

"Supporters of the designation have wielded it most frequently against advocacy groups such as the Council on American-Islamic Relations (CAIR), which regularly files lawsuits on behalf of Muslims over alleged discrimination, as well as against charities. They have also used it to attack Democratic members of Congress, Muslim government officials, longtime Hillary Clinton aide Huma Abedin and the Gold Star father Khizr Khan, who criticized Trump at the Democratic National Convention in the summer."

Just two days after Trump's election, reports of anti-Muslim attacks spike [36A]

Less than 48 hours since Donald Trump became the president-elect, reports of Islamophobia are already on the rise. Attacks on Muslim Americans were already high before Trump clinched enough electoral college delegates to win the presidency on Tuesday night (Nov 8), with hate group experts attributing the uptick to his candidacy. But the situation appears to have worsened since his win. Here are just a few examples of Muslim American reporting instances of harassment and assault this week.

At New York University, Muslim students reportedly awoke to discover that the door to their prayer room had been defaced with the word "Trump!"

This morning at the NYU Tandon School of Engineering, Muslim students found "Trump" scrawled on the door of their prayer room, realizing that our campus is not immune to the bigotry that grips America. We awoke on November 9th to a chilling wakeup call. And as we open our eyes and start to move and organize in the face of these new realities, we ask for your support.

At San Jose State University, a campus-wide alert sent to students reported that a woman had her hijab forcibly removed by a "fair skinned male" with such force that it "caused the victim to lose her balance and choked her."

According to campus police, a student at the University of Louisiana, Lafayette was beaten, robbed, and had her hijab ripped off by two men, one of whom wore a white "TRUMP" hat. The suspects reportedly beat the woman with "something metal."

A Muslim woman in Albuquerque, New Mexico claimed on Twitter that a Trump supporter tried to pull off her hijab at her university. She said school officials are now investigating the incident.

A Muslim woman reported that a woman verbally and physically attacked her at a Walmart, tugging at her hijab while saying that such headwear "is not allowed anymore." She then reportedly suggested the woman hang herself.

Consequences of Negative Rhetoric

To borrow Dr. Craig Considine of Rice University, Houston, it would be naive to think that such divisive, hateful rhetoric could subsist without any consequences. An entire group of people has been degraded and villainized for political gain, and the negative consequences have been quite apparent in American communities.

According to the New York Times, "hate crimes against Muslims have soared to their highest levels since the aftermath of the September 11, 2001, attacks, according to data compiled by researchers." Not only have hate crimes against American Muslims risen by 78 percent over the last year, but "attacks on those perceived as Arab rose even more sharply.

"Muslim Americans have reported being scared living in their own country, and Muslim American students have reported high rates of bullying. In fact, according to the Washington Post, "in one survey, nearly one-third of Muslim students in grades three through 12 said they had experienced insults or abuse at least once because of their faith." As one can see, the results of the hateful anti-Islamic rhetoric being spewed in this election are clear and evident.

2016: The worst year for American Muslims since 2001 [37]

Three mosques in California were sent anonymous hate-mail in November warning them that Donald Trump would "cleanse" Muslims from the US the same way "Hitler did to the Jews." This story best reflects the dilemma of the seven-million-strong Muslim American Community during the presidential election year. The year 2016 was perhaps the worst year for American Muslims since 2001. The New York Times pointed out: Hate crimes against American Muslims have soared to their highest levels since the aftermath of the Sept. 11, 2001 attacks, according to data compiled by researchers, an increase apparently fueled by terrorist attacks in the United States and abroad and by divisive language on the campaign trail.

The trend has alarmed hate crime scholars and law-enforcement officials, who have documented hundreds of attacks — including arsons at mosques, assaults, shootings and threats of violence — since the beginning of 2015. Political rhetoric plays an important role in mitigating or fueling hate crimes. USA Today said Trump's inflammatory rhetoric and policy positions have made many groups feel unsafe on Twitter. Trump has suggested banning Muslims from entering the U.S., has said "Islam hates us," suggested the surveillance of mosques, and has talked about "profiling" of Muslims as a response to terrorism.

According to AOL Global, 15 years after the 2001 terrorist attack, Muslim Americans still face discrimination in their everyday lives. Police and news media reports in recent months have indicated a continued flow of attacks, often against victims wearing traditional Muslim garb or seen as Middle Eastern, the New York Times said adding: "Some scholars believe that the violent backlash against American Muslims is driven not only by the string of terrorist attacks in Europe and the United States that began early last year, but also by the political vitriol from candidates like Donald J. Trump, who has called for a ban on immigration by Muslims and a national registry of Muslims in the United States."

A Georgetown University report released in May 2016 similarly found that threats, intimidation and violence against Muslim Americans have surged over the course of the presidential election. According to the report, in the period between March 2015 and March 2016, there have been 180 reported incidents of anti-Muslim violence. These include 12 murders, 34 physical assaults, 56 acts of vandalisms, nine arsons, and eight shootings and bombings. Last September, a leading Muslim civil advocacy group reported that 2016 is on track to be one of the worst years ever for anti-mosque incidents, with a total of 55 cases recorded as of mid-September. The majority of the 2016 incidents have been violent in tone, characterized by intimidation, physical assault and property damage, destruction or vandalism. In the first two weeks of September, three incidents targeting mosques have occurred. The most destructive of these has been in Florida, where a mosque was intentionally set ablaze and a suspect arrested.

Muslim-Americans receiving anonymous robocalls asking for religious affiliation [38]

The New York Daily News reported on November 22, 2016 that several Muslim-Americans received mysterious robocalls asking them whether they identify as a follower of Islam, some of whom are citing the specter of a proposed Muslim registry as cause for alarm over the confounding calls. The robocall appear to have gone out in the past two days asking Muslim-Americans their religious affiliation and assuring them the call would "be kept strictly anonymous and confidential," according to a Facebook post by Shamsiya Shervani. "Do you identify yourself as a MUSLIM, yes press one no press two," the robocall asked, according to Shervani's post.

A 27-year-old man from outside of Philadelphia who wished to remain anonymous told the Daily News that he and his wife received the calls at the same time around 6 p.m. Monday. "I'm not sure how we were singled out, but the fact that we were is disturbing," he said, adding that he witnessed roughly 5 or 6 of his Muslim-American friends from the Philadelphia area who also received the calls. At least two other Muslim-Americans wrote on social media about receiving the robocalls in the past day. Marisa Stroud wrote on Facebook that she received an email on Monday night from a friend who received the call, reporting that no matter whether the call recipient pressed 'yes' or 'no' in response to whether they identified as Muslim, the call hung up. The calls come amid reports of numerous acts of vandalization and violence against Muslim-Americans in the aftermath of the presidential election. As of Nov. 16, the Southern Poverty Law Center reported more than 700 hate crimes carried out since Election Day. Most of the incidents were designated as anti-immigrant, while 51 of them were anti-Muslim, according to tracking by SPLC.

'Trump will cleanse America':
California mosques sent letters threatening genocide against Muslims [39]

In November 2016, three mosques in California were sent anonymous hate-mail warning them that Donald Trump would "cleanse" Muslims from the US the same way "Hitler did to the Jews." The abusive letters have sparked new fears among Muslims, the Council on American-Islamic Relations (CAIR) said. The Muslim advocacy group called for "stepped-up" police protection of mosques after identical letters were sent to three mosques, calling for the genocide of Muslims earlier this week. The Islamic centers of Long Beach and Claremont, along with the Evergreen Islamic Center in San Jose, were sent the letters.

"There's a new sherriff [sic] in town – President Donald Trump," part of the letter read. "He's going to cleanse America and make it shine again. And, he's going to start with you Muslims." The letter ended with: "Long live President Trump and God bless the USA!" CAIR said there have been over 100 anti-Muslim incidents across America since the US election on November 8, and hundreds of reports of hate crimes against various minority groups were recorded by the Southern Poverty Law Center in recent weeks.

Worries grow that election has 'empowered' bigotry [40]

The 54-year-old white man donning a Pirates cap elbowed and then punched in the head the brown-skinned man who sat at the Red Robin restaurant in South Hills Village."I don't want you sitting next to me ... you people," witnesses said they heard Jeffrey Burgess say in addition to anti-Muslim racial slurs during the incident two days before Thanksgiving, according to a criminal complaint filed by Bethel Park police. The assault marked the first high-profile violent act against a person in Western Pennsylvania believed to be motivated by hate or bias since Donald Trump clinched the U.S. presidency, though reports of hate-fueled acts during and in the aftermath of the presidential campaign have proliferated nationwide.

"Anyone even perceived to be a Muslim now is subject to this kind of public harassment or attack," said Ibrahim Hooper, spokesman for the Council on American-Islamic Relations, the nation's largest Muslim advocacy group. "The election really has empowered bigotry and hatred, and it's not only targeting American Muslims.

When pressed, Trump denounced acts of hate during his first interview as president-elect. "If it helps, I will say this, and I will say right to the cameras: Stop it," Trump told "60 Minutes."Pennsylvania GOP spokeswoman Megan Sweeney acknowledged that the presidential race "was a particularly bruising campaign on both sides." "But just like every other presidential election year," she said, "it's up to us as Americans to come together as we move to a new administration."

Concerns about racial prejudice and inequities have persisted for years. Black and white pastors, Muslim clergy, interfaith groups, foundation executives and Roman Catholic Diocese of Pittsburgh Bishop David Zubik are those who have felt compelled to speak out. Many ramped up efforts following nationwide uprisings spurred by the 2014 deaths of Michael Brown in Ferguson, Mo., and Eric Garner in New York — and again in late 2015 following Trump's call for a ban on Muslim entry into the U.S.On Nov. 10, Pittsburgh's Commission on Human Relations urged people to report "instances of unrest or conflict related to the results of the Nov. 8 election."We want people to know that Pittsburgh is a welcoming city and that we thrive because of our diversity," Chairman Carlos Torres said.

US libraries report spike in Islamophobic hate speech since election [41]

In December 2016, a spate of racist incidents has been reported by US librarians in the aftermath of the presidential election. According to data gathered by the American Libraries Association (ALA), copies of the Qur'an and books about Islam have been defaced with swastikas and hate speech at locations across the US. In the worst incident, four days after the election of Donald Trump, a man attempted to forcibly remove a student's hijab as she studied in the library of the University of New Mexico. In November, in libraries as far apart as Oregon and Illinois, copies of the Qur'an have been defaced. In the Illinois incident, police were called in to investigate after seven books were vandalised in Evanston public libraries. As well as swastikas and comments about the prophet Muhammad in a copy of The Koran for Dummies, copies of the Qur'an, textbooks and conservative commentator Glenn Beck's It's All About Islam were also defaced. ALA president Julie Todaro expressed alarm at the increase in the hate crimes perpetrated in libraries. She laid blame upon divisive rhetoric during the recent presidential election campaign. "These crimes – from defacing library materials in public libraries to offensive graffiti on the walls of academic libraries – have begun to mirror the divisive rhetoric of this campaign season," she said. Until now, the ALA had not collected data on hate crimes based on the legal definition, but Todaro was certain that incidents had risen sharply over the past month. "While libraries have always reported on a wide variety of crimes, and we have always had serious incidents of defacing library materials and graffiti, we are just now beginning to hear of many more specific instances of incidents of bigotry and harassment within libraries," she said. The move of hate crimes into public libraries reflects an overall trend in the US, according to the latest FBI statistics. These revealed a 67% jump in anti-Muslim hate crimes in 2015, rising from 154 incidents in 2014 to 257 a year later during the presidential primaries.

Quran and Islam-themed books defaced at library in Evanston, Illinois [42]

According to a Facebook post from Lorena Neal, an employee at the Evanston Public Library in Evanston, Illinois, staff were picking out books to display during an event about the Quran. The event, held in partnership with Northwestern University's Middle East and North African Studies Program, was about Islam in the United States.When staff picked up the Quran and books about the Quran, hateful messages were written inside. One message read, "Bullshit hatred cover to cover" with a swastika drawn underneath.

"Last night, the Evanston Public Library hosted another of our regular lectures on topics involving the Middle East, cosponsored with Northwestern University's Middle East and North African Studies program (MENA). As usual, I selected some books related to the evening's topic (the Qur'an and Islam in America) for the audience to check out. When I opened one of them, I found this. When the other librarians and I checked the section, we found several others that had also been defaced with swastikas and racial slurs. They were not like this a week ago, when one of the other librarians was showing a Muslim gentleman our collection on this subject. A police report has been filed, and we are reporting the incident to the Southern Poverty Law Center for their database on hate crimes. Evanstonians like to think we are safe in a bubble of tolerance, but none of us can afford to pretend that we are not affected by the hatred that surrounds us now. None of us can afford to sit this out, to hope it goes away, and leaves us untouched. Whatever your politics, if this kind of hatred and intolerance disgusts you, speak out today.

Muslim voters inspired

Washington Post [43] reported "Donald Trump's bigotry has inspired U.S. Muslim voters like no candidate before." Petula Dvorak of the Washington Post wrote "Guess what, Donald Trump? Your bigotry has inspired Muslim American voters like no presidential candidate has done before."

Despite the mounting anti-Islamic rhetoric, the trend towards greater civic engagement continued in 2016. Major American Arab and Muslim organizations, like Council on American-Islamic Relations (CAIR), Muslim Public Affairs Council (MPAC) and Arab American Anti-Discrimination Committee (ADC) began actively campaigning to get Muslims involved in civic life – and particularly in voting.

The US Council of Muslim Organizations launched a three-part campaign to combat Islamophobia in the United States, which includes the goal of registering one million Muslim American voters before the 2016 presidential election – a laudable goal given that the total Muslim American population is estimated at 7 million. The US Council of Muslim Organizations includes the American Muslims for Palestine (AMP), the Council on American-Islamic Relations (CAIR), the Islamic Circle of North America, the Muslim Alliance in North America (MANA), the Muslim American Society (MAS), Muslim Legal Fund of America (MLF), Muslim Umma of North America (MUNA),and Ministry of Imam W. Deen Mohammed (The Mosque Cares).

A poll on Muslim American voters was released by the Council on American-Islamic Relations (CAIR) in February 2016. It found that 73% of those polled plan to participate in the primary elections – a small but steady increase from 2014's 69%, and higher than even New Hampshire's 52% or South Carolina's 30% actual primary turnout. Yet while 30% of respondents listed Islamophobia as the "most important issue to you in the 2016 presidential election" with the economy taking second place at 24%.

Tellingly, while 67% stated that they planned to support the Democratic Party, 15% planned to vote Republican, 11% declined to answer, and 7% planned to support a minor party.

President Trump orders Muslim ban

President Trump signed on January 27, 2017 an executive order that severely restricts immigration from seven Muslim countries, suspends all refugee admission for 120 days, and bars all Syrian refugees indefinitely.

"I'm establishing a new vetting measure to keep radical Islamic terrorists out of the United States of America," Trump said during his signing of the order. "We don't want them here. We want to make sure we are not admitting into our country the very threats our soldiers are fighting overseas." According to the executive action, the order bars people from the Muslim-majority countries of Iraq, Syria, Iran, Sudan, Libya, Somalia or Yemen from entering the United States for 30 days and suspends the U.S. Refugee Admissions Program for 120 days. [44]

In an interview with the Christian Broadcast Network, Trump said he plans to help persecuted Christians. In a statement, the American Civil Liberties Union declared Trump's action "just a euphemism for discrimination against Muslims." And in a strongly worded statement, Rabbi Jack Moline, the Interfaith Alliance president, noted that this decision was announced on International Holocaust Remembrance Day. "For decades, the United States has prided itself as a safe bastion for refugees around the globe escaping war and persecution," he said. "President Trump is poised to trample upon that great legacy with a de facto Muslim ban." [45]

Tellingly, it was a coincidence or deliberate, Trump signed Muslim Ban order on International Holocaust Remembrance Day. During World War II, the United States turned back the S.S. St. Louis, a boat of refugees which sought safety from Nazi persecution. They wanted to reach Cuba and then travel to the U.S., however, they were turned away and forced to return to Europe. At least 250 of those Jewish refugees were killed by Nazis, and the boat was turned away for many of the same xenophobic reasons articulated by Trump in his order. Melanie Nezer, vice president for policy and advocacy of HIAS, which was founded in response to the exodus of Jewish emigrants from Russia in the late 19th and 20th centuries, pointed out the world is experiencing one of the worst global refugee crises in history, with at least 65 million people displaced from their homes. It is a bigger refugee crisis than after World War II. What Trump has done will make the crisis worse. [46]

James Zogby, the president of the Arab American Institute, condemned the section of the order that prioritizes Christian refugees over Muslim refugees. It is a policy of "prejudice and fear" intended to dramatically alter U.S. immigration law and to dramatically transform the U.S. refugee resettlement program. "It is bigotry in its worst form," Zogby declared. "I am an Arab American Christian. I resent my religion being privileged over that of Muslims, and I can tell you having spoken with religious leadership in the Middle East, they are deeply resentful and fearful of this because it will put them at risk in the countries they currently live." "We do not want to see Donald Trump favoring Christians. It will hurt them and put them in a dangerous position," Zogby added. "People like Ted Cruz and Senator [Jeff] Sessions and Donald Trump are not the advocates for Christians in the Middle East. They do not need their advocacy. What they need is to be treated as equal citizens in the states where they are and they have relationships with Muslims in those states working toward that end. This will harm them rather than help them." [47]

What has the order done? [48]
• **Suspends the entire US refugee admissions system for 120 days**, even though it was already one of the most rigorous vetting regimens in the world, taking 18 to 24 months and requiring interviews and background checks through multiple federal agencies.
• **Suspends the Syrian refugee program indefinitely.** The US accepted 12,486 Syrian refugees in 2016, compared with about 300,000 received by Germany the same year. Since the Syrian civil war began, Turkey has received about 2.7 million refugees, Lebanon 1 million refugees and Jordan 650,000.
• **Bans entry from seven majority-Muslim countries – Iran, Iraq, Libya, Somalia, Sudan, Syria and Yemen – for 90 days.** Possibly the vaguest of Trump's orders, in practice this has barred even legal US residents, such as green card holders, from re-entry into the country. The order would let the Department of Homeland Security ban more countries at any time.
• **Dual-nationals who are from those seven countries but have an additional passport will also be barred from entering the country for the next 90 days,** according to the State Department. This means that citizens of Iran, Iraq, Libya, Somalia, Sudan, Syria and Yemen who have a passport from another country, such as Britain or France, are also subject to the ban.
• **Prioritizes refugee claims on the basis of religious persecution,** so long as the applicant belongs to a religion that is a minority in their country of origin. This

provision would allow the Trump White House to prioritize Christians from the Middle East over Muslims. In fiscal year 2016, the US accepted 37,521 Christian and 38,901 Muslim refugees. Since 2001, the US has accepted nearly 400,000 Christian refugees and 279,000 Muslim refugees.

• **Lowered the total of 2017 refugees from anywhere to 50,000, down from 110,000.** It has also ordered a review of states' rights to accept or deny refugees; last year Mike Pence, then governor of Indiana, was slapped down by an appeals court when he tried to stop the resettlement of Syrian refugees in his state.

Federal judges block deportations in emergency rulings on Trump's Muslim ban order [49]

Almost immediately after Trump signed the order, protests erupted around the country, with thousands of demonstrators heading to airports to express outrage over the ban. A wave of demonstrations also took place in cities across the UK, from London to Glasgow.Confusion and concern among immigrant advocates mounted throughout the day (on January 28) as travelers from the Middle East were detained at US airports or sent home.

However, Judges in four cities— Alexandria, Virginia; Boston; New York; and Seattle—ruled against the detention of individuals at airports—in cases filed by the ACLU and others. The rulings appear to be limited to those people already at U.S. airports or in transit. They do not appear to say anything about the legality of the president's actions.

On January 28 evening, a federal judge in Brooklyn, New York issued an emergency ruling to prevent the deportation of travelers from seven Muslim-majority countries who have already entered the country, following President Donald Trump's executive order on immigration.

The ruling, a temporary emergency stay, allowed those who landed in the US and hold a valid visa to remain. Federal judges in Virginia, Massachusetts, and Washington also made emergency rulings on various aspects of the executive order.

The ACLU had filed a habeas corpus petition on behalf of two Iraqi refugees, who were detained by border agents at John F. Kennedy airport in New York City, despite having previously been granted asylum and holding valid visas. Both men were later released.

"There is imminent danger that, absent the stay of removal, there will be substantial and irreparable injury to refugees, visa-holders, and other individuals from nations subject to the January 27, 2017, Executive Order," US District Judge Ann Donnelly said in her ruling.

In Virginia, Judge Leonie M. Brinkema of the U.S. District Court for the Eastern District of Virginia issued a temporary restraining order affecting 63 people detained at Dulles International Airport outside of Washington, D.C. It ordered authorities to "permit lawyers access to all legal permanent residents being detained" at Dulles, and said authorities are "forbidden from removing" the permanent residents for seven days. [NPR]

Judge Thomas S. Zilly of the U.S. District Court of the Western District of Washington at Seattle granted an emergency stay of removal for two people, which orders authorities not to remove them from the country pending a hearing later this week. [NPR]

In Massachusetts, US District Judge Allison Burroughs and Magistrate Judge Judith G. Dein ruled early Sunday morning (January 29) for a temporary seven-day stay on the removal, detainment, or additional screenings of lawful permanent US residents under the authority of Trump's executive order. The judges also expanded the stay to pertain to citizens, visa-holders, approved refugees, and individuals from all nations named in the executive order.

The ACLU of Massachusetts, along with other immigration lawyers, filed the suit in federal court on behalf of two detained Iranian professors. Mazdak Pourabdollah Tootkaboni and Arghavan Louhghalam, two associate professors at the University of Massachusetts-Dartmouth who are both Iranian nationals and lawful permanent US residents were being detained at Logan Airport in Boston.

Reuters reported that a senior Homeland Security official said roughly 375 travelers were affected by the order: One hundred and nine in transit to the United States were denied entry into the country and another 173 people were stopped by airlines from boarding an aircraft to the United States. [NPR]

Border agents defy courts on Trump travel ban [50]

Federal judges in New York, Virginia and Massachusetts **ordered a temporary halt** to the president's deportation of people who had arrived in the US with valid visas.

Customs and Border Protection (CBP) agents defied the orders of federal judges regarding Donald Trump's travel bans, according to members of Congress and attorneys who rallied protests around the country in support of detained refugees and travelers from seven Muslim-majority countries.

Four Democratic members of the House of Representatives arrived at Dulles airport in Virginia on word that people had been detained and denied access to lawyers. "We have a constitutional crisis today," representative Don Beyer wrote on Twitter. "Four members of Congress asked CBP officials to enforce a federal court order and were turned away."

Representative Jamie Raskin, also at the airport, tweeted that the federal agency had given "no answers yet" about whether agents were ignoring the courts. Raskin joined several other attorneys there, including Damon Silvers, special counsel at AFL-CIO, one of the groups trying to help visa holders.

"As far as I know no attorney has been allowed to see any arriving passenger subject to Trumps exec order at Dulles today," Silvers tweeted. "CBP appears to be saying people in their custody not 'detained' technically & Dulles international arrivals areas not in the United States."

"Rogue customs and Border Patrol agents continue to try to get people on to planes," Becca Heller, director of the International Refugee Assistance Project, told reporters at JFK airport in New York. "A lot of people have been handcuffed, a lot of people who don't speak English are being coerced into taking involuntary departures."

At the height of protests at JFK about 5,000 protesters swarmed terminal four after an estimated 17 passengers, including green-card holders, were detained for hours.

In New York, though, lawyers described official resistance to requests for basic information on those being held.

An estimated 400 lawyers have signed up to represent detainees, and dozens flocked to airports, many with signs in Arabic and Farsi to alert relatives that attorneys could help them find lost loved ones. On January 28 and 29, hundreds attended rallies against Trump's "extreme vetting order" at 29 cities and airports across the country.

More reactions to Muslim Ban

Senators Lindsey Graham and John McCain said in a joint statement the move "sends a signal, intended or not, that America does not want Muslims coming into our country. That is why we fear this executive order may do more to help terrorist recruitment than improve our security." [51]

"Tears are running down the cheeks of the Statue of Liberty tonight as a grand tradition of America, welcoming immigrants, that has existed since America was founded has been stomped upon," said Senate Democratic leader Chuck Schumer of New York. [52]

Senator Chris Murphy said Trump is pursuing misguided policies rooted in bigotry and fear.In an opinion piece in Huffington Post he said today's announcement is anchored in his campaign rhetoric, and the fact that every country on today's list is a Muslim-majority nation confirms that he meant what he said – that Muslims are dangerous and need to be treated differently than any other set of people.

Trump has now handed ISIS a path to rebirth. They can and will use his announcement today as confirmation that America is at war with Muslims, especially those Muslims living in desperate circumstances. Their recruitment bulletin boards will light up with new material. Their entreaties to would-be lone wolf attackers in America will have new energy and purpose. All the work we have done to cut down on extremist recruitment at home and abroad now goes out the window. It's a new day for terrorist recruiters. [53]

Attorneys general from 16 U.S. states, including California, New York and Pennsylvania, issued a joint statement condemning President Donald Trump's executive order restricting immigration from seven Muslim-majority countries. "We are committed to working to ensure that as few people as possible suffer from the chaotic situation that it has created," the statement said. [54]

Lawsuits filed challenging Trump's Muslim ban [55]

On January 30, 2017, at least two lawsuits were filed against against President's Trump's "Muslim ban" executive order issued three days ago. In Seattle, Washington, State Attorney General Bob Ferguson announced that he is challenging President Donald Trump's executive order banning Muslim immigrants and refugees, calling it unconstitutional and asking for a temporary restraining order. In Washington DC, the Council on American-Islamic Relations (CAIR) filed the federal lawsuit on behalf of more than 20 "John Doe" individuals who say President Donald Trump's unilateral "Muslim ban" action is unconstitutional. CAIR lists Trump, new Homeland Security Secretary John Kelly, the State Department and the director of national intelligence as defendants in its lawsuit.

Washington State files lawsuit

Washington State Attorney General Bob Ferguson said in a statement that "No one is above the law — not even the President." "And in the courtroom, it is not the loudest voice that prevails. It's the Constitution." In documents filed Jan. 30 against Trump, the U.S. Department of Homeland Security and high-ranking Trump Administration officials, Ferguson argues that the order violates the U.S. Constitution's guarantee of equal protection and the First Amendment's Establishment Clause, infringes individuals' constitutional right to due process and contravenes the federal Immigration and Nationality Act.

Ferguson's complaint asserts that the President's actions are "separating Washington families, harming thousands of Washington residents, damaging Washington's economy, hurting Washington-based companies, and undermining Washington's sovereign interest in remaining a welcoming place for immigrants and refugees."

Tech companies joined the Washington state government to fight against Donald Trump's Muslim ban order. At least three tech companies — Microsoft, Amazon, and Expedia —joined that legal fight. A Microsoft spokesman told Reuters that the company is providing information about the effect of the order in order to "be supportive." They also would "be happy to testify further if needed." Microsoft, Amazon, and Expedia are all based in the Seattle, Washington area. Other tech company executives, ranging from Tesla CEO Elon Musk to Facebook chief Mark Zuckerberg, have spoken out against the order.

CAIR files broadest lawsuit

In Washington DC., the Council on American-Islamic Relations (CAIR), the largest Muslim civil advocacy group, filed the federal lawsuit on behalf of more than 20 "John Doe" individuals who say President Donald Trump's unilateral "Muslim ban" action is unconstitutional. "Our First Amendment is under attack."

The lawsuit, filed in the U.S. District Court - Eastern District of Virginia, states that the order is unconstitutional because its apparent purpose and underlying motive is to ban people of the Islamic faith in Muslim-majority countries from entering the United States.

Twelve anonymous plaintiffs in the suit fear the worst. A Somali on a student visa, a Syrian refugee on asylum, and a Sudanese permanent resident petitioning for his wife to rejoin him are among those arguing that they stand to lose their ability to become U.S. citizens on the basis of religious discrimination.

"It is not a matter of legality; it is a matter of morality and there is a big difference. If you want to play it by law, yes slavery was legal, but it was wrong. Preventing women from voting in America was legal, but it was wrong. Preventing refugees from entering now is wrong," said CAIR National Executive Director Nihad Awad.

"Our First Amendment is under attack. We, as attorneys, are foot soldiers of the American Constitution and took an oath to protect all from being targeted by the government because of their faith," Shereef Akeel, an attorney who is co-counsel on the lawsuit, said in a press release.

The lawsuit comes as the acting Attorney General, Sally Yates, ordered Justice Department lawyers to not defend the controversial executive order in court. "For as long as I am the acting attorney general," Ms Yates said, "the Department of

Justice will not present arguments in defence of the executive order, unless and until I become convinced that it is appropriate to do so." Not surprisingly, Sally Yates was fired by the Trump administration.

Tech companies joined the Washington state government to fight against Donald Trump's Muslim ban order. At least three tech companies — Microsoft, Amazon, and Expedia —joined that legal fight. A Microsoft spokesman told Reuters that the

Donald Trump rolls out Muslim Ban 2.0

On March 6, 2017, President Donald Trump issued a new Muslim ban executive order to temporarily halt entry to the U.S. for people from six Muslim nations who are seeking new visas. The revised Muslim ban order leaves Iraq off the list of banned countries but still affects would-be visitors from Iran, Syria, Somalia, Sudan, Yemen and Libya."

The Washington Post reported that even before the ink was dry Democrats and civil liberties groups asserted that the new order was legally tainted in the same way as the first one: It was a thinly disguised Muslim ban. That seems to portend more litigation — though how soon remains unclear. Washington Attorney General Bob Ferguson, who had successfully sued to have the ban blocked, said in a statement that the rescinding of Trump's first ban showed it was "indefensible — legally, constitutionally and morally." He said the state was reviewing its next legal steps and noted the president had "capitulated on numerous key provisions blocked by our lawsuit."

On March 8, 2017, Hawaii became the first US State to challenge President Donald Trump's new Muslim Ban order. The State of Hawaii lawyers have called the travel ban nothing more than "Muslim Ban 2.0" and asked a federal judge to temporarily block the order. "Nothing of substance has changed: There is the same blanket ban on entry from Muslim-majority countries (minus one)," Hawaii Attorney General Doug Chin said of the new order. "Under the pretense of national security, it still targets immigrants and refugees. It leaves the door open for even further restrictions," Chin added. U.S. District Court Judge Derrick Watson in Hawaii said the state could add to its initial lawsuit, which had challenged Trump's original ban signed in January 2017.

Hawaii says its state universities would be harmed by the order because they would have trouble recruiting students and faculty. It also says the island state's economy would be hit by a decline in tourism. Hawaii asserts that the new order violates the establishment clause of the First Amendment because it is essentially a Muslim ban.

Federal judges in Hawaii and Maryland have blocked President Donald Trump's Muslim Ban 2.0. In their ruling both judges cited Trump's statements about Muslims during the presidential campaign.

On March 15, US District Court Judge Derrick Watson in Hawaii ordered a temporary restraining order nationwide, hours before it was set to go into effect on March 16. Another federal judge in Maryland next day specifically blocked the 90-day ban on immigration for citizens of six Muslim countries.

In a 43-page ruling, Judge Watson concluded that the new executive order failed to pass legal muster at this stage and the state had established "a strong likelihood of success" on their claims of religious discrimination. "The illogic of the Government's contentions is palpable. The notion that one can demonstrate animus toward any group of people only by targeting all of them at once is fundamentally flawed," Watson wrote. "Equally flawed is the notion that the Executive Order cannot be found to have targeted Islam because it applies to all individuals in the six referenced countries," Watson added. "It is undisputed, using the primary source upon which the Government itself relies, that these six countries have overwhelmingly Muslim populations that range from 90.7% to 99.8%."

"It would therefore be no paradigmatic leap to conclude that targeting these countries likewise targets Islam," Watson added. "Certainly, it would be inappropriate to conclude, as the Government does, that it does not." "When considered alongside the constitutional injuries and harms ... and the questionable evidence supporting the Government's national security motivations, the balance of equities and public interests justify granting the Plaintiffs' (request to block the new order)," Watson wrote.

The case in Maryland was brought by three organizations and six people, claiming the order affected their work or prevented their family members from the affected countries from getting visas to enter the United States. Maryland Judge Theodore Chuang blocked only the provision of the new order affecting the issuance of visas to those from the six affected countries. He said those suing had "not provided a sufficient basis" for him to declare the other sections invalid. In Hawaii, U.S. District

Judge Derrick K. Watson went further, also suspending the portion of the order that affected refugees.

Chuang wrote that he "should not, and will not, second-guess the conclusion that national security interests would be served by the travel ban," but if the national security rationale was secondary to an attempt to disfavor a particular religion, he had no choice but to block the executive order. "In this highly unique case," he wrote, "the record provides strong indications that the national security purpose is not the primary purpose for the travel ban."

Judges points to cable news comments

Both Watson and Chuang brought up specific statements made by the President and Stephen Miller, one of his top policy advisers and a reported architect of the original order, in cable news interviews, the CNN reported.

Trump made plain his opposition to Islam in an interview with CNN's Anderson Cooper in 2016, asserting: "I think Islam hates us." Cooper asked then-candidate Trump in the interview to clarify if he meant Islam as a whole or just "radical Islam," to which Trump replied, "It's very hard to separate. Because you don't know who's who." The judge cited this interview as an example of the "religious animus" behind the executive order and quoted Trump telling Cooper: "We can't allow people coming into this country who have this hatred of the United States."

Likewise, the decision cited an interview Miller had on Fox News following the legal struggles of the first executive order last month, which the legal opponents of the ban have emphasized repeatedly. In a February interview, Miller downplayed any major differences the new executive order would have from the first and said it would be "responsive to the judicial ruling" holding it up and have "mostly minor technical differences." "Fundamentally, you're still going to have the same basic policy outcome for the country," Miller added.

"These plainly-worded statements, made in the months leading up to and contemporaneous with the signing of the Executive Order, and, in many cases, made by the Executive himself, betray the Executive Order's stated secular purpose," Watson wrote. "Any reasonable, objective observer would conclude, as does the court for purposes of the instant Motion for TRO, that the stated secular purpose of the Executive Order is, at the very least, 'secondary to a religious objective' of temporarily suspending the entry of Muslims," he added.

Maryland Judge agreed

"These statements, which include explicit, direct statements of President Trump's animus toward Muslims and intention to impose a ban on Muslims entering the United States, present a convincing case that the first executive order was issued to accomplish, as nearly as possible, President Trump's promised Muslim ban," Chuang wrote on Thursday.

"In particular, the direct statements by President Trump and (former New York City Mayor Rudy) Giuliani's account of his conversations with President Trump reveal that the plan had been to bar the entry of nationals of predominantly Muslim countries deemed to constitute dangerous territory in order to approximate a Muslim ban without calling it one precisely the form of the travel ban in the first executive order."

Lee Gelernt, an ACLU lawyer representing those challenging the ban in Maryland, said the ruling in his case was significant in that "two judges have looked at the revised order, and both have come to the same conclusion that it continues to be a Muslim ban." He said he was also encouraged that yet another judge was willing to look beyond the order itself to the president's comments and other potential evidence of discriminatory intent.

Muslim Ban 3.0: Laptops, tablets banned on Middle East-US flights

On March 21, 2017, the United States banned laptops, e-readers, cameras, tablets, printers, electronic games, and portable DVD players on flights from eight Muslim countries. Passengers on flights originating in eight Muslim countries are now prohibited from carrying any electronic device bigger than a mobile phone, the Department of Homeland Security said.

The DHS said the ban was necessary as "terrorist groups continue to target commercial aviation and are aggressively pursuing innovative methods to undertake their attacks, to include smuggling explosive devices in various consumer items.

"Based on this information, Secretary of Homeland Security John Kelly and Transportation Security Administration Acting Administrator Huban Gowadia have determined it is necessary to enhance security procedures for passengers at certain last point of departure airports to the United States," the statement said.

The ban will apply to nonstop flights to the US from 10 international airports serving the cities of Cairo in Egypt; Amman in Jordan; Kuwait City in Kuwait; Casablanca in Morocco; Doha in Qatar; Riyadh and Jeddah in Saudi Arabia; Istanbul in Turkey; and Abu Dhabi and Dubai in the United Arab Emirates, until the threat changes.

The procedures will affect nine airlines: Royal Jordanian Airlines, Egypt Air, Turkish Airlines, Saudi Airlines, Kuwait Airways, Royal Air Maroc, Qatar Airways, Emirates, and Etihad Airways.

In all, an estimated 50 flights each day into the United States would be affected, according to the New York Times. One of the world's busiest airports, in Abu Dhabi, already requires American-bound passengers to undergo strict screening by United States customs officials before boarding flights. Abu Dhabi is one of 15 airports in the world to employ the Homeland Security preclearance techniques.

Britain followed the United States in banning carry-on electronic goods from passenger cabins on inbound flights from Middle Eastern and North African nations.

References

1. Sam Hamod is a former advisor to the U.S. State Dept; founder of 3rd World News (Wash, DC);Director of The Islamic Center (Wash, DC); Professor at Princeton, Michigan, Howard and Iowa (ret.)." He is a Lebanese-American born in Indiana, according to another biography. He is also president of the American-Islamic Institute. He established "Today's Alternative News" in 2000.

2. It really is a crusade By Gary Leupp - Counter Punch, May 27, 2005

3. Ibid.

3A. John Feffer, the co-director of Foreign Policy In Focus at the Institute for Policy Studies in Washington, DC.

4. U.S. military taught officers: Use 'Hiroshima' tactics for 'total war' on Islam by Noah Shachtman and Spencer Ackerman - May 11, 2012

4A. Ibid.

5. Ibid.

6. Ibid.

7. In an Unseen Front in the War on Terrorism, America is Spending Millions...To Change the Very Face of Islam by By David E. Kaplan - U. S. News & World Report, April 17, 2005

8. Ibid.
9. Ibid.
10. Ibid.

10A. "American Jihad:" Representations of Islam in America After 9/11" by Mucahit Bilici, University of Michigan, Ann Arbor. This paper was delivered at the 32nd annual conference of the Association of Muslim Social Scientists of North America, held at Indiana University, Bloomington, Indiana on September 26-28, 2003

11. Civil Democratic Islam: Partners, Resources, and Strategies by the Rand Corporation - March 2004

12. US Neo-Cons: From Nation-Building to Religion-Building by Jim Lobe Inter Press Service, April 7, 2004

13. US strategy in the Muslim World after 9/11 by the Rand Corporation - December 2004

14. Building Moderate Muslim Networks by the Rand Corporation - March 2007

15. The Tennessean, October 24, 2010.]

16. Islamophobia – now in American children's textbooks – American Muslim Perspective – April 12, 2010]

17. Kids' coloring book promotes intolerance ABC-Local Chicago – August 30, 2011

18. The News, Pakistan – September 20, 2012

19. Islamic Invitation Turkey – September 30, 2012

20. The Muslim Times – September 20, 2012

21. Al Jazeera/Associated Press – October 1, 2012

22. Al Manar – September 26, 2012

23. Free Speech or Inciting to Riot? -- An Analysis By Lawrence Davidson – Op Ed News September 17, 2012

24. Hidden causes of the Muslim protests By Robert Wright - The Atlantic – September 16, 2012

25. They dislike us for more than bad movies by Arlen Grossman - OpEd News - September 18, 2012

26. The Reality Behind the "Free Speech" Argument America and the Muslims by Esam Al Amin September 15, 2012

27. Ibid.

28. Conservatives, Democrats and the convenience of denouncing free speech By Glenn Greenwald The Guardian - September 16, 2012

29. The Power plays Behind "The Innocence of Muslims" By Thierry Meyssan – Information Clearance House, September 25, 2012

30. The Moslem World's Rage; Justified or Misplaced? By Soraya Sepahpour-Ulrich – OpEd September 19, 2012

31. Glenn Greenwald Op. Cite.

32. US Media War on Islam: Washington's war on Islam supported by media scoundrels by Stephen Lendman OpEdNews - September 21, 2012

33. Reuters Sept. 21, 2012

34. The Power plays Behind "The Innocence of Muslims" By Thierry Moyooan Information Clearance House, September 25, 2012]

35. US Media War on Islam: Washington's war on Islam supported by media scoundrels by Stephen Lendman OpEdNews - September 21, 2012

36. AMP Report – February 7, 2012

36A. Think Progress – November 10, 2016

37. AMP Report – December 31, 2016

38. The New York Daily News

39. RT November 27

40. Pittsburgh Tribune-Review December 10, 2016

41. The Guardian December 12, 2016

42. Mathew Rodriguez – MIC.COM – November 23, 2016

43. Washington Post, February 25, 2016

44. Washington Post January 28, 2017

Chapter V

Anti-Islam & Anti-Muslim campaign sweeps Europe

- The politics behind the anti-Muslim Dutch cartoons
- The Fitna film
- Council of Europe Commissioner for Human Rights speaks on Islamophobia
- Public opinion response: limit religious freedom of Muslims
- Politicians should not ride the populist wave
- Bigotry is not part of European values
- Amnesty International report also expresses concern
- Nexus of European and US Islamophobists
- Norwegian far right defend Breivik's views on Islam
- Petitions to Stop Muslim Immigration Into Australia, Canada, Japan, Europe & US
- The Israeli connection
- Free to hate: The rise of the right in post-communist eastern Europe
- Pope's thinly veiled attack on Islam

Impact of anti-Islam and anti-Muslim rant in Europe:
- France & Germany
- The Dutch Freedom Party
- French election of 2012 and Islamophobia
- Islam not recognized as a religion in Italy
- Extremist Swede to finance anti-Islam center in Germany
- In search of heterodox (moderate) Muslims
- France likely to close more than 100 mosques
- Anti-Islam movement PEGIDA stages protests across Europe
- Anti-Muslim sentiment in Germany hits record high
- Anti-Muslim sentiment on rise in Europe due to migration and ISIL as continent rejects multi-cultural society
- Why Europe's far-right political parties are gaining ground?
- Europe's Far Right meet in Koblenz, Germany
- Terrorist attacks in France

Anti-Islam & Anti-Muslim campaign sweeps Europe: For centuries European Orientalists have been working to defame and ridicule Islam and demean Muslims through their 'scholarly' enterprises. To borrow Swiss journalist and author, Roger Du Pasquier [1] , "one is forced to concede that Oriental studies in the West have not always been inspired by the purest spirit of scholarly impartiality, and it is hard to deny that some Islamicists and Arabists have worked with the clear intention of belittling Islam and its adherents." At the same time, J.A. Progler, Professor of Social Studies at CUNY, Brooklyn College, says "Critics generally agree that Orientalist pursuits of knowledge are inextricably tied to colonial and imperial power, and that the West's self-image has been cultivated in a binary relationship with Islamic culture. [2]

Similarly, Edward Said interprets orientalism as a European theory that both serves and justifies European and occidental domination of the Orient. In the politics and ideology of orientalism, the Orient is an artificially produced Orient, one produced for European colonial and post-colonial purposes. Edward Said therefore says that representations of Islam and Muslims in the contemporary West are merely the consequences of producing an image of Muslims and of the 'Orient' for domestic purposes. According to Edward Said Western Orientalist writers participated in the construction of an image of the Orient favorable to the political, economic, and cultural interests of Western countries. " A great deal of what was considered learned Orientalist scholarship in Europe pressed ideological myths into service, even as knowledge seemed genuinely to be advancing." [3] Christian picture of Islam was intensified in innumerable ways, including during the Middle Ages and early Renaissance a large variety of poetry, learned controversy, and popular superstition. [4] I wish I could say that general understanding of the Middle East, the Arabs and Islam in the United States has improved somewhat, but alas, it really hasn't...... Twenty-five years after my book's publication Orientalism once again raises the question of whether modern imperialism ever ended, or whether it has continued in the Orient since Napoleon's entry into Egypt two centuries ago. [5]

Islamophobia as neo-orientalism in Europe

Anti-Islam and anti-Muslim articles can be found in very different politically oriented Journals and newspapers, marginal media of sub-cultural streams as well as central organs of the leading intellectual and administrative groups in Europe. These articles and reports have dramatically increased after 9/11 in all the countries in our research focus.

According to Sarajevo Prof. Dr. Enes Karić, hundreds of different publications, books, treatises and newspaper articles now deal with the issue of Islam in the West. These hundreds of publications on Islam in the West had what may be called direct causes. One of these, known is the Rushdie affair, gave rise to dozens of anti-Islamic books, and when a group of Muslims burned Rushdie's book in Bradford as a sign of protest (an unseemly act, certainly, deserving condemnation), throughout the West Muslims were described in abusive terms, and there were frequent and wholly irrelevant comparisons made between Muslims and Nazis. Muslims were described in the media as uncivilized and intolerant, and it was often suggested that Muslims were such 'by the very nature of their faith.' [6]

While the English-speaking regions were particularly inundated with the anti-Muslims campaign that arose from the Rushdie affair, in the French-speaking regions the balance was restored by media coverage in 1994 and 1995 of l'affaire des foulards, when Muslim girls in hundreds of French schools were looked at askance for wearing hijab, and in some parts of the country there were even written decrees banning the wearing of hijab in schools. [7]

To judge from the treatment it receives in many western institutional circles, Islam is being promoted as the 'new enemy of the liberal democracies of the West', a trend culminating in the jejune study by Samuel Huntington entitled The Clash of Civilizations, of which much has been said in this part of the world too. [8]

In the post-9/11 world, like the USA, the neo-orientalism in Europe came in the shape of Islamophobia according to Frank Ejby Poulsen, doctoral student at the European University Institute, Italy.

In an article - Islamophobia as neo-orientalism - Poulsen says: "Islamophobia can be described as attitudes or actions. As attitudes it sees Islam e.g. as a retarded monolithic block remote from Western values and permeable to progressive change. This conception is spreading in the West, by means of neo-orientalism. Islamophobia is threatening to flourish, particularly in Western societies. It is a concept that is difficult to define, and the attempts to define it have been criticized. " [9]

Tracing the terminology of Islamophobia, Poulsen pointed out that a UK-based NGO, The Runnymede Trust, published a study in 1997 entitled "Islamophobia: A Challenge for Us All" where it defines Islamophobia with the following characteristics: Islam is seen as a monolithic bloc, static and unresponsive to change; Islam is seen as separate and "other"; it does not have values in common with other cultures, is not affected by them and does not influence them; Islam is seen as inferior to the West; it is seen as barbaric, irrational, primitive, and sexist; Islam is seen as violent, aggressive, threatening, supportive of terrorism, and engaged in a clash of civilizations; Islam is seen as a political ideology, used for political or military advantage; criticisms made of 'the West' by Islam are rejected out of hand; hostility towards Islam is used to justify discriminatory practices towards Muslims and exclusion of Muslims from mainstream society; anti-Muslim hostility is seen as natural and normal [10].

Another pertinent publication on Islamophobia comes from the European Union Monitoring Centre on Racism and Xenophobia, Poulsen says adding: "Thus, *JP* (*Jyllands-Posten*) and co. are not actively discriminating Muslims, but the publication of the cartoons – for the reasons they were published, and precisely in the context they were publish – contributes to the spread of Islamophobia as an attitude."

Paulson argues that this Islamophobia is perhaps fashioned by an already existing orientalism – orientalism in literature that transformed into orientalism and neo-orientalism in political science.

"Orientalism was characterised, as in the famous book by Edward Said, by old-fashioned and prejudiced Western interpretations of Eastern cultures and peoples. In a romantic vein, it is e.g. *The Turkish Bath* by Ingres: Orient associated with lascivious eroticism," Paulin pointed out.

Nowadays, the same prejudiced interpretations persist, albeit in a negative form, he says adding that many see Islam as limited to the Middle-East, oppressing women, as corresponding to a less advanced stage of Western civilization (i.e. the Middle-Ages), as a unity, epitomized by the radicals and extremists, etc.

"Orientalism and Neo-orientalism appeared in Middle-East academic experts circle as two ways to explain the alleged impossible democratization of Muslim countries," Paulin quotes Yahya Sadowski, the author of "The New Orientalism and the Democracy Debate," and says: For orientalists, it was the "weak society" that explained this. With the "weak society" making a revolution in Iran in 1979, the paradigm had to be thought anew. Neo-orientalists now believe that the reason why Muslim countries are resilient to democratization is exactly the opposite: a "weak state".

Paulin pointed out that Neo-orientalists such as Daniel Pipes, Patricia Crone, Michael Mann, José Ghilerme Merquior, and John Hall are influential in US policy circles.

But why is Neo-orientalism so influent?, he questions and went on to say: " One possible answer is that seeing Muslim countries this way and associating them with barbarism, provide a strong symbolic violence in Western imaginaries. This serves as a hegemonic strategy for legitimizing colonialist economic or political projects (8). In other words, since the end of the cold war and 9/11, there is a hegemonic Western centre that is facing "irrationality", and "anarchy" in the non-Western periphery, which has to be "rationalized" and "ordered" in order to avoid a "clash of civilizations." [11]

In another article titled, "for a West-Islam dialogue instead of cartoons," Paulin said freedom of speech shall not serve as a folding-screen to the spread of Islamophobic feelings. He went on to say:

"Furthermore, publishing cartoons representing Muhammad or Muslims as extremists is spreading Islamophobia by blurring nuances, enmeshing extremists with moderates, avoiding the presentation of moderate Muslims' opinions, spreading the image of a Middle-Age Islam as the only existing Islam, thus maintaining ignorance about Islam and the Islamic world by focusing on negative aspects, and perpetuating the conception that Islam is necessarily remote from Western values. This was the work of a tabloid and not of a responsible newspaper." [12]

The politics behind the anti-Muslim Dutch cartoons

Many analysts in the West argue that if Adolf Hitler and Joseph Goebbels could persuade an entire nation to hate Jewish citizens, and using the same methods, the Western Civilization should be able to evoke worldwide loathing, hatred, and contempt for Islam and Muslims.

Goebbels believed that arguments that will not persuade (and may even alienate) an educated person are often effective in persuading the masses. Hence, according to Hitler, all propaganda has to be popular and has to adapt its spiritual level to the perception of the least intelligent of those towards whom it intends to direct itself." [13]

In the post-9/11 era we are witnessing an indiscriminate propaganda campaign that uses the most inflammatory language possible, in effective and synergistic combination with pictures and often distorted facts, to dehumanize Muslims and evoke worldwide hatred of Islam and Muslims.

As the modern psychology suggests, the human brain is designed to process images, not words. Hence Napoleon Bonaparte was right when he said, "a picture is worth a thousand words." This adage refers to the notion that a complex idea can be conveyed with just a single still image.

Political cartoons are among the most effective means of communication and propaganda. Perhaps one of the most effective hate cartoons ever created was Grant Hamilton's "The Spanish Brute." It is said that this cartoon and material like it, were instrumental in goading the United States into the Spanish-American War. Since the abuse of women is particularly offensive to Euro-American audiences, First World War propagandists eagerly added this theme to their cartoons.

The same principle was applied when on September 30, 2005, a Danish newspaper, *Jyllands-Posten,* published cartoons denigrating Prophet of Islam, Mohammad. The cartoons utilize the common anti-Islam and anti-Muslim propaganda themes to incite hatred against the faith of 1.5 billion people. Bluntly linking Islam with terrorism, one cartoon shows Muhammad with a bomb in his turban, with a lit fuse and the Islamic creed (shahadah) written on the bomb. Another cartoon shows Muhammad wearing an imamah (turban) and prepared for battle, with a sword in his hand. He is flanked by two women in niqabs. Yet another cartoon shows Muhammad, dressed like a mullah, stands on a cloud as if in Heaven, greeting freshly arrived dead suicide bombers with "Stop Stop vi er løbet tør for Jomfruer!" Translated in English: "Stop, stop, we have run out of virgins!", an allusion to the neo-orientalists claim that seventy two virgins promised to martyrs (known as Shaheed).

On 27 October 2005, a number of Muslim organizations filed a complaint with the Danish police saying that Jyllands-Posten had committed an offence under section 140 and 266b of the Danish Criminal Code. On 6 January 2006, the Regional Public Prosecutor in Viborg discontinued the investigation as he found no basis for concluding that the cartoons constituted a criminal offence. His reason is based on his finding that the article concerns a subject of public interest.

Two imams who had been granted sanctuary in Denmark, dissatisfied with the reaction of the Danish Government and Jyllands-Posten, created a dossier containing a forty-three-page document entitled "Dossier about championing the prophet Muhammad peace be upon him." This consisted of several letters from Muslim organizations explaining their case including allegations of the mistreatment of Danish Muslims.

Appended to the dossier were multiple clippings from Jyllands-Posten, multiple clippings from Weekendavisen, some clippings from Arabic-language papers. The imams said that the three additional images were sent anonymously by mail to Muslims who were participating in an online debate on Jyllands-Posten, and were apparently included to illustrate the perceived atmosphere of Islamophobia in which they lived.

At the December 6, 2005 summit of the Organisation of the Islamic Conference (OIC), with many heads of state in attendance, the dossier was handed around on the sidelines first session. The OIC eventually issued an official communiqué, demanding that the United Nations impose international sanctions upon Denmark.

Four months later, In February, 2006,Muslims protested across the Islamic world, some of which escalated into violence with instances of firing on crowds of protestors resulting in a total of more than 100 reported deaths, including the bombing of the Danish embassy in Pakistan and setting fire to the Danish Embassies in Syria, Lebanon and Iran, storming European buildings, and burning the Danish, Dutch, Norwegian, French and German flags in Gaza City.

Under the title, Don't Be Fooled This Isn't an Issue of Islam versus Secularism, Robert Fisk said: "It's not about whether the Prophet should be pictured. The Koran does not forbid images of the Prophet even though millions of Muslims do. The problem is that these cartoons portrayed Mohamed as a bin Laden-type image of violence. They portrayed Islam as a violent religion. It is not. Or do we want to make it so? [14]

However, in the West the publication of cartoons was supported as a free-speech right. The Western newspapers insisted that the whole thing was an exercise of the sacred human right to freedom; in this case freedom of expression. The European papers that published the cartoons in solidarity with the Danish paper said they wanted Muslims to know they cannot be exempt from satire. But for Muslims the cartoons were sheer ridicule.

What is critical to know is that it was not some random cartoonist drawing one cartoon and an editor who decided to publish it. Rather, a neo-con newspaper chose to commission artists to draw these images that depict the Prophet as a terrorist. These cartoons were not an ignorant mistake. The intent was to insult and inflame.

The New York Times on a February 12, 2006 quoted the cultural editor of Jylland-Postens, Flemming Rose—the supposed champion of free speech and Western values—who vented his own nationalist venom and anti-Muslim bias in the following manner: "People are no longer willing to pay taxes to help support someone called Ali who comes from a country with a different language and culture that is 5,000 miles away." [15]

Dr. Habib Siddiqui is right when he says that Europe talks about freedom of speech, but she wastes no time to gang up on others' right to such expressions. "Why is it a crime in France, Germany and some other European states to express views that question the Holocaust? Why such selective use of law limiting the so-called freedom of speech when it comes to Holocaust but nonchalant about materials that are offensive to nearly one quarter of humanity?" [16]

Interestingly, the British newspaper The Guardian reported on February 6, 2006 that the Danish newspaper that initially ran the cartoons defaming Muhammad had refused to run drawings lampooning Jesus Christ three years ago on the "grounds that they could be offensive to readers and were not funny." With this revelation, the newspaper's intent became clear. In today's polarized world, newspapers hiding behind freedom of speech in an effort to provoke and demean a disenfranchised European Muslim minority is nothing to celebrate.

The Fitna film

Taking cue from the Hollywood anti-Arab and anti-Muslim "crusade," in March 2008, Geert Wilders, leader of the anti-Islam and anti-Muslim Dutch Freedom Party, released the film Fitna on internet. The Jyllands-Posten cartoon of Muhammad with a bomb in his turban was shown during the 15-minute film's opening and closing scenes.

Wilders described the film as "a call to shake off the creeping tyranny of Islamization," and a push for a Leitkultur, a culture that "draws on Christian, Jewish, humanistic traditions and that poses a challenge to the Islamic problem." [Wikipedia]

Wilders' film Fitna uses verses from the Quran alongside images of the terrorist attacks in the US on September 11, 2001, Madrid in March 2004 and London in July 2005. The film equates Islam's holy text with violence and ends with a call to Muslims to remove "hate-preaching" verses from the Quran.

Not surprisingly, provoked protests in Muslim-majority countries including Indonesia and Pakistan. The Organisation of the Islamic Conference (OIC) protested the film saying "The film is solely intended to incite and provoke unrest and intolerance among people of different religious beliefs and to jeopardize world peace and stability, U.N. Secretary-General Ban Ki-moon condemned the film as "offensively anti-Islamic" and U.N. High Commissioner for Human Rights Louise Arbour said it was "hateful".

Council of Europe Commissioner for Human Rights speaks on Islamophobia

In October 2010, in a powerful indictment, the Council of Europe Commissioner for Human Rights, Thomas Hammarberg, posted a blog about how European Muslims are stigmatised by populist rhetoric. "European countries appear to face another crisis beyond budget deficits - the disintegration of human value. One symptom is the increasing expression of intolerance towards Muslims. Opinion polls in several European countries reflect fear, suspicion and negative opinions of Muslims and Islamic culture," he wrote.

Thomas Hammarberg's blog post in part said:

"These Islamophobic prejudices are combined with racist attitudes – directed not least against people originating from Turkey, Arab countries and South Asia.

Muslims with this background are discriminated in the labour market and the education system in a number of European countries. There are reports showing that they tend to be targeted by police in repeated identity controls and intrusive searches. This is a serious human rights problem.

"Recent elections have seen extremist political parties gaining ground after aggressively Islamophobic campaigns. Even more worrying is the inertia or confusion which seems to have befallen the established democratic parties in this situation. Compromises are made which tend to give an air of legitimacy to crude prejudices and open xenophobia.

Public opinion response: limit religious freedom of Muslims

"When the German President Christian Wulff in a recent speech confirmed the obvious, that Islam – like Christianity and Judaism - is part of the national context, this was seen as controversial. One newspaper reported that two thirds of the population disagreed.

"A more ambitious survey initiated by Friedrich Ebert Stiftung showed that 58 per cent agreed that "religious practices for Muslims in Germany should be seriously limited". Though not totally clear, this statement appears to reject freedom of religion for one group – Muslims. The broad support for this opinion is a bad sign.

Politicians should not ride the populist wave

"This appears to be a general phenomenon: lack of knowledge feeds prejudices. Political leaders have on the whole failed to counter Islamophobic stereotypes. Of course, this became more difficult after the terrorist attacks in New York, Madrid, London, Amsterdam and also Beslan and Moscow. However, the emotions caused by these horrible crimes called for systematic efforts to establish a distinction between the evildoers and the overwhelming majority of Muslims. These efforts were rarely made.

"Neither has sufficient priority been given to analyzing what makes some people listen to hateful propaganda against Muslims. Part of the explanation appears to be the same ignorance, fear and frustration which have caused bigotry against Roma and immigrants in general. We have learnt that minorities are sometimes turned into scapegoats by people who feel alienated and ignored by those in power. It is important to seek full explanations.

"President Wulff was of course right: Islam is already part of our culture. Muslims in Europe – including the approximately 1.6 million Muslims in the United Kingdom,

3.8 million in Germany, 5 million in France and 15-20 million in Russia - contribute to our economies and societies. They belong. Most of them are in fact born in these countries, the majority are not particularly religious and very few can be characterised as Islamists.

Bigotry is not part of European values

"The diverse groups of Muslims are now blamed by politicians in some countries for not "assimilating". However, integration is a two-way process based on mutual understanding. Anti-Muslim bigotry has in fact become a major obstacle to respectful relationships. Indeed, the Islamophobic atmosphere has probably been a factor enabling extremists in some cases to recruit young and embittered individuals who lack a sense of belonging.

"Instead of discussing such problems seriously, we have had a debate about methods to penalise women wearing the niqab and to prevent the building of minarets. This is hardly the way to give depth to our European values."

Amnesty International report also expresses concern

Thomas Hammarberg was not alone in giving Europeans this warning; many people across British politics and media have shared similar sentiments for some time. Amnesty International has shared this concern. In its April 23, 2012 report "Choice and prejudice: discrimination against Muslims in Europe", Amnesty exposes the impact of discrimination on Muslims. Marco Perolini, Amnesty's expert on discrimination, says: "Muslim women are being denied jobs and girls prevented from attending regular classes just because they wear traditional forms of dress, such as the headscarf. Men can be dismissed for wearing beards associated with Islam... Rather than countering these prejudices, political parties and public officials are all too often pandering to them in their quest for votes."

The report finds the impact of discrimination on the ground of religion or belief on Muslims in several aspects of their lives, including employment and education. It focuses on Belgium, France, the Netherlands, Spain, and Switzerland where Amnesty International has already raised issues such as restrictions on the establishment of places of worship and prohibitions on full-face veils. The report documents numerous individual cases of discrimination across the countries covered.

"Wearing religious and cultural symbols and dress is part of the right of freedom of expression. It is part of the right to freedom of religion or belief – and these rights must be enjoyed by all faiths equally." said Marco Perolini. While everyone has the right to express their cultural, traditional or religious background by wearing a specific form of dress no one should be pressurized or coerced to do so. General bans on particular forms of dress that violate the rights of those freely choosing to dress in a particular way are not the way to do this."

The report highlights that legislation prohibiting discrimination in employment has not been appropriately implemented in Belgium, France and the Netherlands. Employers have been allowed to discriminate on the grounds that religious or cultural symbols will jar with clients or colleagues or that a clash exists with a company's corporate image or its 'neutrality'. In the last decade, pupils have been forbidden to wear the headscarf or other religious and traditional dress at school in many countries including Spain, France, Belgium, Switzerland and the Netherlands.

"Any restriction on the wearing of religious and cultural symbols and dress in schools must be based on assessment of the needs in each individual case. General bans risk adversely Muslims girls' access to education and violating their rights to freedom of expression and to manifest their beliefs." Marco Perolini said.

The right to establish places of worship is a key component of the right to freedom of religion or belief which is being restricted in some European countries, despite state obligations to protect, respect and fulfill this right. Since 2010, the Swiss Constitution has specifically targeted Muslims with the prohibition of the construction of minarets, embedding anti-Islam stereotypes and violating international obligations that Switzerland is bound to respect. In Catalonia (Spain), Muslims have to pray in outdoor spaces because existing prayer rooms are too small to accommodate all the worshippers and requests to build mosques are being disputed as incompatible with the respect of Catalan traditions and culture. This goes against freedom of religion which includes the right to worship collectively in adequate places. "There is a groundswell of opinion in many European countries that Islam is alright and Muslims are ok so long as they are not too visible. This attitude is generating human rights violations and needs to be challenged," said Marco Perolini.

In the last decade, pupils have been forbidden to wear the headscarf or other religious and traditional dress at school in many countries including Spain, France, Belgium, Switzerland and the Netherlands. "Any restriction on the wearing of religious and cultural symbols and dress in schools must be based on assessment of the needs in each individual case. General bans risk adversely Muslims girls' access to education and violating their rights to freedom of expression and to manifest their beliefs." Marco Perolini said. [17]

Nexus of European and US Islamophobists

The Oslo massacre on July 22, 2011 exposed the nexus of European and US Islamophobes. Prominent US Islamophobists, Pamela Geller and Robert Spencer, just happen to be among the heroes cited in the 1,500-page manifesto written by Andrew Behring Breivik, the Norwegian terrorist whose anti-Muslim paranoia apparently drove him to kill 77 people, most of them kids. According to the New York Times, Breivik was deeply influenced by a small group of American bloggers lacing his manifesto with quotations from them, as well as copying multiple passages from the tract of the Unabomber. [18]

Breivik is apparently an avid fan of the U.S. anti-Muslim activists such as Pamela Geller, Robert Spencer and Daniel Pipes. He lauds the Stop Islamization of America co-founded by Geller and Spencer. Jihad Watch of Robert Spencer was cited 112 times. Breivik cited Robert Spencer 54 times in his manifesto. Pamela Geller, and her blog, Atlas Shrugs, was mentioned 12 times. Daniel Pipes is cited 11 times and his blog danielpipes.org 14 times.

2083: A European Declaration of Independence, the manifesto of Anders Behring Breivik includes a lengthy discussion of and support for the "Eurabia" theory advocated by Bat Ye'Or, anti-Muslim Jewish writer. It also contains several articles on the Eurabia theme by Bat Ye'Or. Pamela Geller promotes her "Eurabia" theory on her blog. "Eurabia" predicted a coming a tsunami of Islam that will make Europe unrecognizable, where Muslim birth rates overwhelm older populations, mosques are as plentiful as McDonald's restaurants, and Islamic sharia law supplants European constitutions.

The nexus of Islamophobia and right-wing extremism was clearly on display during 2010 summer's "Ground Zero mosque" hysteria, which culminated in a rally where Geller and Geert Wilders addressed a crowd that included members of the the English Defense League (EDL) waving Israeli flags. Geert Wilders' whose anti-Islam Party for Freedom (PVV) is currently the third-largest party in the Netherlands.

It may be pointed out that Stop Islamisation of America was founded in 2010, according to Wikipedia, at the request of Anders Gravers Pedersen, the leader of Stop Islamisation of Europe, of which it is the American affiliate. In February 2011 when the Southern Poverty Law Center named it a hate group.

Norwegian far right defend Breivik's views on Islam

Not surprisingly, defense witnesses from the far right in Norway backed terrorist Anders Behring Breivik's views on Islam in court on (June 5, 2012) Day 31 of his murder trial. They said Norway was threatened by Muslim immigration, an argument used by Breivik in an attempt to justify massacring 77 people and injuring 242 on July 22, 2011.

Arne Tumyr, who heads an organisation called Stop the Islamisation of Norway, described Islam as "a religion of violence, a religion of wars," and the Muslim Prophet Mohamed, who he called "a sexual delinquent, a looter of caravans, an assassin, a war criminal." His organisation, he said, considered Islam "a threat to Norwegian society and values." If nothing was done, he said, Norway would be "taken over by Muslims." "We consider Islam as a threat to the Norwegian society and values," he said, claiming for instance that a daycare centre had been forced to remove a reference to Piglet, Winnie-the-Pooh's friend, so as not to offend Muslim children.

Tore Tvedt, founder of far-right group Vigrid, said on Muslim immigration: "When they get their will, the Nordic race will be exterminated." "The constitution has been cancelled, we're at war now," he told the court. "Norway is at war. It is in the process of being Balkanised," Tore Tvedt said.

In response to lawyers for survivors and family members of Breivik's victims, defense lawyer Geir Lippestad said the far-right testimony was necessary to show his client was sane. "Our aim is not to argue in favor of a political opinion but to show that the way the accused views the world is shared by others," he told the court.

Members of Islamic communities currently make up just under 2% of Norway's population of 4.9 million, according to data from Statistics Norway quoted by BBC. [19]

Petitions to Stop Muslim Immigration Into Australia, Canada, Japan, Europe and US

Borrowing a page from the well-known American Islamophobe, David Yerushalmi's template of the so-called anti-Sharia bills, two shady websites - www.loganswarning.com and www.citizenwarrior.com - have uploaded templates of petitions to Stop Muslim immigration into Australia, Canada, Japan, Europe and the US.

The petitions are tailored to the situation in individual country but some of the arguments are common:

Islam is both a religion and a political ideology, and its politics are supremacist. That is, the doctrines of mainstream Islam command Muslims to work toward the dominance of their religion over all other religions, and the subjugation of all people to the Islamic political system (Shari'a).

When Muslims move into any country, a certain percentage of them will start agitating for special considerations. They start to organize and influence the nation politically in a way that is good for Islam and bad for freedom and equality. When the percentage of the Muslims in a nation's population becomes high enough, they gain so much political power that freedoms and rights begin to disappear.

Some want to follow Mohammad's example (as it says they should in the Quran) and make the governments of their adopted home eventually follow Sharia law rather than the already existing laws. We could ask them on their immigration application, but another Islamic principle (known as "taqiyya") allows Muslims to deceive non-Muslims if it helps the spread or dominance of Islam. Until we find some way to determine who genuinely rejects the political goals of Islam and who does not, we should stop all immigration.

The situation is urgent because at some point Muslims will comprise too large a voting block for politicians to ignore. We must stop immigration soon. The first step is to show political leaders there is widespread support for such a policy. So please sign the petition for your country. And get all your friends to sign it. Post it on Facebook. Do whatever you can to get the word out. Let's get this done.

The Israeli connection [20]

Geert Wilders, whose anti-Islam Party for Freedom (PVV) is currently the third-largest party in the Netherlands, has visited Israel numerous times, including in 2008, the year his anti-Muslim film Fitna made international headlines, according to investigative journalist Asa Winstanley. In 2010 he met with far-right Israeli foreign minister (and settler) Avigdor Lieberman and gave a speech in Tel Aviv in which he called for more Israeli colonization of the Palestinian West Bank. Speaking to Reuters, he explained the counter-jihad ideology that so many in Europe's far right are now adapting: "Our culture is based on Christianity, Judaism and humanism and [the Israelis] are fighting our fight...If Jerusalem falls, Amsterdam and New York will be next."

Here are excerpts from Asa Winstanley's article Europe's Islamophobes and Israel: The Right Alliance published by Al Akhbar of Lebanon on January 2, 2012:

The day after Wilders spoke in Tel Aviv, a delegation of politicians from European anti-Islam parties toured West Bank colonies, reported settler news site Arutz Sheva. They included leaders from Germany, Austria and Belgium; "and yet these parties had by no means abandoned their anti-Semitic roots" according to Lerman.

In October 2009, the British National Party leader Nick Griffin made a controversial appearance on Question Time, the BBC's flagship political talk show. He used the occasion to express enthusiastic support for Israeli war crimes in the Gaza Strip: "I have brought the British National Party from being, frankly, an antisemitic and racist organization into being the only political party which, in the clashes between Israel and Gaza, stood full square behind Israel's right to deal with Hamas terrorists."

The BNP won almost a million votes in 2009 elections to the European parliament, so Griffin cannot be dismissed as a totally unrepresentative quack. Nonetheless, he clearly is an extremist in mainstream political terms. But the leading British parties feed into BNP rhetoric on issues like immigration.

The English Defence League, an anti-Muslim street gang that contains many football hooligan elements, regularly waves Israeli flags during its demonstrations. Since it rose to prominence in 2009, it was open about its counter-jihadist orientation. EDL leader Tommy Robinson said that one of the main principles the group was founded on was "support for Israel's right to defend itself...Israel is a shining star of democracy. If Israel falls, we all fall."

In 2010 the EDL launched a so-called Jewish Division. Although this sub-group is thought to be numerically insignificant, it is emblematic of the EDL's counter-jihadist, pro-Zionist ideology. There are also more recent reports that the EDL may be developing links with the Jewish Defense League, founded in America by Meir Kahane the extremist American rabbi who later settled in occupied Palestine and founded the Kach party (later banned under US terrorism legislation).

While visiting Berlin in July this year Israeli deputy minister Ayoob Kara met Patrik Brinkmann, who has ties with the German neo-Nazi party. Brinkman has reportedly visited Kara in Israel several times. In November, Israel's new UN ambassador Ron Prosor was photographed smiling next to Marine Le Pen, the leader of the French National Front (laughably, he later claimed this was an accident).

And then there is the Islamophobic Norwegian terrorist Anders Breivik, who reportedly confessed to the murder of 77 people in a combined bombing and mass-shooting in July, press reports noted that some of his young leftist victims had held Palestine solidarity workshops at their summer camp on Utøya island.

From what he's written, it's clear Breivik is a big fan of Israel. His rambling online book is full of flattering references to the state. For example: "let us fight together with Israel, with our Zionist brothers against all anti-Zionists," he wrote, "against all cultural Marxists/multiculturalists." This is from page 1163 of his "compendium," large chunks of which were reportedly copied from other Islamophobic sources.

These connections and affinities between Zionism and the far-right do not stop at Europe of course. In the US, right-wing fundamentalist Christianity is a far bigger political factor, and this current very much tends to side with Israel. It has even been argued that this Christian Zionism the greatest factor fueling political support for Israel in the United States. John Hagee of Christians United for Israel is openly anti-semitic, with his fundamentalist rantings about how Hitler was supposedly sent by God and so forth.

Free to hate: the rise of the right in post-communist eastern Europe *[21]*

Paul Hockenos, the author of "Free to hate: the rise of the right in post-communist eastern Europe" says that in recent (2011) elections Islamophobes like France's right-wing National Front and the anti-EU True Finn Party racked up their best numbers ever, the latest strides in a surging movement that is recasting the political landscape of Western Europe. "These elements have every reason to thank mainstream politicians, who, in the hope of exploiting the phenomenon for their own gain, have paved the way for the far right. In April, for example, France's ridiculous "burqa ban" went into effect with overwhelming popular support, while EU leaders pushed the panic button over Tunisian refugees landing in Italy and Malta, turning the image of peaceful revolutionaries across the Mediterranean into one of an impoverished mob besieging Fortress Europe, he said adding:

"Where (Islamophobia) manifests itself in electoral parties, such as in France, the Netherlands, Denmark, Switzerland, Austria and now even Sweden and Finland, its advocates fare much better than old-school far-right parties ever did, with their vulgar anti-Semitism and expansionist fantasies.

The Berlin-based writer Paul Hockenos emphasizes that Islamophobia is solidly mainstream; there is no politically correct taboo against it, as there is with overt racism or other strains of xenophobia. In fact, some of Europe's highest-profile Islamophobes justify their attacks on Islam and Europe's Muslims in the name of women's and gay rights. "Conservative, liberal and even leftist parties tap into it, partly out of opportunism and partly out of conviction. Invoking secularism and Enlightenment values, some centrists and leftists propagate a cultural racism that instead of using skin color imputes immutable characteristics to cultures and assigns them a hierarchy, with Western civilization at the top. This is Islamophobia, which functions just as racism does, and serves the purposes of those who have long sought to stem immigration, keep Turkey out of the European Union and secure a white Christian Europe."

Paul Hockenos in his article "Europe's Rising Islamophobia" published by Middle East Online on April 24, 2011, went on to say:

"Not every European country has anti-Muslim parties as successful as two of Islamophobia's poster boys, the Dutch Freedom Party and the Danish People's Party, both of which put the clash of cultures and the Islamic menace at the center of their programs. Yet these cases are instructive, because they represent a new generation of the European right, and the conditions of their rise exist across Western Europe. Surveys and opinion polls, for example, indicate that anti-Muslim sentiment in Holland and Denmark is about the same as in most other Western European countries. In one recent study, between 34 and 37 percent of French, Dutch, Portuguese and Danes say they have a negative opinion of Muslims. In Germany the figure is 59 percent.

"Even in EU countries that don't have growing anti-Muslim parties, Islamophobic sentiment is potent. In Germany, for example, one survey after another attests to widening hostility directed at the Muslim population and Islam in general. One recent study showed 58 percent of Germans in favor of restricting religious freedom for Muslims. This included more than 75 percent of those in eastern Germany, where the Muslim population is negligible. Thirty-seven percent of Germans feel the Federal Republic would be better off "without Islam." The surveys underscore the steady rise of these sentiments since 2004, with a significant jump from 2009 to 2010. They also show that while attitudes are particularly strong in traditional right-wing milieus, they have also become more pronounced in the middle and upper classes and among Germans with higher education. They also reveal that anti-Muslim feelings are far stronger than homophobia, classic racism, sexism or anti-Semitism -- the latter long the measure for illiberal thinking in Germany."

Paul Hockenos argues that this mainstreaming of Islamophobia would have been inconceivable without the post-9/11 anti-Muslim discourse in European media; Islamophobic websites like Germany's Bürgerbewegung Pax Europa and Politically Incorrect have tens of thousands of visitors a day. "In large part the trail was blazed by intellectuals, a surprising number of whom had roots in progressive politics. Hugely influential was the late Italian writer Oriana Fallaci, whose bestselling books insisted that Islam is a thoroughly violent and totalitarian creed striving for world domination. The former antifascist partisan and left-wing journalist once likened the Koran to Hitler's Mein Kampf."

According to Paul Hockenos other intellectuals include French writer and activist Bernard-Henri Levy ("the veil is an invitation to rape"), British novelist and former New Statesman editor Martin Amis, Dutch intellectual and Labor Party member Paul Scheffer, and in Germany such figures as Ralph Giordano, Necla Kelek, Alice Schwarzer and Henryk Broder, all leftists or former leftists of one stripe or another. Schwarzer, for example, is the mother of Germany's feminist movement, and with her flagship quarterly EMMA she has fought for women's liberation since the early 1970s. She denounces Islam as misogynistic and misanthropic, accusing it -- and those who defend it -- of betraying the universality of human rights. For her, and for many other critics of Islam, "tolerating" the religion means tolerating forced marriages, honor killings, burqas, female genital mutilation and polygamy. Schwarzer now argues for measures that conservatives and the far right have pursued for decades. In the past it was coalitions comprising liberal intellectuals, feminists and Christian churches that waged fierce opposition to such legislation.

Pope's thinly veiled attack on Islam [22]

The European Islamophobes a boost when Pope Benedict hit out at Islam and its concept of Jihad. The thinly veiled attack on Islam came during a theological lecture on Sept. 12, 2006 to the staff and students at the University of Regensburg, where he taught theology in the 1970s.

Just like a cheap shot against Islam - packaged in western free speech clichés and marketed as innocent satire – launched in the form of cartoons of Prophet Muhammad printed by a Danish daily and republished by European newspapers, Pope's anti-Islam remarks are touted as an invitation to open dialogue with Muslims.

However, this was no casual slip. Beneath his scholarly rhetoric, the Pope's logic seemed to be that Islam is dangerous and godless. Though many are inclined to see this debate as a fresh maneuver to keep the Muslims engaged in controversies.

Using the words, "jihad" and "holy war", the Pope quoted criticisms of Prophet Muhammad by a 14th century Byzantine Christian emperor, Manuel II, during a debate with a learned Persian. "Show me just what Mohammed brought that was new, and there you will find things only evil and inhuman, such as his command to spread by the sword the faith he preached," Benedict quoted the emperor as saying. "The emperor goes on to explain in detail the reasons why spreading the faith through violence is something unreasonable," the Pope said and added: "Violence is incompatible with the nature of God and the nature of the soul."

Manuel II (1350-1425) was the second-to-last emperor of the East-Roman (Byzantine) Empire. As a boy, he had been held prisoner by the Turks, and his dialogues took place as his inheritance lay in jeopardy to the Ottoman empire, and his capital under siege. Only 28 years after his death, Constantinople, the capital of Byzantine Empire fell to the Ottomans under Sultan Mehmed II.

Giles Fraser, a lecturer in philosophy at Wadham College, Oxford, - quoting Christopher Tyerman's latest book on the Crusades, "God' s War" - argues that analogies between the Crusades and the present global conflict are often overdrawn and historically dubious. After all, it was one of Benedict's predecessors, Urban II, who first summoned a Christian jihad against Islam. And it's Born-Again Christians who have been at the forefront of support for the invasion of Iraq, the occupation of Palestinian lands by Israel, and the whole "reorganization" of the Middle East - a catastrophe in which many thousands of Muslims have lost their lives.

But what makes his comments from Bavaria doubly insensitive is that Munich and its surrounding towns are home to thousands of Gastarbeiter, many from Turkey, who are often badly treated by local Germans and frequently subjected to racism, Fraser pointed out. "It won't be lost on them that Manuel II ran his Christian empire from what is now the Turkish city of Istanbul. And reference to that time, in circumstances such as these, has the unmistakable whiff of Christian triumphalism," he concluded.

Another report in the Guardian gives some insight into the thinking of Vatican about Islam. John Hooper of Guardian reports from Rome that Pope believes his church should take tougher line on Islam. Writing under the title, After a quiet first year as pontiff, God's Rottweiler shows his teeth, Hooper says the key word in the Vatican now is "reciprocity". The leadership of the Roman Catholic Church is increasingly of the opinion that a meaningful dialogue with the Muslim world is not possible while Christians are denied religious freedom in Muslim states.

As a cardinal in the Holy See, he was known to be skeptical of John Paul II's pursuit of conversation. One of his earliest decisions as pope was to move Archbishop Michael Fitzgerald, one of the Catholic Church's leading experts on Islam, and head of its council on inter-religious dialogue, away from the center of influence in Rome, and send him to Egypt as papal nuncio.

Benedict has spoken publicly of Christianity as the cornerstone of Europe and against the admission of Turkey into the European Council. Renzo Guolo, a professor of the sociology of religion at the University of Padua, believes that this is maybe the strongest criticism because he doesn't speak of "fundamentalist Islam" but of Islam generally.

Impact of anti-Islam and anti-Muslim rant in Europe

France & Germany

Jean-Marie le Pen, leader of a French nationalist party, le Front National, calls for a 'halt to the Islamization of France'. His colleague in anti-Islamic conviction, Franz Schonhuber (leader of the right-wing Republikaner Party of Germany), says, 'Never will the green flag of Islam fly over Germany'. The election slogan of the Denmark Progressive Party, 'Denmark without Muslims', is much the same thing. Many more such examples could be cited, but that is not the purpose of this essay. [23]

The year 2009 has a brought a wide range of anti-Islamic measures. Switzerland passed a referendum to ban minarets on mosques. Belgium has prohibited the burqa, or full-length veil worn by Muslim women, and France is about to. In June 2010, voters in the Netherlands – whose second-largest city, Rotterdam, has a majority population of ethnic minorities – made the party of anti-Islam political figure Geert Wilders the third largest in Dutch politics. Mr. Wilders's platform calls for banning the Koran and new mosques, taxing head scarves, and ending immigration from Muslim countries. [24]

The Dutch Freedom Party

The Dutch Freedom Party is a one-man outfit led by 47-year-old Geert Wilders, immediately recognizable by his wavy mane of platinum-blond hair. Since October the party has been an unofficial partner in the center-right governing coalition (it has no cabinet seats, but it can dictate terms to a minority government that ultimately needs its votes). In the Netherlands, previously renowned for its tolerance, Wilders's party more than doubled its numbers last year, to 16 percent of the electorate, on a platform to stop the "Islamization of the Netherlands." The party pledged to halt immigration from "Muslim countries," to tax women wearing headscarves and to ban the Koran as well as the construction of mosques. Wilders blames the easygoing model of Dutch multiculturalism for exposing the Netherlands to Islam, and thus for undermining the very tolerance it naïvely extended to Muslim peoples. Over the past two years he has consistently polled as one of the country's most popular politicians, despite being put on trial on charges of inciting hatred against Muslims (the case is ongoing). [25]

Danish People's Party

As for the Danish People's Party, it has worked hand-in-hand with the country's center-right government since 2001. The party -- one leading MP likens the hijab to the swastika -- took 15 percent of the vote in the 2009 European Parliament elections and is now Denmark's third-biggest party. Its guiding light, Pia Kjaersgaard, originally belonged to one of Denmark's establishment parties, as

Wilders did in the Netherlands. Unlike the old right, with its blood-and-soil chauvinism and anti-Semitism, new rightists like Kjaersgaard couch their nationalism as a defense of Western civilization and even "Judeo-Christian values." One of her quotes: "Not in their wildest imagination would anyone [in 1900] have imagined that large parts of Copenhagen and other Danish towns would be populated by people who are at a lower stage of civilization, with their own primitive and cruel customs like honor killings, forced marriages, halal slaughtering, and blood-feuds. This is exactly what is happening now.... [They] have come to a Denmark that left the dark ages hundreds of years ago." [26]

In both countries the governments have caved in to Islamophobes by dramatically tightening immigration requirements for non-Westerners. The once proudly open-minded Denmark now has the strictest such laws in Europe. [27]

The Netherlands and Denmark, like most of Western Europe, have significant numbers of foreign-born immigrants and second-generation inhabitants from Arabic or majority-Muslim countries. (Many have Turkish backgrounds and -- as with many Bosnians, Moroccans and Iraqis -- may or may not practice Islam. But thanks to the new discourse, which conflates ethnicity with religion, they're all called Muslims.) These communities make up 5 and 4 percent of their populations, respectively (3.2 percent is the European Union average), and have a positive birth rate, in contrast with sagging demographics across almost all of traditionally Christian Europe, a trend that has Islamophobes sounding the alarm bells. It is also the case -- though the root causes are hotly disputed -- that segments of these minorities are poorly integrated, unemployment among them is higher than the national average and 1 to 2 percent hold radical views. [28]

French election of 2012 and Islamophobia

Alarmingly, while anti-Islam and anti-Muslim political parties are gaining ground in a number of European countries the anti-Islam New York-based Gatestone Institute is claiming that in May 6, 2012, French election the incumbent president Nicolas Sarkozy was defeated by the Socialist rival François Hollande because of Muslim vote. Hollande is the first Socialist president of France was elected since1995.

The Gatestone Institute of report titled "Muslim voters change Europe" claimed:

According to a survey of 10,000 French voters conducted by the polling firm Opinion Way for the Paris-based newspaper Le Figaro, an extr-aordinary 93% of French Muslims voted for Hollande on May 6. By contrast, the poll shows that only 7% of French Muslims voted for the incumbent, Nicolas Sarkozy. An estimated 2 million Muslims participated in the 2012 election, meaning that roughly 1.7 million Muslim votes went to Hollande rather than to Sarkozy. In the election as a whole, however, Hollande won over Sarkozy by only 1.1 million votes. This figure implies that Muslims cast the deciding votes that thrust Hollande into the Élysée Palace. France, home to between five and six million Muslims, already has the largest Muslim population in the European Union, and those numbers are expected to increase exponentially in coming years. According to conservative estimates, the Muslim population is projected to exceed 10% of the overall French population within the next decade-and-a-half.

During the campaign, Hollande offered an amnesty to all of the estimated 400,000 illegal Muslim immigrants currently in France. He also pledged to change French electoral laws so that Muslim residents without French citizenship would be allowed to vote in municipal elections as of 2014. These measures, if implemented, would enable the Socialist Party tighten its grip on political power, both at the regional and national levels. Muslims in France — and across Europe as a whole — tend to support the Socialists for a variety of demographic, socio-economic and ideological reasons.

The Gatestone Institute said although Hollande has not articulated his views on Israel — he has said he wants to visit Israel and the Palestinian territories this summer — many observers fear that Hollande will surround himself with a coterie of leftwing advisors who will push him to distance France from the pro-Jewish, pro-Israel course established by Sarkozy. Hollande has also said he is opposed to Israeli or American military action against Iranian nuclear facilities and many analysts believe the new French government will seek to weaken international sanctions against Iran.

The report said that political changes in France have many Jews concerned about the future of the Jews. On the day that French voters elected Hollande as their new president, more than 5,000 French Jews participated in an Aliyah (immigration of Jews to Israel) fair in Paris. The annual event, organized and run by the Jewish Agency, usually attracts about 2,000 visitors. [29]

Islam Not Recognized as a Religion in Italy

According to a AKI online report of August 27, 2010, Mosques in Italy will not receive a share of income tax revenue the Italian government allocates to religious faiths each year. Hindu and Buddhist temples, Greek Orthodox churches and Jehovah's Witnesses will be eligible for the funds, according to a bill approved by the Italian cabinet in May and still must be approved by parliament. Until now, the government had earmarked 8 percent of income tax revenue for Italy's established churches. The great majority of these funds go to the Catholic Church, although if they wish, individual tax payers may elect to give the money to charities and cultural projects instead.

Islam is not an established religion in Italy and there is only one official mosque in the country, Rome's Grand Mosque. Politicians from the ruling coalition cite radical imams, polygamy and failure to uphold women's rights by Muslims immigrants as obstacles to recognizing Islam as an official religion in Italy.

Until now, only the Catholic Church, Judaism and other established churches including Lutherans, Evangelists, Waldensians and 7th-day Adventists have received the income tax revenue from the Itallain government.

There are between one million and 1.5 million Muslims in Italy and 130 mosques linked the Muslim umbrella organization UCOII across the country, according to AKI report.

Extremist Swede to finance anti-Islam center in Germany [30]

On January 24, 2010, it was reported that Swedish far-right businessman Patrik Brinkmann has announced he will pour 5 million Euro into the coffers of Pro NRW, an anti-Islam populist party based in Cologne.

In an interview with Germany's public broadcaster WDR Brinkmann said he fears Germany is becoming "too foreign" and that Sharia law will be introduced in the country. "However, there are no, or very few, politicians who take this seriously," Brinkmann said.

"That's why I believe that a new right wing (in Germany) can not only succeed, but in five or ten years be as large as the FPÖ in Austria or the SVP in Switzerland," he added, referring to Austria's Freedom Party and the Swiss People's Party, two far-right groups which have enjoyed a certain amount of electoral success. The millionaire, who reportedly already has ties to Germany's extreme-right NPD and DVU parties, will finance a building for Pro NRW to be used as an anti-Islam centre.

In search of heterodox (moderate) Muslims [31]

An anti-Islam website - www.inquiryintoislam.com - claims that the so-called radicalized Muslims are not really radical but in reality they are orthodox. The Inquiry Into Islam argues:

"The first definition for "orthodox" in Answers.com is: Adhering to the accepted or traditional and established faith, especially in religion. That's perfect. And it is easily understood by most Westerners. It's a term we're already familiar with. "And in Answers.com, heterodox means: Not in agreement with accepted beliefs, especially in church doctrine or dogma. You can delete the word "church" and that's a great definition for what has been termed "moderate" Muslims. It's accurate and makes the distinction very clear.

"So I'll be using the term "orthodox" to describe someone who strictly follows the teachings in the Quran and the Hadith, and who tries — as a good Muslim is supposed to do according to the doctrines — to follow Mohammad's example."

Anti-Islam Muslims in Europe

The European Orientalists have been working zealously against Islam since the 18th century, however, during the second half of the 20th century the European anti-Islam campaign got a boost from a number of Muslims who were used to speak and write against their own faith.

As Yasemin Karakasoglu, Professor for Intercultural Education at University of Bremen (Germany) pointed out, a criticism from the inside of Muslim society is regarded as authentic and plausible because individuals like Ayaan Hirsi Ali in the Netherlands or Necla Kelek in particular or in some respect also Seyran Ates in Germany have a Muslim family background, hold academic or political titles or mandates which seem to give them legitimization and authorization to analyze phenomenon like: forced marriages, honor killings, female circumcision, and domestic violence. "The value of their opinion derives also from the fact that leading politicians declare them as noteworthy experts. Some of them like Necla Kelek or Chardott Djavann (France) have gained status as official advisers to Ministers. Necla Kelek is advisor to the Ministry of Interior in questions of Muslim affairs (she is a permanent member of the recently established German wide Islamkonferenz) and also for migrant issues to the Ministry of Integration," Yasemin said adding:

Chardott Djavann was among the selected few invited for an audition at the Stasi Commission set up by Jacques Chirac to reflect upon the applications of laïcité. For all of these authentic criticizers the above-mentioned phenomena in Muslim families are directly based on Islam itself. The protagonists mentioned become especially valuable because they are without any restrictions willing to share the harsh critique on Islam as expressed by representatives of the non-Islamic majority society. Here I want to draw your attention to an interesting metamorphose they are undergoing in the process. [32]

"While Hirsi Ali and Kelek at the beginning of their media career as Islam-Experts stated they no longer regarded themselves as Muslims even though those in the media and politics continuously address them as examples of independent secular Muslims. With their critical approach to Islam they are regarded as ideal representatives of a modern form of Islam and thus defined as authentic ´good´ Muslims. Interestingly – when addressed as Modern Muslim women none of them rejects the classification of being a Muslim. Because it is this combination of being both an ´authentic Muslim´ and a women that makes them authoritative and powerful voices in the discourse on Islam as being oppressive against women. Their main topics are the abolition of the headscarf, the fight against domestic violence, against arranged or forced marriages, honor killings and, in the case of Ayaan Hirsi Ali, against female circumcision. Their bestselling books oscillate between the currently very famous ´veil literature´ and political pamphlets. The rhetoric is sharp. In their statements no special interpretations of Islam but only that Islam itself is incompatible with democracy and sexual equality. [33]

"To make their argumentation more convincing to the masses they mix empirical data and novel-like elements with narrations of their own family history. All the three women mentioned regard themselves as the voice of the oppressed women who cannot speak or are afraid to do so. Their common assumption is that all these phenomena are based on Islam itself and are covered by Islamic law, disregarding that in several of the cases of forced marriages, honour killings and female circumcision that became public, that the individuals were members of Oriental or African religious minorities, not Muslims. And also not taking into consideration the Fatwas of the leading European Ulemas who point out that these practises are not at all covered by Islamic law. [34]

"Like Hirsi Ali in the Netherlands Seyran Ates faces serious death threats because of her publicly expressed opinions on Islam and Muslim men. This has understandably led on the one hand to further discussions on the value of freedom of speech in the respective societies but it has also strengthened the symbolic role of the threatened criticizers of Islam (a newly established term for a profession created by media) in the discourse. Ironically it has also strengthened their role as authentic informants on the "real face of Islam" because it was then regarded as evident that Islam, as represented by the offenders, really is a religion of violence. [35] "In this respect even assaultive and openly aggressive assertions against Islam can be expressed without showing any evidence for what is stated as the "hidden face of Islam". Some of these protagonists (like Ayaan Hirsi Ali, Necla Kelek, Chardott Djavann) have been awarded several times for their engagement for freedom of speech, intercultural understanding and world freedom. Thus they gained some kind of official status as the "Oriental confirmer

in July" for the superiority of Western culture to Islam. This is a figure that is well known in the modern Literature of the East where the "Western confirmer in duty" has the role to confirm that he who is part of the western culture and knows oriental culture very well can confirm that oriental culture is superior (Wieland 1980). The mechanism here is the same: if in the eyes of an alien we are regarded as superior we must be superior." [36]

Not surprisingly Ayaan Hirsi Ali was hired as a resident scholar at the extra-right-wing American Enterprise Institute in Washington DC when her Dutch citizenship was temporarily withdrawn because of telling lie in her asylum application when she came to the Netherlands in 1992. She is currently researching the relationship between the West and Islam.

France likely to close more than 100 mosques [37]

France is likely to close up to 160 mosques in the coming months as part of a nationwide police operation under the state of emergency which allows places of worship that promote radical views to be shut down, one of the country's chief imams has said. Following news that three mosques have already been closed since the November 13, 2016 attacks on the capital, Hassan El Alaoui, who is in charge of nominating regional and local Muslim imams and mediating between the imams and prison officials, told Al Jazeera on November 30, 2016 that more were set to be shut. "According to official figures and our discussions with the interior ministry, between 100 and 160 more mosques will be closed because they are run illegally without proper licenses, they preach hatred, or use takfiri speech," he said. There are a total of 2,600 mosques in France, El Alaoui said. France's extended emergency rule has seen a surge in arrests, house arrests and raids on homes and private property in the wake of the Paris attacks - including at mosques and Muslim-owned businesses - and has raised alarm among rights organisations that the law could curb civil liberties.

Anti-Islam movement PEGIDA stages protests across Europe [38]

Germany's anti-Islam PEGIDA movement staged rallies in several cities across Europe on February 6, 2016 to protest against the arrival of hundreds of thousands of migrants from the Middle East and Africa. The movement, whose name stands for Patriotic Europeans Against the Islamisation of the West, originated in the eastern German city of Dresden in 2014, with supporters seizing on a surge in asylum seekers to warn that Germany risks being overrun by Muslims.

After almost fizzling out in early 2010, the movement has regained momentum amid deepening public unease over whether Germany can cope with the 1.1 million migrants who arrived in the country during 2015. Far-right groups see Europe's refugee crisis as an opportunity to broadcast their anti-immigrant message. There were 208 rallies in Germany in the last quarter of 2015, up from 95 a year earlier, Interior Ministry data showed.

The February 6 protests also took place in other cities, including Amsterdam, Prague and the English city of Birmingham.

Anti-Muslim sentiment in Germany hits record high [39]

The number of Germans with negative attitudes towards Muslims has hit its highest mark yet, according to results of a recent study by Leipzig University released in Berlin on June 15, 2016. Some 50 percent of those surveyed said that they "sometimes feel like a foreigner in their own country due to so many Muslims living here," while nearly 41 percent advocated a ban on Muslim migration.

The representative study revealed a significant increase in negative attitudes towards Muslims and refugees in Germany, as the country is trying to cope with the biggest refugee influx since World War II.

Europe's largest economy accepted more than one million refugees last year; most of these were Syrians, Iraqis and Afghans. The research results showed that the refugee crisis has further increased worries over migration.

The amount of Germans who complained about the number of Muslim migrants living in their country rose to 50 percent this year compared to 32.2 percent in 2009. Those who advocated a ban against migration by Muslims into Germany increased from 36.6 percent to 41.4 in a year. Those who favored such a ban were 21.4 percent in 2009.

Ayhan Şimşek of Anadolu Agency of Turkey Germany has witnessed growing anti-refugee and anti-Muslim sentiment in recent years, triggered by the propaganda by far-right and populist parties, which have exploited the refugee crisis and fears of religious extremist and terrorist groups.

German far-right movements like Pegida and Alternative for Germany (AfD) have been calling for measures to curb migration and restrict the rights of Muslims, for what they perceive as a potential "threat of the Islamization of Germany".

Germany has a total population of 81.1 million; around five percent are Muslims. Among the nearly four million Muslim residents in the country, three million are of Turkish origin. Many of these people migrated to Germany in the 1960s.

Anti-Muslim sentiment on rise in Europe due to migration and ISIL as continent rejects multi-cultural society [40]

The Daily Telegraph quoting a new Europe-wide survey released on July 11, 2016, Europe is rejecting the idea that multi-culturalism is beneficial to cooioty following a year in which the migrant crisis and ISIL-inspired terror attacks have boosted anti-Muslim sentiment across the continent. The data from Pew Research, the leading non-partisan US social attitudes survey company, will serve as another sharp warning to Europe's political elites about the growing strength of grassroots sentiment over the migration issue. It also highlights Europe's stark political and geographical divisions, with Hungary, Poland and Greece all showing themselves to be fiercely anti-Muslim, while a rising base of Right-wing parties are hugely more anti-Muslim than supporters on the European Left.

When asked if diversity had made their country "a better place to live" only 33 per cent of Britons agreed, mirroring sentiment across the EU where more than 70 per cent of people in 10 EU countries surveyed said multi-culturalism made their country either a "worse" place to live, or made "no difference" at all. The survey uncovered lingering suspicions among non-Muslim Europeans that a portion of their Muslim population harbors sympathies for so-called Islamic State of Iraq and the Levant (ISIL), or Da'esh.

Even in the relatively more "tolerant countries" – Germany, Netherlands, UK, and Sweden – fewer than half of respondents believed "very few" Muslims supported Isil, with the majority saying that at least "some" Muslims did sympathize with the terrorists. In the past year unfavorable opinions of Muslims have increased in the UK by 9 percentage points, in Spain by 8 per cent and in Italy and Greece – where migrants have been arriving - per cent and in Italy and Greece – where migrants have been arriving - negative views of Muslims are up by 8 per cent and 12 per cent respectively. "Attitudes toward Muslims and refugees loom large in the European political debate, and this is reflected in current public opinion. Majorities in Greece, Hungary, Italy and Poland express negative attitudes toward both Muslims and refugees," the survey authors wrote.

"Even in countries with more positive views, such as Germany, Sweden and the Netherlands, at least half believe Muslims do not want to integrate into the larger society and majorities express concerns that refugees increase the chance of domestic terrorist attacks." The Pew Research, drawn from surveys conducted in April-May this year, covered 10 countries that account for 80 per cent of the European Union population and 82 per cent of the EU's gross domestic product.

The Pew Survey also revealed the depth of Right-Left political divisions in Europe over attitudes to Muslims and immigrants, with sympathizers of Right-wing parties markedly more concerned than voters on the Left. In Britain some 64 per cent of Ukip supporters believed a more diverse society made the UK a "worse" place to live, compared with only 32 per cent of Conservative Party supporters and 19 per cent of Labor Party supporters. This basic trend was mirrored across Europe with 51 per cent of French National Front supporters believing diversity is bad for France, compared with just 34 per cent of mainstream conservative Republicans and 11 per cent of Socialist Party adherents.

In Germany, which took in nearly one million migrants in 2015, some 62 per cent of people who support the Right-wing party Alternative for Germany (AfD) believe increased racial diversity was bad for Germany, a number echoed in Sweden where 65 per cent of supporters of the anti-immigrant Swedish Democrats believed the same.

Why Europe's far-right political parties are gaining ground? [41]

The refugee crisis, escalating terrorism and dissatisfaction with the political elite are blamed for the current rise of Europe's far-right political parties. Such a revival has not been seen since World War II. What's uniting the parties is an "imagined Muslim enemy in Europe," according to Farid Hafez, a sociology and political science professor at Austria's Salzburg University. The ideology of Europe's far-right parties is rooted in several things, said Cas Mudde, a Dutch political scientist and an associate professor at the University of Georgia's School for Public and International Affairs. "The refugee crisis speaks to a fear of aliens taking the native land," Mudde said. "Authoritarianism is a reaction to the terrorism, and the connection made between refugees and terrorism. Populism plays into the European Union and its inability to deal with terrorism and the refugee crisis."

Over the last 17 years, Europe has seen the number of seats for far-right parties double in each election, from 11 percent in 1999 to 22.9 percent in 2014, according to a report by European Parliament research fellow Thilo Janssen. If the trend continues, the far-right could win 37 percent of European Parliament seats in the next election, the same percentage that Adolf Hitler's National Society party won in 1932, resulting in the rise of the Nazi regime.

When large numbers of foreign workers began streaming into Europe in the early 1990s, the far-right tried to re-establish prominence through economic nationalism, a feeling of loyalty and pride in their own country. They also felt native-born citizens should be given job preferences and welfare support over non-natives. But their efforts were largely unsuccessful.

However, after 9/11, and in the wake of Muslim refugees flooding into Europe, the far-right found its ticket, Islamophobia, according to Ayhan Kaya, director of the European Institute at Istanbul Bilgi University in Turkey. He calls what's happening in Europe "Islamophism" and likens it to the anti-Semitism of the 19th century. "Muslims have become global scapegoats, blamed for all negative social phenomena, such as illegality, crime, violence, drug abuse, radicalism, fundamentalism," Kaya wrote in a recent paper. "There is a growing fear in Europe that Muslims will demographically take over sooner or later."

Europe's Far Right meet in Koblenz, Germany [Euro News]

On January 21, 2017, Europe's Far-Right nationalist parties gathered in the German city of Koblenz under the banner "Europe of Nations and Freedom" -- their political bloc in the European Union parliament. ENF is a political grouping in the European Parliament launched on June 15, 2015. With 40 members, the group is the smallest in the European Parliament.
The Koblenz meeting brought together Greet Wilders, the head of the Dutch Freedom Party (PVV), Frauke Petry of the anti-immigrant Alternative for Germany (AfD), Marine Le Pen of National Front of France and Matteo Salvini of Italy's Northern League. The meeting was organized by Germany's Alternative für Deutschland (AfD) party, under the slogan 'Freedom for Europe'.

According to the Euro-News, Wilders has been leading the major polls and is expected to cause an upset in March's parliamentary elections. Le Pen, leader of France's anti-EU and anti-immigrant National Front, is seen as highly likely to make a two-person runoff vote for the French presidency in May. And Petry's anti-immigration Alternative for Germany party (AfD) is expected to unsettle the established order by entering the Bundestag in September as the third largest bloc.

Marine Le Pen repeated her promise to hold a referendum on France's EU membership if she enters the Elysee Palace as president. "The day after my election I will address the European Union and ask for the return of the four sovereign powers. The sovereignty of the territory, that is the borders, the sovereignty of the money, the economic sovereignty and the legislative sovereignty."

"Without those there is no freedom for the people and no capacity to implement the necessary reforms," Le Pen said. "Because it is not about allowing a self-declared supranational structure to remove the laws that the people decided on." She also cited similarities between Trump's inauguration speech and the message of the conference leaders to reclaim national sovereignty.

For **Greet Wilders**, the popularity of Petry's party is a sign that Germans are wising-up to the folly of their current leader. "Europe needs a strong Germany, a confident and proud Germany, a Germany that stands for its culture, its identity and civilization. Europe needs Frauke instead of Angela," he said. Wilders said if patriots fail to act to preserve freedom and national identity in Europe, "we cease to exist". "The year of liberation, the year of a patriotic spring. In two months, next

March, we will give the Dutch people a chance to liberate the Netherlands. And next April, Marine, as I said, will become the next president of France. And next autumn, it is your turn, my dear German friends. I am convinced that with Frauke Petry, the future of Germany is secured". About perceived threat of Islam in Europe, Wilders said: "blonde" Europeans were in danger of becoming "strangers in their own countries" because of "islamization."

Frauke Petry predicts a bleak future for the EU and has drawn parallels with Napoleon's France, Nazi Germany and the Soviet Union. "And we stand together with our opinion that every country has to decide by itself what is best, and furthermore the commonalities are crucial for us. Together with parties represented here we want a subsidiary Europe of the free home countries. We agree on this even if there are some differences in the details. This doesn't mean a contradiction," she told a press conference afterwards. Frauke Petry said "Mass migration is sold to us as 'diversity.' Well, we don't want this 'diversity' that Brussels dictates to us." "Together with patriots of Europe, the nation state will come back," Petry told the crowd. "But we have to be courageous to rethink Europe and Europe's freedom." Interestingly, several leading German media outlets were barred from attending the gathering.

Terrorist attacks in France

In 2015 Paris witnessed two major terrorist attacks. On January 7, 2015, the French satirical weekly newspaper Charlie Hebdo in Paris was attack apparently for publishing anti-Islam cartoons. Twelve people were killed in the attack. On November 13, 2015, around 129 people were killed in an attack in central and northern Paris – at the Bataclan Theater and Stade de France – and that the attack was allegedly perpetrated by Muslim terrorists.

Makia Freeman, the editor of Alternative News *The Freedom Articles*, argues that these were false flag operations. to borrow Dr. Eowyn, the founder of Fellowship of the Minds, the term "false flag" has its origins in naval warfare where a flag other than the belligerent's true battle flag is used as a *ruse de guerre* or pretext for war. As the term is used in contemporary America, a false flag is an event that is contrived and manipulated by the authorities to achieve a covert agenda. The public is given an untruthful version of the event by government and/or the media. The intended result is a "rallying around the flag" effect, wherein an inflamed populace is mobilized to support the government's preconceived agenda.

Makia Freeman enumerates 10 ways that Paris shooting of November 13, 2015 has a hallmark false flag operation:

Sign #1: Drills on Same Day

Sign #2: Terrorist Passport Magically Found

Sign #3: Terrorists Already Known to French Authorities

Sign #4: Terrorist Declares he is from ISIS

Sign #5: Terrorist States Reason for the Shooting

Sign #6: Shooting Occurs Right Before G20 Summit

Sign #7: Shooting Also Occurs Before COP 21 (Paris UN Climate Change Summit)

Sign #8: Charlie Hebdo Precedent(Many researchers have done a great job compiling evidence that Charlie Hebdo was a false flag attack)

Sign #9: Numerology (The number 13 being a very significant number for the Illuminati, Freemasons and other secret society initiates).

Sign #10: A Long List of Beneficiaries. Cui Bono? Who Benefits? The answer is that the following groups benefit:

– **the French Government** (who can now push through harsher laws under the guise of fighting terrorism, especially while people are in a state of shock and fear; A state of emergency was imposed after the November 2015 attack. It was extended to six month in July 2016 after the Riviera city of Nice terrorist attack, on Bastille Day, killing 84 people.)

– **Islamophobes** (who have more ammunition to denounce an entire religion based on the actions of a tiny, tiny number of extremists);

– **Zionist Israel** (who will no doubt use the Paris attack to strengthen their claim that all Muslims are crazy, dangerous terrorists);

– **New World Order manipulators** (who follow the general rule of thumb that the more division and infighting there is, the more opportunity for profit and control there is).

References

1. From Unveiling Islam, by Roger Du Pasquier, pages 5-7

2. The Utility of Islamic Imagery in the West by J.A. Progler - Al-Tawhid http://www.al-islam.org/al-tawhid/islamicimageryinwest.htm

3. Orientalism, by Edward Said, page 63

4. Ibid page 61

5. Orientalism 25 Years Later: Worldly Humanism v. the Empire-builders by Edward Said

6. Debate: Islam in Europe by Prof. Dr. Enes Karić (Sarajevo)

7. Ibid.

8. Ibid.

9. Fries Magazine - July 6, 2007

10. The Runnymede Trust report

11. Fries Magazine - July 6, 2007

12. Ibid.

13. Adolf Hitler, Mein Kampf ("My Struggle"), Vol. I

14. ROBERT FISK is a reporter for The Independent and author of Pity the Nation. He is also a contributor to Counter Punch's collection, The Politics of Anti-Semitism. Fisk's new book is The Conquest of the Middle East. http://www.counterpunch.org/2006/02/06/don-t-be-fooled-this-isn-t-an-issue-of-islam-versus-secularism/

15. In their own words: The politics behind the anti-Muslim cartoons By Barry Grey February 15, 2006 http://www.wsws.org/articles/2006/feb2006/cart-f15.shtml

16. Danish cartoons – Expression of freedom or abuse of speech? By Dr. Habib Siddiqui February 15, 2006

17. Amnesty Press Release - April 23, 2012

18. New York Times – July 24, 2011

19. http://www.bbc.co.uk/news/world-europe-18332442?print=true

20. http://english.al-akhbar.com/node/2987/

21. Europe's Rising Islamophobia by Paul Hockenos - Middle East Online, April 24, 2011 http://www.middle-east-online.com/english/?id=45735

22. *Pope's attack on Islam was no casual slip* by Abdus Sattar Ghazali – The Milli Gazette – September 17, 2006

23. Debate: Islam in Europe by Prof. Dr. Enes Karić (Sarajevo)

24. Why 'Islamophobia' is less thinly veiled in Europe CSM September 5, 2010

25. Op. cite.

26. Ibid.

27. Ibid.

28. Ibid.

29. Muslim voters change Europe by Soeren Kern - The Gatestone Institute May 17, 2012

30. http://loganswarning.com/2010/01/24/germany-political-party-to-open-anti-islam-center/

31. http://www.inquiryintoislam.com/2010/07/orthodox-versus-heterodox-muslims.html

32. Anti-Islamic Discourses in Europe: Agents and Contents by Yasemin Karakasoglu of University of Bremen
http://www.ces.fas.harvard.edu/conferences/muslims/Karakasoglu.pdf]

33. Ibid.
34. Ibid.
35. Ibid.
36. Ibid.

37. Al Jazeera Dec 2, 2016

38. Reuters February 6, 2016

39. Anadolu June 15, 2016
40. PEW Survey reported by Telegraph July 12, 2016
41. Jewish News Service - August 25, 2016

Chapter VI

The fake Arab Spring

- The truth about the "Arab Spring"
- AFP: US trains activists to evade security forces
- Arab regimes alarmed at the US "Democracy" groups
- Pro-West Moncef Marzouki elected President of Tunisia
- Autocrat Mubarak quits but Egyptian army remains the arbiter of power
- Manufacturing a facade of democracy in Egypt
- Egypt's infamous emergency law re-imposed
- Egyptian-Israeli relations
- Who is Mohammed Morsi?
- The West's 'humanitarian' invasion of Libya
- Responsibility to Protect R2P
- US groups spreading 'democracy'
- Centre for Applied Non Violent Actions and Strategies
- Alliance of Youth Movements
- International Republican Institute
- National Democratic Institute for International Affairs
- National Endowment for Democracy
- Arab regimes alarmed at the US "Democracy" groups
- Emirates Detain Pair From U.S.-Backed Group
- Egypt bars US-based civil society groups
- Responsibility to Protect R2P

In 2011, the world witnessed a new phenomenon - nearly simultaneous demonstrations against authoritarian pro-US regimes in many Arab countries. This has become known as the Arab Spring. On December 17, 2010, the Tunisian fruit vendor, Mohamed Bouazizi, 26, set himself on fire in protest at his treatment by local authorities. The ensuing public outrage eventually ousted a 23-year old dictatorship. After weeks of demonstrations and clashes Tunisian president Zine el-Abidinde Ben Ali steps down and flees to Saudi Arabia on January 14. Two days later, witnessing the departure of Ben Ali demonstrators take to the streets in Egypt chanting; "Ben Ali, tell Mubarak there is a plane waiting for him too." Amid violent demonstrations, Hosni Mubarak resigned on February 10, 2011, after 30 years in power. He handed over power to the Armed Forces Supreme Council. On January 27, 2011, 16 000 protesters gather in the streets of the Yemeni capital of

Sana'a demanding the resignation of President Ali Abduhllah Saleh. After ten months demonstrations, President Ali Abdullah Saleh resigned on November 23, 2011 after 33 years in power.

On January 21, 2011, 5000 people take to the streets in the Jordanian capital of Amman; demonstrating against increases in fuel prices as well as higher level of taxation imposed by the government. On February 1, the Jordanian King, King Abdullah, dissolves the government, and nominates Marouf al-Bakhit, a former army general to create a new cabinet. On January 22, 2011, In Algeria 42 people are injured as protesters march to the parliament building in Algiers; the protesters are not granted permission for their march and are subsequently met by reinforced police. One month later, on February 24, 2011, Algerian President Abdelaziz Bouteflika lifts the emergency rule, in place since 1992, after pressure from protesters and oppositional powers within Algeria.

On February 14, 2011, crowds gathered in the Bahraini capital of Manama to protest corruption, unemployment and to generally voice their discontent with the ruling monarchy in Bahrain. The protesters gathered at the Pearl Roundabout, and the traffic circle became, just as the Tharir Square in Cairo, a symbolic congregation point for the protesters. On February 17, 2011, a day of revolt is organized in Libya, encouraging people to gather in the streets and voice their disapproval of Muammar Gaddafi and his regime. On March 16, 2011, Syrian security forces break up a peaceful gathering in the Marjeh square of Damascus. The approximately 150 protesters were holding up pictures of imprisoned relatives and friends. On March 24, 2011 Syrian President Bashar al-Assad announces the lifting of emergency laws, in effect over the past 48 years; he also announced the formation of a committee whose sole purpose is to increase living standards in Syria.

The so-called Arab Spring was initially received with hope for positive democratic change. However, it soon became clear that any interpretation that what was happening in the Arab countries was the result of an internal dynamic of revolution was not only false but a distortion of the real stakes involved. It was simply amounted to more political manoeuvring through soft power, i.e. a matrix of tools and methods to reach foreign policy goals without the use of arms but by exerting information and other levers of influence.

The truth about the "Arab Spring"

The so-called Arab Spring was neither spontaneous, nor indigenous but a premeditated US geopolitical plot as the New York Times reported on April 14, 2011. In its article, "U.S. Groups Helped Nurture Arab Uprisings," the paper reported, "a number of the groups and individuals directly involved in the revolts and reforms sweeping the region, including the April 6 Youth Movement in Egypt, the Bahrain Center for Human Rights and grass-roots activists like Entsar Qadhi, a youth leader in Yemen, received training and financing from groups like the International Republican Institute, the National Democratic Institute and Freedom House, a nonprofit human rights organization based in Washington."

"The Republican and Democratic institutes are loosely affiliated with the Republican and Democratic Parties. They were created by Congress and are financed through the National Endowment for Democracy, which was set up in 1983 to channel grants for promoting democracy in developing nations. The National Endowment receives about $100 million annually from Congress. Freedom House also gets the bulk of its money from the American government, mainly from the State Department, the New York Times said adding:

Some Egyptian youth leaders attended a 2008 technology meeting in New York, where they were taught to use social networking and mobile technologies to promote democracy. Among those sponsoring the meeting were Facebook, Google, MTV, Columbia Law School and the State Department.

Some of the leaders of the protests had been trained in Belgrade, Serbia, by activists of Canvas (the Center for Applied Non-Violent Actions and Strategies) and Otpor (a youth movement that played a significant role ousting the former Serbian president Slobodan Milosevic), organizations financed by the US State Department.

AFP: US trains activists to evade security forces

On April 8, 2011 AFP reported that the United States is training thousands of cell phone and Internet pro-democracy campaigners worldwide to evade security forces in what it calls a "cat-and-mouse game" with authoritarian governments. The

AFP quoted the US State Department's Michael Posner as saying: the "US government has budgeted $50 million in the last two years to develop new technologies to help activists protect themselves from arrest and prosecution by authoritarian governments." The report went on to explain that the US "organized training sessions for 5,000 activists in different parts of the world. A session held in the Middle East about six weeks ago gathered activists from Tunisia, Egypt, Syria and Lebanon who returned to their countries with the aim of training their colleagues there." Posner would add, "They went back and there's a ripple effect." That ripple effect of course, is the "Arab Spring."

According to F. William Engdahl, the template for such covert regime change has been developed by the Pentagon, US intelligence agencies and various think-tanks such as RAND Corporation over decades, beginning with the May 1968 destabilization of the de Gaulle presidency in France. This is the first time since the US-backed regime changes in Eastern Europe some two decades back that Washington has initiated simultaneous operations in many countries in a region. [1]

"The strategy had been in various State Department and Pentagon files since at least a decade or longer. After George W. Bush declared a War on Terror in 2001 it was called the Greater Middle East Project. Today it is known as the less threatening-sounding "New Middle East" project. It is a strategy to break open the states of the region from Morocco to Afghanistan, the region defined by David Rockefeller's friend Samuel Huntington in his infamous Clash of Civilizations essay in Foreign Affairs. [2]

"The protests that led to the abrupt firing of the entire Egyptian government by President Mubarak on the heels of the panicked flight of Tunisia's Ben Ali into a Saudi exile are not at all as "spontaneous" as the Obama White House, Clinton State Department or CNN, BBC and other major media in the West make them to be. [3]

"They are being organized in a Ukrainian-style high-tech electronic fashion with large internet-linked networks of youth tied to Mohammed ElBaradei and the banned Muslim Brotherhood. It has all the footprints of another US-backed regime change along the model of the 2003-2004 Color Revolutions in Georgia and Ukraine and the failed Green Revolution against Iran's Ahmedinejad in 2009. [4]

"April 6 is headed by one Ahmed Maher Ibrahim, a 29-year-old civil engineer, who set up the Facebook site to support a workers' call for a strike on April 6, 2008. According to a New York Times account from 2009, some 800,000 Egyptians, most "youth, were already then Facebook or Twitter members. In an interview with the Washington-based Carnegie Endowment, April 6 Movement head Maher stated, "Being the first youth movement in Egypt to use internet-based modes of communication like Facebook and Twitter, we aim to promote democracy by encouraging public involvement in the political process." [5]

Arab regimes alarmed at the US "Democracy" groups

Not surprisingly, the work of the US "pro-democracy groups" often provoked tensions between the United States and many autocrat Middle Eastern leaders, who frequently complained that their leadership was being undermined.

According to the New York Times, interviews with officials of the nongovernmental groups and a review of diplomatic cables obtained by WikiLeaks show that the democracy programs were constant sources of tension between the United States and many Arab governments. The cables, in particular, show how leaders in the Middle East and North Africa viewed these groups with deep suspicion, and tried to weaken them. Today the work of these groups is among the reasons that governments in turmoil claim that Western meddling was behind the uprisings, with some officials noting that leaders like Ms. Qadhi (a youth leader in Yemen) were trained and financed by the United States. Diplomatic cables report how American officials frequently assured skeptical governments that the training was aimed at reform, not promoting revolutions. [6]

Pro-West Moncef Marzouki elected President of Tunisia

On December 17, 2010, grocery vendor Mohammed Bouazizi who on the previous day was arrested and had his cart confiscated sets himself on fire after being ignored by the Tunisian authorities when complaining to authorities about police brutality. He died of his wounds on January 4 2011. As the death of Bouazizi is announced over 5000 people take to the streets in his home town of Sidi Bouazid, the demonstrators demand better living conditions and a stop to police brutality and corruption in Tunisia. After weeks of demonstrations and clashes Tunisian president Zine el-Abidinde Ben Ali steps down and flees to Saudi Arabia, on

January 14, 2011. Ben Ali's ousting came at the price of dozens of lives caused by clashes between security forces and demonstrators mainly in the capital Tunis. Ben Ali is replaced by the ruling party's parliamentary speaker.

On January 26, 2011, the interim Tunisian government issued an international arrest warrant for Ben Ali, accusing him of taking money out of the nation illegally and illegally acquiring real estate and other assets abroad, Justice Minister Lazhar Karoui Chebbi said. Videos showed that the president stashed cash and jewelry in the president's palace. The gold and jewelry will be redistributed to the people by the government. The Swiss government announced that it was freezing millions of dollars held in bank accounts by his family. On Jan. 28, 2011, Interpol issued an arrest warrant for Ben Ali and his six family members, including his wife Leila. [7]

After Ben Ali fled Tunisia, he and his wife were tried in absentia for his suspected involvement in some of the country's largest businesses during his 23-year long reign. On June 20, 2011, Ben Ali and his wife were sentenced to 35 years in prison after being found guilty of theft and unlawful possession of cash and jewelry. The verdict also includes a penalty of 91 million Tunisian dinars (approximately 50 million Euro) that Ben Ali has to pay. [8]

Ben Ali's Prime Minister Gannouchi stepped down on February 27, being replaced by Fouad Mebazaa who immediately announced that new elections to assemble a council of representatives to rewrite the constitution would be held on July 24. The elections were ultimately held on October 23, 2011 in which once-banned Ennahda party won 89 of the 217 seats. The runners up in the first free elections in the north African country were the left-wing Congress for the Republic (CPR) with 29 seats, and the Popular Petition with 26 seats. The left-wing Ettakatol party won 20 seats, the Progressist Democratic Party took 16, and the Democratic Modernist Pole took five. Some of the remaining seats went to very small parties, including the Communists who won three. Sixteen seats went to candidates from independent lists. [9]

In December 2011, Moncef Marzouki was elected president with 153 of the 202 votes cast. He was elected president as part of a power-sharing deal between the Ennahda party and its smaller secularist coalition partners, Ettakatol and Marzouki's Congress for the Republic. Under the coalition deal, Ennahda's secretary-general, Hamadi Jebali, will hold the most powerful position, of prime minister, while the Ettakatol leader, Mustafa Ben Jaafar, becomes speaker of the constitutional assembly. Days after protests forced Ben Ali to flee on January 14, 2011, Marzouki flew home from Paris where he spent two decades in exile. Marzouki's organization, the Tunisian League for Human Rights, was a US National Endowment for Democracy and George Soros Open Society-funded International Federation for Human Rights (FIDH) member organization.

The myriad of NGOs and opposition organizations that worked with Marzouki to overthrow the government of Tunisia were fully subsidized and backed by the US government and US corporate-funded foundations. Marzouki was also founder and head of the Arab Commission for Human Rights, a collaborating institution with the US NED World Movement for Democracy (WMD) including for a "Conference on Human Rights Activists in Exile" and a participant in the WMD "third assembly" alongside Marzouki's Tunisian League for Human Rights, sponsored by NED, Soros' Open Society, and USAID.

Autocrat Mubarak quits but Egyptian army remains the arbiter of power

On January 16, 2011, two days after the departure of Tunisian president Zine el-Abidinde Ben Ali to Saudi Arabia, demonstrators take to the streets in Egypt chanting; "Ben Ali, tell Mubarak there is a plane waiting for him too." One week later, on January 25, tens of thousands of Egyptians take to the streets demanding the end of the pro-US regime of Hosni Mubarak in power since 1981. The initiative that started as a Facebook group enjoyed widespread support in all tiers of Egyptian society. Further the Muslim Brotherhood, a long since banned oppositional group in Egypt announced its support for the 'day of rage' marches, as did former head of the IAEA (International Atomic Energy Agency) Mohammed El-Barardei, who returned to Egypt from his home in Vienna. The protesters marched towards the central Tahrir Square, where they set camp. The Square became a symbolic stronghold of the protesters throughout the struggle against Mubarak.

After weeks of protests and numerous deaths due to clashes between protesters and pro-Mubarak elements, on February 11, 2011 Mubarak announced that he would step down as Egyptian President. Mubarak handed power to all powerful military junta upon his resignation. Preliminary death tolls of the tumultuous events that led to the resignation of Mubarak were put to over three hundred.

After months of violent demonstrations against the ruling junta, the head of the Egyptian national election committee, Abdel Moez Ibrahim announced on September 18, 2011 that the first elections in Egypt since the ouster of Mubarak will take place in a time period of several months beginning on November 21, 2011 and continue through to January 3.

The first part of the complicated and stretched out Egyptian elections was held On November 28, 2011. The second round of the elections for the lower house of the Egyptian parliament was held, on December 14, 2011.

The final results of the parliamentary elections were announced on January 21, 2012. Religious parties constituted a large majority of the newly elected People's Assembly, with the Muslim Brotherhood's Freedom and Justice Party winning about 47 percent of the seats in the assembly and the Nūr Party winning 25 percent. The first session of the People's Assembly was held on January 23, 2012. The secretary-general of the Freedom and Justice Party, Muḥammad Saʿad al-Katātnī, was appointed speaker of the assembly.

Manufacturing a facade of democracy in Egypt

On June 24, 2012, Mohammed Mursi of the Muslim Brotherhood, was declared the winner of Egypt's presidential election run-off. He won 51.73% of the vote, beating former Prime Minister Ahmed Shafiq. However, shortly before the presidential vote, with the help of a Mubarak-era judiciary, the Supreme Council of the Armed Forces (SCAF), dissolved the parliament and gave itself the legislative power, which cuts into Mursi's powers to act.

The pro-US army, which receives $1.3 billion in U.S. military aid yearly for maintaining ties with Israel, has ruled Egypt since February 2011 revolution that toppled former president Hosni Mubarak. The military council had promised to oversee a transition to democracy, however, a series of decrees has led many to believe it intends to cling on to power. On June 13, the justice ministry gave soldiers the right to arrest civilians for trial in military courts until the ratification of a new constitution.

The SCAF then issued a decree on June 15 dissolving parliament in line with a Supreme Constitutional Court ruling that the law on elections to the lower house was invalid because party members had been allowed to contest seats reserved for independents.

On June 19, just as the polls were closing in the presidential run-off, the generals issued an interim constitutional declaration that granted them legislative powers and reinforced their role in the drafting of a permanent constitution. The military was also exempted from civilian oversight. Field Marshal Tantawi has also announced the re-establishment of a National Defense Council, putting the generals in charge of Egypt's national security policy.

The exact powers of Egypt's incoming president, and of the parliament, remain undefined, and the court-ordered disbandment of the lower house appeared to abort a committee appointed to draft a new constitution that would define them.

Ahram Online pointed out that the Muslim Brotherhood's Mohamed Mursi will be sworn in to a truncated presidency. According to CNN, for the moment, the presidency is largely a figurehead position as Egypt's Supreme Council of the Armed Forces (SCAF) maintains widespread control over the country including the power to make laws and budget decisions. Egypt Independent says Mursi faces a daunting struggle for power with the country's still-dominant military rulers who took over after Mubarak's ouster in the uprising.

On the 14 June 2012, just two days before the second round of the presidential elections was due to take place, the Higher Constitutional Court declared the election unconstitutional, on the grounds that political party candidates had been permitted to contest one-third of the parliamentary seats reserved for individual, non-partisan candidates.

One of the key legislative changes the SCAF made after the ouster of Mubarak, was that the heads of courts were appointed by the General Assembly of Judges, on the grounds of seniority, not by the president as was the case before. This allowed the SCAF to confirm the appointment of the constitutional court's new head, Judge Maher El-Beheiry. El-Beheiry will start his new role on 1 July; the day after the president is sworn in.

The president will not be able to change El-Beheiry, as according to Article 57 of the Constitutional Declaration, "judges... are not subject to removal." This also means the majority of Egypt's judges, including El-Beheiry, are Mubarak-appointees. Mubark raised the number of judges over the last 12 years which has ensured that the court is stacked in favor of the former regime.

The constitutional addendum announced by the SCAF on 18 June, as the presidential runoff polling stations closed, assigned yet more authorities to the SCAF. It was called by many as another military coup. Under the addendum, the SCAF would be responsible for deciding on all issues related to the armed forces including appointing its commanders and extending the terms in office of the aforesaid commanders, effectively making the military council immune.

The president cannot declare war without the approval of the SCAF. In addition, should there be domestic unrest within the country the president would have to ask permission of the military council for assistance. Now that the president is no longer head of the police, effectively the president has absolutely no control over weaponry or an armed force.

Egypt's infamous emergency law re-imposed

It may be recalled that Egypt's infamous emergency law, which had given President Hosni Mubarak and his police forces vast authority to crack down on dissent, expired on May 31, 2012 and officials said they were disinclined to extend it.

Suspension of the law, which had been in effect for more than 30 years, was among the key demands of revolutionaries who toppled Mubarak on Feb. 11, 2011. Human rights activists hailed its expiration as a historic milestone and among the most important dividends of last year's popular revolt. "It's a law that symbolized the extraordinary powers given to the police, which created an environment in which forced disappearances and torture happened regularly," said Heba Morayef, a Cairo-based researcher for Human Rights Watch.

The Brotherhood, a venerable organization, was among the opposition groups in the country that suffered most from the law. Many of the organization's leaders were imprisoned for years, without due process, based on the government's contention that they posed a security threat. However, just days before the presidential vote, on June 13, the Egyptian government announced that military police and intelligence officers have been given the right to detain civilians.

The decree was dated June 4, meaning it was issued just four days after the expiration of Egypt's infamous emergency law, which for decades gave the state broad powers to imprison political activists which posed a threat to the ruling party. The new edict authorizes military and intelligence officials to detain civilians for numerous alleged offenses, including disobeying orders, blocking traffic and going on strike.

Egyptian-Israeli relations

Not surprisingly, on March 12, 2012, the new Egyptian parliament unanimously voted in support of the expulsion of Israel's ambassador in Cairo and for a halt to gas exports to Israel. The motion was largely symbolic because only the ruling military council can make such decisions, and it was not likely to impact Egypt's relations with Israel. But the move signaled the seismic change in Egypt after the ouster of longtime leader and Israeli ally Hosni Mubarak a year ago. The vote was taken by a show of hands on a report by the chamber's Arab affairs committee that declared that Egypt will "never" be a friend, partner or ally of Israel. The report described Israel as the nation's "number one enemy." The parliamentary report also called for a revision of Egypt's nuclear power policy in view of the widespread suspicion that Israel has a nuclear arsenal of its own.

Earlier on May 4, 2011, he Palestinian organizations Hamas and Fatah, bitter rivals and enemies agreed, under the mediation of the new Egyptian government to bury the hatchet and reconcile peacefully. On May 28, 2011, Egypt reopens its Rafah border crossing with the Gaza Strip, enabling the citizens of Gaza to freely cross the border for the first time in four years. This move was a sharp departure from the politics enforced by Mubarak.

And on September 10, 2011, Egyptian protesters attacked the Israeli embassy in Cairo, demolishing one outer wall and wreaking havoc within the building. The Israeli staff and ambassador were flow back to Israel. The attacks were, according to interviews with participants a reaction to the shooting to death of five Egyptian border police men as Israeli forces hunted a group of attackers across the Israeli/Egyptian border.

Who is Mohammed Morsi? A U.S.-educated engineer, Mr. Mursi will be the Arab world's first freely elected president, the Wall Street Journal said adding: " That he hails from a conservative Islamist party, with offshoots in nearly every Muslim country, is certain to reverberate beyond Egypt's borders—particularly in other Arab states still in the throes of revolution."

Mursi was born in 1951 in the Delta province of Sharqiya. He studied engineering at Cairo University before he went to the University of South California to pursue a PhD. According to his resume posted on a Muslim Brotherhood's website, Mursi worked as assistant professor at California State University Northridge in the early 1980s.

He returned to Egypt in the mid-1980s to teach at Zagazig University's Faculty of Engineering.

In 2006, Mursi was detained for seven months on grounds of participating in a protest denouncing Mubarak's interference with the judiciary. On the early morning of 28 January 2011, Mursi was arrested along with several Muslim Brotherhood leaders as part of Mubarak's last desperate measure to pre-empt the sweeping protests that were set to kick off on that day.

During his parliamentary tenure from 2000 to 2005, Mursi initiated several motions to expose government corruption. He also called for several political reforms including the abolition of the notorious political parties law, the empowerment of municipal councils, the lifting of the state of emergency and all restrictions on the press and student political activities. Mursi was also an outspoken critic of the Egypt-Israel gas deal.

He also had filed an information request alleging that there are pro-American forces within the government seek to weaken Al-Azhar and religious education.

Hours after the result, Mr Mursi resigned from his positions within the Muslim Brotherhood including his role as chairman of its Freedom and Justice Party (FJP) as he had pledged to do in the event of his victory.

The West's 'humanitarian' invasion of Libya

"War and the "free market" go hand in hand... War physically destroys what has not been dismantled through deregulation, privatization and the imposition of "free market" reforms, says Prof. Michel Chossudovsky, the author of "The Globalization of Poverty and the New World Order" [10]

Perhaps this is true in the case of Libya where unlike the autocratic rulers of Egypt and Tunisia, Gaddafi had secured a mass regional base among a substantial sector of the Libyan population. This support was based on the fact that almost two generations of Libyans have benefited from Gaddafi's petroleum-financed welfare, educational, employment and housing programs, none of which existed under America's favorite, King Idris.

Unlike Tunisia or Egypt where it can be argued that the population was suffering from exploding food prices and a vast wealth gap, Gaddafi's Libya was very different.

To borrow historian F. William Engdahl, Libyans enjoyed the highest living standard on the Continent. "Gaddafi did not stay on top for 42 years without ensuring that his population had little room to complain. Most health services, education and fuel was state-subsidized. Gaddafi's Libya had the lowest infant mortality rate and highest life expectancy of all Africa. When he seized power from ailing King Idris four decades ago literacy was below 10% of the population. Today it is above 90%, hardly the footprint of your typical tyrant. Less than 5% of the population is undernourished, a figure lower than in the United States. In response to the rising food prices of recent months, Gaddafi took care to abolish all taxes on food. And a lower percentage of people lived below the poverty line than in the Netherlands. Gaddafi calls his model a form of Islamic socialism. It is secular and not theocratic, despite its overwhelmingly Sunni base in the population."

Why is the United States so opposed to Gadaffi? Clearly because he is simply "not with the program." Gaddafi has shown repeatedly and not without grounds that he deeply distrusts Washington. He has constantly tried to forge an independent voice for an Africa that is increasingly being usurped by the Pentagon's AFRICOM. In 1999 he initiated creation of the African Union, based in Addis Abbaba, to strengthen the international voice of Africa's former colonial states. At a pan-African summit in 2009 he appealed for creation of a United States of Africa to combine the economic strengths of what is perhaps the world's richest continent in terms of unexploited mineral and agricultural potentials [11]

Many are convinced intervention in Libya is all about Gaddafi's plan to introduce the gold dinar, a single African-Muslim currency made from gold, a true sharing of the wealth. According to Ministry of Peace founder Dr James Thring. "There were two conferences on this, in 1986 and 2000, organized by Gaddafi. everybody was interested, most countries in Africa were keen." Gaddafi did not give up. In the months leading up to the military intervention, he called on African and Muslim nations to join together to create this new currency that would rival the dollar and euro. They would sell oil and other resources around the world only for gold dinars. It is an idea that would shift the economic balance of the world. A country's wealth would depend on how much gold it had and not how many dollars it traded. And Libya has 144 tons of gold.

Gaddafi has been working for decades to build an independent voice for African states not controlled by either the US or former European colonial powers, his United States of Africa. [12]

So long as he remains, Libya poses an embarrassing economic alternative to Washington's 'free market' globalization template which it is now desperate to impose on the one billion peoples of the Islamic world from Morocco across Africa and the Middle East to Afghanistan. For the powers driving this spreading war, it is a question of survival of the American Century, or what the quaint neo-conservatives called the New American Century, of the future survival of a sole American Superpower through spreading war and chaos as its own economy disintegrates more by the day. [13]

Libyan "revolution" was actually a civil war brokered by Western powers - US, UK, and France - and some Arab countries like Egypt, UAE, and Qatar. Egypt and Qatar were the main arms suppliers to the Libyan rebels. Under American pressure Arab League urged UN to impose a no-fly zone over Libya, and Qatar offered to cover all expenses of NATO forces to bomb alleged Gaddafi's forces.

The NATO operation purports to enforce the neoliberal economic agenda. Countries which are reluctant to accept the sugar coated bullets of IMF "economic medicine" will eventually be the object of a responsibility to protect [R2P] NATO humanitarian operation. [14]

The objective of the NATO bombings of Libya from the outset was to destroy the country's standard of living, its health infrastructure, its schools and hospitals, its water distribution system. And then "rebuild" with the help of donors and creditors under the helm of the IMF and the World Bank. [15]

About nine thousand strike sorties, tens of thousands of strikes on civilian targets including residential areas, government buildings, water supply and electricity generation facilities. [16]

According to the NATO press release of September 5, 2011, since the beginning of the NATO operation (31 March 2011) a total of 21,662 sorties including 8,140 strike sorties have been conducted.

Not surprisingly, the World Bank announced on September 13, 2011, that it has been asked to lead the effort in the areas of public expenditure and financial management, infrastructure repair, job creation for young people and service delivery. "The World Bank joins the United Nations and the European Union as one of the three institutions invited by Libya's National Transitional Council (NTC) to coordinate assistance for the north African nation as it forges a path forward after months of violent conflict."

Specifically, the Bank has been asked to examine the need for repair and restoration of services in the water, energy and transport sectors and, in cooperation with the International Monetary Fund, to support budget preparation and help the banking sector back on to its feet. Employment generation for young Libyans has been added as an urgent need facing the country.

"We are ready to support the people in Libya. Our experts have started coordinating with their partners already and we are moving fast to begin work," said Sri Mulyani Indrawati, Managing Director of the World Bank. "The areas we have been requested to help with reflect our comparative advantage and we will work closely with the EU, the UN and our Arab partners." [17]

Libya's frozen overseas financial assets are estimated to be of the order of $150 billion, with NATO countries holding more than $100 billion. Prior to the war, Libya had no debts. In fact quite the opposite. It was a creditor nation investing in neighboring African countries. The R2P military intervention is intended to spearhead the Libyan Arab Jamahiriya into the straightjacket of an indebted developing country, under the surveillance of the Washington based Bretton Woods institutions. [18]

In a bitter irony, after having stolen Libya's oil wealth and confiscated its overseas financial assets, the "donor community" has pledged to lend the (stolen) money back to finance Libya's post-war "reconstruction".   Libya is slated to join the ranks of indebted African countries which have driven into poverty by IMF and the World Bank since the onsalught of the debt crisis in the early 1980s. [19]

Responsibility to Protect R2P

The Responsibility to Protect (R2P) principle calls for the international community to intervene with diplomatic and, if necessary, military action, in cases of genocide, ethnic cleansing, war crimes, and crimes against humanity. Since its contested adoption at the UN's World summit in 2005, the R2P doctrine's well-funded lobbyists have by and large insulated themselves from scrutiny and have generally evaded debates with their detractors.

In February 2011, R2P was invoked by the Security Council, the Secretary-General's Special Advisers on the Prevention of Genocide and the responsibility to protect, and a number of civil society organizations. Whereas the uprisings in Tunisia and Egypt were primarily considered an internal matter with significant repercussions for the region, the need for appropriate international engagement has been more broadly discussed in relation to the situation in Libya.

During the July 2009 debate at the UN on the principle of the Responsibility to Protect (R2P)Noam Chomsky began by stating, "The discussions about R2P, or it's cousin, humanitarian aid, are regularly disturbed by a skeleton in the closet, history" He then listed imperialist genocides committed under the guise of humanitarian aid throughout history, dating back to the 17th century. Belgian academic Jean Bricmont stated that, "The main obstacle to the implementation of a genuine and acceptable R2P, are precisely the policies and the attitudes of the countries that are most enthusiastic for R2P, namely the western countries and in particular the United States."

[20]   "They're not double standards; they're the single standard of maximizing power and wealth and privilege, and that applies in different ways in different times. So Palestine is particularly significant for the United Nations because these are protected people under the Geneva Conventions. So it's like the Iraq sanctions, which were in fact administered by the Security Council. So yeah, those are real responsibilities by the United Nations..and to answer your question about why nothing can be done, it's because the United States and its allies don't want anything to be done." [21]

As Michael Barker, an Australian analyst of the use of humanitarian rhetoric and US-based NGOs to advance a Washington agenda noted, "Perhaps if 'evil' Qaddafi had been a bona fide US-backed dictator...the US government could have exerted more influence over Qaddafi's political choices, and encouraged him to back down and allow himself to be replaced with a suitably US friendly leader. However, it is precisely because Qaddafi is not a Western-backed dictator that external powers cannot force his hand so easily: this helps explain why the world's leading...elites were so keen to use the humanitarian pretext to support his opponents in the civil war." [22]

On October 20, 2011, Gaddafi was captured and killed in mysterious circumstances. On October 25, a National Transitional Council (NTC) official told the BBC that the bodies of Gaddafi, his son Mutassim and former Defense Minister Abu Bakr Younis Jabr have been buried in secret in the desert.

On October 31, 2011, Abdurraheem el-Keib, a dual U.S.-Libyan citizen, was chosen by members of the Transitional National Council as prime minister. El-Keib, a resident of Tripoli, earned his PhD at North Carolina State University in 1984 and was a longtime professor at the University of Alabama. He joined the interim council last spring. El-Keib's election came just hours before NATO formally ended its seven-month bombing campaign in Libya. El-Keib replaced Mahmoud Jibril, an American-educated political scientist.

On July 7, 2012, elections were held for 80 seats of the 200-member General National Congress (GNC). The rest so-called independent 120 seats will be filled through a controversial process. These individual seats will all be filled with independent candidates not affiliated with any political party, but nothing prevented candidates from being endorsed by a political party.

Former interim Prime Minister Mahmoud Jibril's National Forces Alliance won 39 seats, or nearly half of those allocated for parties. The Muslim Brotherhood's Justice and Construction party came in second with 17 seats. Smaller factions won the other 24 seats set aside for parties. Jibril's party is comprised of dozens of parties and civil society groups. In its political platform, the alliance states that Islamic Shariah law should be the main source of legislation, but adds that the state must respect all religions and sects.

US groups spreading 'democracy'

Centre for Applied Non Violent Actions and Strategies

The Centre for Applied Non Violent Actions and Strategies (CANVAS) is a non-profit, non-governmental, educational institution focused on the use of nonviolent conflict to promote human rights and democracy. It was founded in 2004 by Srđa Popović and Slobodan Đinović, former members of the Serbian youth resistance movement, Otpor!, which played a key role in the overthrow of Slobodan Milošević in October 2000. Drawing upon the Serbian experience, CANVAS seeks to educate pro-democracy activists around the world in what it regards as the universal principles for success in nonviolent struggle. [Wikipedia]

Established in Belgrade, CANVAS has worked with pro-democracy activists from more than 50 countries, including Iran, Zimbabwe, Burma, Venezuela, Ukraine, Georgia, Palestine, Western Sahara, West Papua, Eritrea, Belarus, Azerbaijan and Tonga and, recently, Tunisia and Egypt. It works only with groups with no history of violence and only in response to requests for assistance. CANVAS' training and methodology has reportedly been successfully applied by groups in Georgia (2003), Ukraine (2004), Lebanon (2005), The Maldives (2008) and Egypt (2011). [23]

Alliance of Youth Movements

The Alliance of Youth Movements was an event in 2008 which led to the creation of Movements.org, a nonprofit organization dedicated to identifying, connecting, and supporting, digital activists. Founders of Movements.org include Jared Cohen, former advisor to both Secretaries of State Condoleezza Rice and Hillary Clinton and a director at Google, Jason Liebman, CEO and co-founder of Howcast, the How-to website, and Roman Tsunder, co-founder of Access 360 Media. Movements.org hosts annual conferences, events, and trainings that link influential leaders in technology, media, in the private and public sectors with the some of the world's most promising digital activists. The organization's website, Movements.org, serves as a hub for discussion, resources, and news about digital activism around the world. [Wikipedia]

Movements.org began with a December 2008 summit in New York City to identify, convene, and engage 21st century movements online for the first time in history. The US Department of State partnered with Facebook, Howcast, MTV, Google, YouTube, AT&T, JetBlue, Gen-Nex, Access 360 Media, and Columbia Law School to launch a global network and empower young people mobilizing against violence and oppression. The inaugural summit was called the Alliance of Youth Movements Summit. Later when the organization launched its website in 2011, Movements.org, they began to refer to the organization as Movements.org. Speakers at the inaugural 2008 summit included actress Whoopi Goldberg, Facebook co-founder Dustin Moskovitz, the Obama Campaign's New Media Team, and then-current Under Secretary of State for Public Diplomacy and Public Affairs of the United States James K. Glassman. [Wikipedia]

In March 2009 U.S. Secretary of State Hillary Clinton announced and endorsed the Second Alliance for Youth Movements Summi, held October 14–16, 2009 in Mexico City. This Summit explored the role of technology in mobilizing young people working to end violence throughout Latin America and around the world. Young delegates, described by Secretary Clinton as "the vanguard of a rising generation of citizen activists," were joined by more than 15 private and public partners, including the world's leading technology companies. Together they launched discussions on how best to use the latest technological tools to catalyze change, build movements, and transform lives. [24]

In June 2012, Movements.org formally became a division of Advancing Human Rights (AHR), created in 2010 by Robert L. Bernstein, the founder of the New York-based Human Rights Watch Human Rights Watch with offices in Berlin, Beirut, Brussels, Chicago, Geneva, Johannesburg, London, Los Angeles, Moscow, Paris, San Francisco, Tokyo, Toronto, and Washington.

As of June 2011, the organization's annual expenses totaled $50.6 million. The George Soros Open Society Foundation is the primary donor of the Human Rights Watch, contributing $100 Million of $128 Million of contributions and grants received by the HRW in the 2011 financial year. The $100 Million contribution from the Open Society Foundation will be paid out over ten years in $10 Million annual installments. [25]

International Republican Institute

Founded in 1983, the International Republican Institute (IRI) is an ideologically right-wing organization, funded by the United States government, that conducts international political programs, sometimes called 'democratization programs'. [26]

Initially known as the National Republican Institute for International Affairs, the IRI's stated mission is to expand freedom throughout the world. Its activities include teaching and assisting with right-wing political party and candidate development in their values, "good governance" practices, civil society development, civic education, women's and youth leadership development, electoral reform and election monitoring, and political expression in closed societies. It has been chaired by former presidential candidate John McCain since January 1993. [27]

At first, IRI focused on democratic institutions and processes in Latin America but has expanded its focus worldwide since the end of the Cold War. IRI has conducted programs in more than 100 countries and is currently active in 70 countries. IRI was involved in Haiti prior to the 2004 Haitian coup d'état, in Honduras following the 2009 Coup d'état,, attempting to normalise and legitimise it, organised right-wing political parties in Poland, and has been involved in political activities in Egypt during the Arab Spring. [28]

The majority of the IRI's funding comes from the US Agency for International Development (USAID), the US State Department, and the National Endowment for Democracy. The IRI operates as a political organization abroad, providing training and assistance to favored political parties. As a 501(c)(3) tax-exempt organization, it plays no part in domestic U.S. politics. However, the majority of its board, staff and consultants are drawn from the Republican Party. Its sister organization, the National Democratic Institute for International Affairs, draws mainly from the Democratic Party. [29]

National Democratic Institute for International Affairs

The National Democratic Institute for International Affairs (NDIIA or NDI) is an organization created by the United States government by way of the National Endowment for Democracy (NED) to channel grants for furthering democracy in developing nations. It was founded in 1983, shortly after the U.S. Congress created the National Endowment for Democracy. Taxpayer funding is provided by the

Federal Government, both directly from the United States Agency for International Development and the Department of State and indirectly through the National Endowment for Democracy. [30]

NDI has worked in 125 different countries and territories since it was created and its six main areas of work are citizen participation, election processes, political parties, women in politics, democracy and technology, and democratic governance. [31]

NDI is loosely associated with the Democratic Party of the United States and maintains ties with the Liberal International of UK, Socialist International, and the Centrist Democrat International (formerly Christian Democrats). Its board of directors is chaired by Madeleine K. Albright. [32]

National Endowment for Democracy

The National Endowment for Democracy, or NED, is a U.S. non-profit organization that was founded in 1983 to promote democracy. It is funded primarily through an annual allocation from the U.S. Congress, within the budget of USAID, the U.S. agency for development assistance, which is part of the U.S. State Department. Although administered as a private organization, its funding mostly comes from a governmental appropriation by Congress but was created by The Democracy Program as a bipartisan, private, non-profit corporation. In addition to its grants program, NED also supports and houses the Journal of Democracy, the World Movement for Democracy, the International Forum for Democratic Studies, the Reagan-Fascell Fellowship Program, the Network of Democracy Research Institutes, and the Center for International Media Assistance. [33]

NED is structured to act as a grant-making foundation, distributing funds to private non-governmental organizations for the purpose of promoting democracy abroad. Approximately half of NED's funding is allocated annually to four main U.S. organizations: the American Center for International Labor Solidarity (ACILS), the Center for International Private Enterprise (CIPE), the National Democratic Institute for International Affairs (NDI), and the International Republican Institute (IRI). The other half of NED's funding is awarded annually to hundreds of non-governmental organizations based abroad which apply for support. NED's long time president is Carl Gershman, former Senior Counselor to the United States Representative to the United Nations and former Executive Director of Social Democrats USA. [34]

F. William Engdahl Freedom House and Washington's government-funded regime change NGO, National Endowment for Democracy (NED) are at the heart of the uprisings now sweeping across the Islamic world. They fit the geographic context of what George W. Bush proclaimed after 2001 as his Greater Middle East Project to bring "democracy" and "liberal free market" economic reform to the Islamic countries from Afghanistan to Morocco. When Washington talks about introducing "liberal free market reform" people should watch out. It is little more than code for bringing those economies under the yoke of the dollar system and all that implies. [35]

The list of where the NED is active is revealing. Its website lists Tunisia, Egypt, Jordan, Kuwait, Libya, Syria, Yemen and Sudan as well, interestingly, as Israel. Coincidentally these countries are almost all today subject to "spontaneous" popular regime-change uprisings. [36]

The International Republican Institute and the National Democratic Institute for International Affairs mentioned by the RAND document study of Kefaya are subsidiary organizations of the Washington-based and US Congress-financed National Endowment for Democracy. [37]

The NED is the coordinating Washington agency for regime destabilization and change. It is active from Tibet to Ukraine, from Venezuela to Tunisia, from Kuwait to Morocco in reshaping the world after the collapse of the Soviet Union into what George H.W. Bush in a 1991 speech to Congress proclaimed triumphantly as the dawn of a New World Order. [38]

As the architect and first head of the NED, Allen Weinstein told the Washington Post in 1991 that, "a lot of what we do today was done covertly 25 years ago by the CIA." [39]

The NED Board of Directors includes or has included former Defense Secretary and CIA Deputy head, Frank Carlucci of the Carlyle Group; retired General Wesley Clark of NATO; neo-conservative war hawk Zalmay Khalilzad who was architect of George W. Bush's Afghan invasion and later ambassador to Afghanistan as well as to occupied Iraq. Another NED board member, Vin Weber, co-chaired a major independent task force on US Policy toward Reform in the Arab World with former

US Secretary of State Madeleine Albright, and was a founding member of the ultra-hawkish Project for a New American Century think-tank with Dick Cheney and Don Rumsfeld, which advocated forced regime change in Iraq as early as 1998.20 [40]

The NED is supposedly a private, non-government, non-profit foundation, but it receives a yearly appropriation for its international work from the US Congress. The National Endowment for Democracy is dependent on the US taxpayer for funding, but because NED is not a government agency, it is not subject to normal Congressional oversight. [41]

NED money is channeled into target countries through four "core foundations"—the National Democratic Institute for International Affairs, linked to the Democratic Party; the International Republican Institute tied to the Republican Party; the American Center for International Labor Solidarity linked to the AFL-CIO US labor federation as well as the US State Department; and the Center for International Private Enterprise linked to the free-market US Chamber of Commerce. [42]

Significantly the NED details its various projects today in Islamic countries, including in addition to Egypt, in Tunisia, Yemen, Jordan, Algeria, Morocco, Kuwait, Lebanon, Libya, Syria, Iran and Afghanistan. In short, most every country which is presently feeling the earthquake effects of the reform protests sweeping across the Middle East and North Africa is a target of NED. [43]

Arab regimes alarmed at the US "Democracy" groups

Not surprisingly, the work of the US "pro-democracy groups" often provoked tensions between the United States and many autocrat Middle Eastern leaders, who frequently complained that their leadership was being undermined.

According to the New York Times, interviews with officials of the nongovernmental groups and a review of diplomatic cables obtained by WikiLeaks show that the democracy programs were constant sources of tension between the United States and many Arab governments. The cables, in particular, show how leaders in the Middle East and North Africa viewed these groups with deep suspicion, and tried to weaken them. Today the work of these groups is among the reasons that governments in turmoil claim that Western meddling was behind the uprisings, with some officials noting that leaders like Ms. Qadhi (a youth leader in Yemen) were trained and financed by the United States. Diplomatic cables report how American officials frequently assured skeptical governments that the training was aimed at reform, not promoting revolutions. [44]

Last year, for example, a few months before national elections in Bahrain, officials there barred a representative of the National Democratic Institute from entering the country. In Bahrain, officials worried that the group's political training "disproportionately benefited the opposition," according to a January 2010 cable. [45]

In Yemen, where the United States has been spending millions on an anti-terrorism program, officials complained that American efforts to promote democracy amounted to "interference in internal Yemeni affairs." [46]

But nowhere was the opposition to the American groups stronger than in Egypt. Egypt, whose government receives $1.5 billion annually in military and economic aid from the United States, viewed efforts to promote political change with deep suspicion, even outrage. Hosni Mubarak, then Egypt's president, was "deeply skeptical of the U.S. role in democracy promotion," said a diplomatic cable from the United States Embassy in Cairo dated Oct. 9, 2007.

In 2005, under a Bush administration initiative, local groups were given direct grants, much to the chagrin of Egyptian officials. According to a September 2006 cable, Mahmoud Nayel, an official with the Egyptian Ministry of Foreign Affairs, complained to American Embassy officials about the United States government's "arrogant tactics in promoting reform in Egypt."

The main targets of the Egyptian complaints were the Republican and Democratic institutes. Diplomatic cables show that Egyptian officials complained that the United States was providing support for "illegal organizations." The Egyptian government even appealed to groups like Freedom House to stop working with local political activists and human rights groups. When their appeals to the United States government failed, the Egyptian authorities reacted by restricting the activities of the American non-profit organizations.

In the face of government opposition, some groups moved their training sessions to friendlier countries like Jordan or Morocco. They also sent activists to the United States for training, the New York Times report concluded.

Emirates Detain Pair From U.S.-Backed Group

On April 3, 2012, the United Arab Emirates detained two employees of an American-financed pro-democracy organization and barred one of them from leaving the country. The United Arab Emirates, one of the closest American allies in the Persian Gulf, In March ordered the closing of the organization, the National Democratic Institute, and then detained its two employees as they prepared to leave the country. The institute's local director, Patricia Davis, an American, was ultimately allowed to leave. The detentions appeared to be part of a broader crackdown on nongovernmental organizations in the country, which also shut down a German advocacy group, the Konrad Adenauer Foundation, which has close ties to the government of Chancellor Angela Merkel. [47]

Egypt bars US-based civil society groups

In April 2012, Egypt rejected a request from eight US-based civil society groups for licences to operate in the country. Egyptian state news agency MENA said requests from the Carter Center for Human Rights, Coptic Orphans, Seeds of Peace and other groups had been rejected.

The Egyptian decision came on the same day that Interpol's headquarters in France refused a request by Egypt to issue worldwide arrest warrants for 15 employees of a number of US-based non-governmental organizations that operate in Egypt. Interpol's statement said the request for arrest warrants for the 15, of whom 12 were Americans, was not in line with its rules that forbid "political, military, religious or racial" interventions. [48]

Washington had threatened to withdraw $3 billion in military aid until an Egyptian judge lifted a travel ban on several American democracy activists in March 2012 and allowed them to leave the country and avoid possible imprisonment. But just after the United States announced it was resuming aid to Egypt in March, Cairo asked Interpol to issue "red notices" for 15 other NGO workers who were not in Egypt when the charges against the organizations were made.

Twelve of the 15 whose arrest was sought by Egypt were American, two were Lebanese and one was Jordanian, Interpol said in its statement.

Egyptian police raided the offices of Freedom House and other pro-democracy groups in late December2011. Prosecutors later charged 43 people including 16

Americans - one of them the son of U.S. Transportation Secretary Ray LaHood - with working for organizations that received illegal foreign funding.

On June 3, 2012, a dual U.S.-Egyptian citizen, Sherif Mansour, was detained on arrival at Cairo airport because he faces trial in a case of pro-democracy groups receiving foreign funds. According to the Egyptian officials Sherif Mansour was detained as one of 43 defendants, including 16 Americans, on trial in the case that has shaken Cairo's ties with Washington. The trial began in February, with only 14 Egyptian defendants attending. The defendants are facing charges over their groups' receiving foreign funds without permits. Six Americans charged in the case were allowed to leave the country in March. [49]

Responsibility to Protect R2P

In February 2011, R2P was invoked by the Security Council, the Secretary-General's Special Advisers on the Prevention of Genocide and the responsibility to protect, and a number of civil society organizations. Whereas the uprisings in Tunisia and Egypt were primarily considered an internal matter with significant repercussions for the region, the need for appropriate international engagement has been more broadly discussed in relation to the situation in Libya.

The Responsibility to Protect (R2P) principle calls for the international community to intervene with diplomatic and, if necessary, military action, in cases of genocide, ethnic cleansing, war crimes, and crimes against humanity. Since its contested adoption at the UN's World summit in 2005, the R2P doctrine's well-funded lobbyists have by and large insulated themselves from scrutiny and have generally evaded debates with their detractors.

The Global Centre for the Responsibility to Protect, much like the famous wooden Russian dolls, was created by other human rights NGOs including by the International Crisis Group, Human Rights Watch, Oxfam International, Refugees International, typically financed by a small network of donors. Gareth Evans is co-chair of the Global Centre for the Responsibility to Protect's International Advisory Board, as well as being President Emeritus of the International Crisis Group which he led from 2000 to 2009. [50]

What is ICG? In addition to getting government funds from the US and UK governments, Evans' International Crisis Group also gets generous support from the Rockefeller, Ford and MacArthur foundations.[xi] George Soros, founder of the Open Society Institute sits on the ICG Board of Trustees. Until he made his dramatic and well-timed return to Egypt in January 2011, Mohamed El Baradei also sat on the board of the Brussels-based ICG. [51]

The ICG was previously headed by Zbigniew Brzezinski, adviser to US presidents and long-time associate of David Rockefeller. Among other leading figures linked to Evans' International Crisis Group have been founder, Morton Abramowitz, former board member of the National Endowment for Democracy. [52]

During the July 2009 debate at the UN on the principle of the Responsibility to Protect (R2P)Noam Chomsky began by stating, "The discussions about R2P, or it's cousin, humanitarian aid, are regularly disturbed by a skeleton in the closet, history" He then listed imperialist genocides committed under the guise of humanitarian aid throughout history, dating back to the 17th century. Belgian academic Jean Bricmont stated that, "The main obstacle to the implementation of a genuine and acceptable R2P, are precisely the policies and the attitudes of the countries that are most enthusiastic for R2P, namely the western countries and in particular the United States." [53]

"They're not double standards; they're the single standard of maximizing power and wealth and privilege, and that applies in different ways in different times. So Palestine is particularly significant for the United Nations because these are protected people under the Geneva Conventions. So it's like the Iraq sanctions, which were in fact administered by the Security Council. So yeah, those are real responsibilities by the United Nations..and to answer your question about why nothing can be done, it's because the United States and its allies don't want anything to be done." [54]

Chomsky and Bricmont provided a laundry list of historical 'R2P-like' interventions carried out by imperial powers (they could have mentioned Afghanistan's recent transformation to an R2P-like occupation under Stanley McChrystal's 'population-centric' COIN approach). Many of the General Assembly's R2P-friendly delegates were uncomfortable with Chomsky, Bricmont, and Ngugi's constant drudging up of history. [55]

In the post-dialogue press conference, a reporter asked Chomsky if and how he thinks R2P can be applied to R2P in Gaza:

"It's very simple, it doesn't apply. It doesn't apply because of...the U.S. is backing the destruction of Gaza so therefore R2P doesn't apply; it's very simple...And it's not just Gaza, it's also the West Bank. In fact in the West Bank...read the New York Times, they're very upbeat about the fact, as they put it, Israel finally has a legitimate partner for peace, maybe, in the Palestinian Authority. Why? Because of a big achievement. During the attack on Gaza, which was a U.S.-Israeli attack, not an Israeli attack; it was a U.S.-Israeli attack on Gaza, during that attack there was concern that there might be protests in the West Bank, but they were put down; they were put down by an army run by General Keith Dayton, U.S. General; trained and armed by Jordan and Israel, which is imposed in order to control the population of the West Bank." [56]

What is emerging, with the aggression against Libya as a major test case in the reframing of military intervention as responsibility to protect, is acceptance of radical new forms of US-orchestrated military intervention, with or without UN Security Council sanction, a radical new form of neo-colonialism, a major new step on the road to a New World Order, the Pentagon's much-sought Full Spectrum Dominance. [57]

Reference

1. Egypt's Revolution: Creative Destruction for a 'Greater Middle East'? by F. William Engdahl, February 4, 2011

2. Ibid.

3. Ibid.

4. Ibid.

5. Ibid.

6. U.S. Groups Helped Nurture Arab Uprisings – New York Times April 14, 2011

7. Wikipedia

8. Ibid.

9. Al Jazeera Nov 14, 2011

10. The Globalization of Poverty and the New World Order" by Michel Chossudovsky, 2003, paperback [first edition 1997 - p10]

11. Creative Destruction Part II: Libya in Washington's Greater Middle East Project By F. William Engdahl, March 26, 2011

12. Ibid.

13. Ibid.

14. Destroying a Country's Standard of Living: What Libya Had Achieved, What has been Destroyed By Prof. Michel Chossudovsky September 20, 2011

15. Ibid.

16] Ibid.

17. http://web.worldbank.org/WBSITE/EXTERNAL/NEWS/0,,contentMDK:22998913~pagePK:34370~piPK:34424~theSitePK:4607,00.html

18. Chossudovsky op. cit.

19. Ibid.

20. How Far Should U.N. Go to Protect Civilians by Henry Parr – IPS July 24, 2009

21. Ibid.

22. Humanitarian Neo-colonialism: Framing Libya and Reframing War By F. William Engdahl, 3 May 2011

23. Wikipedia

24. Ibid.

25. Ibid.

26. Ibid.

27. Ibid.

28. Ibid.

29. Ibid.

30. Ibid.

31 Ibid.

32. Ibid.

Chapter VII

The Muslim World in 2030/2050

- Muslim countries fire power
- The World in 2050 will shift in global economic power continue?
- The PWC projections for Muslim countries for 2030 & 2050
- Price Waterhouse Coopers projection for Indonesia
- The HSBC expects the emerging world to overtake developed economies
- Here are more highlights of the HSBC study
- The HSBC projections for Muslim countries
- Dramatic religious and economic shifts to impact planet

This chapter is based on the western projections for 2030/2050 which presume that the current political and economic structure created by the West after the Second World War will prevail. Not surprisingly, for the Islamic world economic and political forecasts are notoriously weak.

At 1.6 billion Muslims comprise one-fifth of the world's population. By 2050, that number is expected to rise to 2.76 billion, according to PEW projections. Sixty percent of the world's Muslims fall between the ages of 15 and 59 years, with the median age being 24 years. 317 million of the world's Muslims live in the Middle East and North Africa region (MENA) and 344 million in India and Pakistan.[1]

The Muslim countries collectively account for approximately 20 percent of the world's population, but only 7 percent of global output. The 23 Arab countries had a combined GDP of $1.9 trillion in 2010, compared with the European Union's GDP of $17.5 trillion. Spain alone produced $1.43 trillion in GDP, without the benefit of natural resources, such as oil and gas. [2]

Roughly half of the world's illiterate adults are Muslims, and two-thirds of that number are women. Greece, with a population of 11 million, translates more books from other languages into Greek than the entire Arab world, which has a cumulative population of 360 million, does into Arabic. More books are published in Danish, the mother tongue of 5.6 million people, than in Urdu, which is the language of at least 300 million South Asian Muslims. Since the 9th century, when the Abbasid rulers of Baghdad patronized learning and built a huge library for its time, only 100,000 books have been translated from other languages into Arabic. The same number of books are translated from other languages into Spanish every year. [3]

Muslim countries fire power [4]

As of April 1, 2016, there were a total of (126) countries included in the Global Fire Power database.

Four Muslim countries are listed in the first 15 countries:
Turkey (8), Egypt (12), Pakistan (13) and Indonesia (14).

First seven countries were: The United State (1), Russia (2), China (3), India (4), France (5), United Kingdom (6) and Japan (7). Germany (9), Italy (10) and South Korea (11) are followed by Turkey (8). Brazil (15) is followed by Turkey (8), Egypt (12), Pakistan (13) and Indonesia (14).

No projections were available for the military power of the Muslim countries in 2030/2050.

The World in 2050 will shift in global economic power continue? [5]

The global economic power shift away from the established advanced economies in North America, Western Europe and Japan will continue over the next 35 years. China has already overtaken the US in 2014 to become the largest economy in purchasing power parity (PPP2) terms. In market exchange rate (MER) terms, we project China to overtake the US in 2028 despite its projected growth slowdown.
India has the potential to become the second largest economy in the world by 2050 in PPP terms (third in MER terms), although this requires a sustained program of structural reforms.

We project that the gap between the three biggest economies (i.e. China, India and the US) and the rest of the world will widen over the next few decades. In 2014, the third biggest economy in PPP terms (India) is around 50% larger than the fourth biggest economy (Japan). In 2050, the third biggest economy in PPP terms (the US) is projected to be approximately 240% larger than the fourth biggest economy (Indonesia).

We project new emerging economies like Mexico and Indonesia to be larger than the UK and France by 2030 (in PPP terms) while Turkey could become larger than Italy. Nigeria and Vietnam could be the fast growing large economies over the period to 2050.

The rise of Indonesia and Nigeria through the world rankings throughout the period to 2050 is very striking: Indonesia rises from 9th in 2014 to 4th in 2050, and Nigeria rises from 20th in 2014 to 9th in 2050.

However, average income per capita (i.e. GDP per capita) will still be significantly higher in the advanced economies than the emerging economies in 2050. The current gap in income per capita between developing and developed countries is just too large to bridge fully over this period.

Colombia, Poland and Malaysia all possess great potential for sustainable long-term growth in the coming decades according to our country experts.
At the same time, recent experience has re-emphasized that relatively rapid growth is not guaranteed for emerging economies, as indicated by recent problems in Russia and Brazil, for example. It requires sustained and effective investment in infrastructure and improving political, economic, legal and social institutions. It also requires remaining open to the free flow of technology, ideas and talented people that are key drivers of economic catch-up growth.
We think that overdependence on natural resources could also impede long term growth in some countries (e.g. Russia, Nigeria and Saudi Arabia) unless they can diversify their economies.

The PWC projections for Muslim countries for 2030 & 2050 [6]

Ranking of Muslim countries out of 32 in 2014 according to GDP at purchasing power parity (PPP):

Indonesia (9), Saudi Arabia (14), Turkey (17), Iran (18), Nigeria (20), Egypt (22), Pakistan (25), Malaysia (27), Bangladesh (31).

Ranking of Muslim countries out of 32 in 2030 according to GDP at purchasing power parity (PPP):

Indonesia (5), Saudi Arabia (12), Turkey (14), Nigeria (16), Iran (19), Egypt (20), Pakistan (22), Malaysia (24), Bangladesh (29).

Ranking of Muslim countries out of 32 in 2050 according to GDP at purchasing power parity (PPP):

Indonesia (4), Nigeria (9), Saudi Arabia (12), Turkey (14), Pakistan (15), Egypt (16), Bangladesh (23), Malaysia (24), Iran (25)

Price Waterhouse Coopers projection for Indonesia [7]

A report by Price Waterhouse Coopers predicts that by 2050 the Indonesian economy will have grown to almost 20% the size of the US economy. Currently Indonesian GDP is 7% the size of the world giant America in purchasing power parity terms and 2% in current exchange rate terms.

Indonesia is included in a group called 'E7' which also is comprised of China, India, Brazil, Russia, Mexico and Turkey. By 2050, the report says, the 'E7' economies will have outstripped the current 'G7' (US, Japan, Germany, UK, France, Italy and Canada) "by between 25% when comparing GDP using market exchange rates to around 75% when using purchasing power parity (PPP) exchange rates".

Indonesia, along with Mexico, is also predicted to have eclipsed both Germany and the UK by 2050 even at market exchange rates terms.

The HSBC expects the emerging world to overtake developed economies [8]

The HSBC research finds that 19 of the world's top 30 economies in 2050 are emerging markets today.

China will be the world's biggest economy in 2050, the report predicts, having pushed the United States into second place. India will be third. Japan, Germany, Britain, Brazil, Mexico, France and Canada make up the remainder of the top 10.

The research bases its projections on the work of Harvard Professor Robert Barro, who found that the three key determinants of economic growth are economic governance (monetary stability, the rule of law, political rights and size of government), human capital (education, health and fertility rate) and the starting level of income per capita.

Countries that were strong in these areas effectively had a strong framework for growth, the report found. Aside from China and India, others expected to surge up the global economic league table include Mexico, Turkey, the Philippines and Peru.

Between now and 2050, around 2.6 billion people are expected to move up into the middle class in the emerging markets.

Here are more highlights of the HSBC study: [9]

* Massive demographic change: in 2050 there will be almost as many people in Nigeria as in the United States, and Ethiopia will have twice as many people as projected in the UK or Germany. The population of many African countries will double. Pakistan will have the sixth-largest population in the world. Even if some of these countries remain relatively poor on a per-capita basis, they could see a dramatic increase in the size of their economies thanks to population growth.

* By contrast, the Japanese working population looks set to contract by 37% and the Russian one by 31%. The eurozone faces similar problems with working population declines of 29% in Germany, 24% in Portugal, 23% in Italy and 11% in Spain, adding a whole new perspective to the sovereign debt crisis.

* It is not just about population. Ukraine is set to jump 19 places to fortieth because of its education system and rule of law, even though its population is set to fall to 36m from 45m.

* HSBC study divided the Top 100 into three categories: 1) **fast growth** – with expected average annual growth of more than 5%; 2) **growth** – with expected annual growth of between 3% and 5%; and 3) **stable** – those countries expected to expand less than 3% a year.

* HSBC study identified 26 **fast-growth** countries. They share a very low level of development but have made great progress in improving fundamentals. As they open themselves to the technology available elsewhere, they should enjoy many years of 'copy and paste' growth ahead. Besides China, India, the Philippines and Malaysia, this category includes Bangladesh, the central Asian countries of Uzbekistan, Kazakhstan and Turkmenistan, Peru and Ecuador in Latin America, and Egypt and Jordan in the Middle East.

* The **growth category** extends to 43 countries. It includes 11 Latin American countries such as Brazil, Argentina, Chile, El Salvador, Costa Rica and the Dominican Republic; Turkey, Romania and the Czech Republic in central and eastern Europe; as well as the war-ravaged Iraq and Yemen.

* Africa will finally start to emerge from economic obscurity. Five of our fast-growth countries come from Sub-Saharan Africa and three are in the growth category.

* Most of the economies in our 'stable' group are in the developed world. The West is not getting poorer, but high levels of income per capita and weak demographics will limit growth. It is the small-population, ageing economies in Europe that are the big relative losers, seeing the biggest moves down the table.

* Peru, the Philippines and Pakistan leapfrog into the Top 30. Pakistan makes it into the top league, less because of individual prosperity, than because of population size.

The HSBC projections for Muslim countries [10]

According to the HSBC 2050 list of top economies the ranks of the Muslim countries is (change in rank from 2010):

Turkey (12 +6), Indonesia (17 +4), Egypt (20 +15), Malaysia (21 +17), Saudi Arabia (22 +1), Iran (27 +7), Pakistan (30 +14).

12. Turkey – $2.15 trillion [11]

Turkey will enjoy the biggest leap of all the countries on this list, rising six spots to become one of the 15 richest nations in 2050. The country will move past the Netherlands, Russia, Australia, South Korea, Spain and Argentina.

Turkey will experience a healthy increase in the working population due to above average fertility rates. This allows the country to take advantage of fundamental economic strengths moving forward.

Over the past decade, the income of Turkish citizens per capita has almost tripled, surviving and even thriving throughout the 2008 global economic crisis. In the past five years, foreign direct investment has increased by $13 billion, further encouraging growth.

Dramatic religious and economic shifts to impact planet [12]

A new study by the Religious Freedom & Business Foundation says that the world will see dramatic shift in economic and religious affairs.

Globally, economic growth among the Muslim population is expected to significantly outpace global economic growth, in large part because the number of Muslims in the world is expected to nearly double between 2010 and 2050. Indeed, Muslims are expected to lead the world in population growth compared with other religious groups, despite global trends among Muslim populations for lower fertility, the study says adding: For instance, in Iran today, the total fertility rate has dropped below replacement level of 2.1 children per woman. The largest share of the world's Muslims lived in the Asia-Pacific region as of 2010 and will continue to live in this region in the decades ahead, making this region the engine of economic growth for Muslim populations. [13]

The RFBF report also said that to some extent, a part of global Muslim economic advance will also ride on India's economic coattails. India is expected to have the world's largest Muslim population by 2050, surpassing Indonesia. This, along with the growing economies of countries like Indonesia, will make Asia the Muslim world's center of economic power. The study finds that more than half of the economic influence associated with Muslim populations will come from the Asia-Pacific region in the decades ahead.

Other findings of the RFBF report [14] are:

"Aside from Hindu and Muslim populations, the demographic and economic forecasts for other large religious blocks is mixed. Christian populations are expected to increase in size and economic power, but slower than the demographic and economic growth of the world as a whole. This is in part because the growth of the global Christian population is projected to be about the same rate as overall global population growth between 2010-2050. And much of the growth of Christianity will occur in Africa, which is projected to grow economically, but not commensurate with the demographic growth. Half of the world's demographic growth will occur in Africa, but a significantly smaller share of the world's economic growth will occur there.

" By 2050, only one of the five leading economies is projected to have a majority Christian population – the United States. The other mega economies in 2050 are projected to include, as mentioned, India (Hindu majority), as well as Indonesia (Muslim majority), and China and Japan countries with high levels of religious diversity.

"China's religious landscape, in particular, present a clear picture of the importance of successfully navigating religious diversity. Aside from India, China has more religious believers than any other country – some 600 million.

" Almost one-in-two people in China follow a faith. This includes about 300 million practicing folk religions, 244 million separately following Buddhism (half of all on the planet), 68 million Christians (the world's seventh-largest population), and approximately 25 million Muslims, constitute the world's 17th largest Muslim population, right after Saudi Arabia and before Yemen. Certainly, China's economic success would not have been possible had the country kept religion and other forms of identity completely suppressed. And its future success requires the un-coerced buy-in of all these groups.

" The globe's growing religious diversity might be one of the 21st century's most important developments, especially as it is backed up by growing and shifting wealth. This could be very good for innovation and sustainable development – if accompanied by increases in human rights and interfaith understanding.
If not, social hostilities involving religion ranging from discrimination and hate crimes to terrorism and conflict may continue to rise, as documented by an ongoing Pew Research study." [15]

References

1. Pew Research Center Religion & Public Life, "The Future of World Religions: Population Growth Projections, 2010-2050 Muslims," Pew Research Center, April 5, 2012, <http://www.pewforum. org/2015/04/02/muslims/>.

2. The World Bank, World Development Indicators, <http://databank.worldbank.org/data/reports.aspx?so urce=2&country=ESP&series=&period=>.

3. United Nations Development Programme Arab Fund for Economic and Social Development, 3 and 78.

4. http://www.globalfirepower.com/countries-listing.asp

5. Power Waterhouse Coopers study of February 2015.
6. Ibid.
7. Ibid.

8. HSBC 2050 list of top economies, 2012 study.

Chapter VIII

C o n c l u s i o n

- Wreck and ruin policy of the Western imperialism
- The grand western strategy of a fractured and divided Middle East
- Who created ISIL?

Wreck and ruin policy of the Western imperialism

For hundreds of years Western colonialism pursued a strategy of "divide and conquer" to maintain colonial rule, deliberately setting religious and ethnic groups against each other and in some cases even inventing ethnic or racial categories. Today, Western imperialism appears to be pursuing a strategy of "wreck and ruin," apparently having concluded that if it can no longer install puppet regimes to do its bidding, at least it can fragment and weaken any nation that hews to an independent foreign policy or aligns with a rival hegemonic bloc. [1]

Following its invasion of Iraq, the US government believed it could install a puppet regime in Baghdad. Initial meetings for a provisional government were held as if an Iraqi presence was not even necessary. That arrogance proved catastrophic for US planners. Cockburn offers a telling anecdote: as the last American ground forces prepared to leave Iraq in June 2009, a US general attempted to attend a meeting of top-ranking Iraqi government and military officials. He was asked to leave. As a result of Western intervention, the entire Middle East now faces "the possibility of an endless cycle of indecisive wars and an era of instability." [2]

The cumulative effect of Western intervention has meant 'chaos and conflict are spreading in a great swath of Islamic countries between north-west Pakistan and north-east Nigeria' (p.9). Cockburn calculates there are now eight wars underway as a consequence of Bush and Blair's misconceived 'War on Terror'. The renewal of hostilities between Turkey and the Kurds is the latest addition to a list that already includes Afghanistan, Iraq, Syria, Yemen, Libya, Somalia and Nigeria (p.402). [3]

The grand western strategy of a fractured and divided Middle East   [4]

Not surprisingly, similar views were expressed by Steven MacMillan. He wrote in June 2014 under the title: The Grand Western Strategy of a Fractured and Divided Middle East: "Western imperial powers have used a policy of divide and conquer, coupled with chaos, to fracture regimes along sectarian and ethnic lines in order to destroy nation states that resist Anglo-American-European hegemony. Iraq is part of a wider strategy for the Middle East which is advocated by western geopolitical strategists Zbigniew Brzezinski and Bernard Lewis. Historian and author Webster Tarpley crystallises the Brzezinski-Lewis blueprint for a "New Middle East" during an interview in 2012: "The US strategic goal in the Middle East is the destruction of all existing national states. There's an outline for this that has been known for many years as the Bernard Lewis plan, [and] it's been expressed again by people like Zbigniew Brzezinski; micro states, mini-states, rump-states, secessionism, chaos, war lords and NATO feels free to seize whatever assets they think are important."

Bernard Lewis gave a glimpse into the strategy of Western powers in an article published in the 1992 issue of "Foreign Affairs" titled: Rethinking the Middle East, where he outlines the possibility of a future Mideast comprised of warring sects and tribes: "Another possibility, which could even be precipitated by fundamentalism, is what has of late become fashionable to call "Lebanonization." Most of the states of the Mideast—Egypt is an obvious exception—are of recent and artificial construction and are vulnerable to such a process. If the central power is sufficiently weakened, there is no real civil society to hold the polity together, no real sense of common national identity or overriding allegiance to the nation state. The state then disintegrates—as happened in Lebanon—into a chaos of squabbling, feuding, fighting sects, tribes, regions and parties. If things go badly and central governments falter and collapse, the same could happen, not only in the countries of the existing Mideast, but also in the newly independent Soviet republics, where the artificial frontiers drawn by the former imperial masters left each republic with a mosaic of minorities and claims of one sort or another on or by its   neighbors."

Who created ISIL? [5] "As Tony Cartalucci has reported for New Eastern Outlook, ISIL is a creation of the US and its Sunni Gulf Monarch allies in the region. It is designed to create a Sunni

Islamic state within Iraq and increase sectarian tensions across the Middle East which will weaken the Shia powers of Iran, Syria and Hezbollah. World Net Daily has also received leaks from Jordanian officials which reveal that the US military trained the militants in secret bases inside Jordan in 2012, to then be deployed to fight against the regime in Syria. ISIL has been destabilising Iraq for years and in March the Iraqi Prime Minister Nouri al-Maliki asserted that Saudi Arabia and Qatar were funding the ISIL to weaken the government in Bagdad. In the run up to the Iraqi elections in April, ISIL was fighting in the western Anbar region of Iraq which resulted in approximately 300 deaths in February. [6]

Imperious powers have always feared a strong, unified and cohesive people who can form organized resistance movements to oppose colonial forces. Classical divide and conquer doctrine has been implemented in the Middle East over the previous few decades in order to engineer a state of chaos which destroys nation states. Destabilization, chaos and balkanization is the policy of today, which weakens regimes who are hostile to Western geostrategic interests and allows multinational corporations to rape the region of its resources. [7]

The Age of Disintegration [8] Patrick Cockburn provides a deep insight into the ongoing wars the Middle East and elsewhere. Writing under the title - The Age of Disintegration: Neo-liberalism, Interventionism, the Resource Curse, and a Fragmenting World – Cockburn wrote in June 2016: "The question for our moment: Why is a "mass extinction" of independent states taking place in the Middle East, North Africa, and beyond? Western politicians and media often refer to such countries as "failed states." The implication embedded in that term is that the process is a self-destructive one. But several of the states now labeled "failed" like Libya only became so after Western-backed opposition movements seized power with the support and military intervention of Washington and NATO, and proved too weak to impose their own central governments and so a monopoly of violence within the national territory.

"In many ways, this process began with the intervention of a U S -led coalition in Iraq in 2003 leading to the overthrow of Saddam Hussein, the shutting down of his Baathist Party, and the disbanding of his military. Whatever their faults, Saddam and Libya's autocratic ruler Muammar Gaddafi were clearly demonized and blamed for all ethnic, sectarian, and regional differences in the countries they ruled, forces that were, in fact, set loose in grim ways upon their deaths."

"A question remains, however: Why did the opposition to autocracy and to Western intervention take on an Islamic form and why were the Islamic movements that came to dominate the armed resistance in Iraq and Syria in particular so violent, regressive, and sectarian? Put another way, how could such groups find so many people willing to die for their causes, while their opponents found so few? When IS battle groups were sweeping through northern Iraq in the summer of 2014, soldiers who had thrown aside their uniforms and weapons and deserted that country's northern cities would justify their flight by saying derisively: "Die for [then-Prime Minister Nouri] al-Maliki? Never!", Cockburn wrote adding:

"A common explanation for the rise of Islamic resistance movements is that the socialist, secularist, and nationalist opposition had been crushed by the old regimes' security forces, while the Islamists were not. In countries like Libya and Syria, however, Islamists were savagely persecuted, too, and they still came to dominate the opposition. And yet, while these religious movements were strong enough to oppose governments, they generally have not proven strong enough to replace them.

"In Iraq with a population of 33 million people, for instance, no less than seven million of them are on the government payroll, thanks to salaries or pensions that cost the government $4 billion a month. This crude way of distributing oil revenues to the people has often been denounced by Western commentators and economists as corruption. They, in turn, generally recommend cutting the number of these jobs, but this would mean that all, rather than just part, of the state's resource revenues would be stolen by the elite. This, in fact, is increasingly the case in such lands as oil prices bottom out and even the Saudi royals begin to cut back on state support for the populace."

Cockburn argues, "Neo-liberalism was once believed to be the path to secular democracy and free-market economies. In practice, it has been anything but. Instead, in conjunction with the resource curse, as well as repeated military interventions by Washington and its allies, free-market economics has profoundly destabilized the Greater Middle East."

"Encouraged by Washington and Brussels, twenty-first-century neo-liberalism has made unequal societies ever more unequal and helped transform already corrupt regimes into looting machines. This is also, of course, a formula for the success of the Islamic State or any other radical alternative to the status quo. Such movements are bound to find support in impoverished or neglected regions like eastern Syria or eastern Libya, Cockburn said adding:

"Note, however, that this process of destabilization is by no means confined to the Greater Middle East and North Africa. We are indeed in the age of destabilization, a phenomenon that is on the rise globally and at present spreading into the Balkans and Eastern Europe (with the European Union ever less able to influence events there). People no longer speak of European integration, but of how to prevent the complete break-up of the European Union in the wake of the British vote to leave."

Cockburn was on the view that the U.S. remains a superpower, but is no longer as powerful as it once was. It, too, is feeling the strains of this global moment, in which it and its local allies are powerful enough to imagine they can get rid of regimes they do not like, but either they do not quite succeed, as in Syria, or succeed but cannot replace what they have destroyed, as in Libya. An Iraqi politician once said that the problem in his country was that parties and movements were "too weak to win, but too strong to lose." This is increasingly the pattern for the whole region and is spreading elsewhere. It carries with it the possibility of an endless cycle of indecisive wars and an era of instability that has already begun.

Reference Conclusion

1. The West's "wreck and ruin" strategy in the Middle East by Rod Such - The Electronic Intifada July 8, 2016.

2. Ibid.

3. Chaos and Caliphate: Jihadis and the West in the Struggle for the Middle East review by Sean Ledwith – Counterfire.org June 30, 2016.

4. The Grand Western Strategy of a Fractured and Divided Middle East By Steven MacMillan - The Analyst Report - June 26, 2014.

5. Ibid.

6. Ibid.

7. Ibid.

8. The Age of Disintegration: Neoliberalism, Interventionism, the Resource Curse, and a Fragmenting World by Cockburn - Tomgram.com June 2016]

Appendix-I

Who is an enlightened Muslim By Dr. Ali Shariati

Third World countries, and particularly Islamic societies, have witnessed mistakes and deviations committed by the so-called enlightened thinkers. An unfortunate development, which I call the history of "confusing the issues" (awadi gereftanha) constitutes the story of the fundamental errors committed by the educated Muslims as well as those of other Eastern societies, Like a scientist who imports medicine to his country, these people believed that enlightenment could be imported to their home while they themselves played the role of enlightened persons. The tragic result was that the Eastern and Islamic societies were deprived of their best minds, individuals who could help their countries to recover from their backwardness. For years the feelings. consciences, and thoughts of our people were directed by the so called "enlightened," who delivered the wrong messages while thinking they were showing the path to salvation. Following their incorrect diagnoses, struggles and strivings, o pportunities were lost, and people's potentials were wasted. The end result was hopelessness, desperation, hatred, evasion of responsibility, isolation, mysticism, and various games of existentialism. This continued until it was gradually replaced by another wrong direction, inappropriate objective, or mistaken diagnosis. The cycle repeated itself with the result that the people wasted their talents gathering around these social prophets.

Our greatest and most pressing responsibility is to see, historically speaking, where the Muslim society is. Do Muslims live under the same conditions as those of twentieth century Europe, and is it thus possible for European solutions, ideologies and writers to be useful? Do Muslims live in an industrial age, and so experience the same problems as those of industrial societies? Have Muslim societies reached the modern bourgeois era? Have they passed the era of the rule of religion? Are they experiencing some kind of religious reform! Are Muslims living under the same conditions as were the Europeans during the Renaissance or during the French Revolution? How does one characterize Muslim culture? Once the historical condition and the culture of the society are understood, both the enlightened and the general public will know what their responsibilities and duties are.

Historically speaking, the present condition of Muslims, as compared to that of the West, is where the latter was at the end of the Middle Ages and the beginning of the Renaissance. Similar to that time, Muslims are in a period of social and intellectual transformation. Economically, the dominant system in the Islamic societies is an "agricultural market" or the intermediate bourgeoisie. In other words, the largest and the basic foundation of the economy is agricultural production and not urban-market economy and bourgeois capitalism, as commonly understood. The reason is that European bourgeoisie, which contributed greatly to the French Revolution, was completely different from that of the present Iranian or other Islamic societies. The bourgeoisie in the Islamic Societies includes the bazaar merchants and not the modern industrial and banking capitalists. To be more exact, the bazaar merchants lack the vigor and dynamism of the modern bourgeoisie. They only act as a mediator between the agricultural sector and the consumer. There is, no doubt, a newly evolving bourgeoisie resembling that of eighteenth century Europe, but it has not had the same influence that the latter had.

An enlightened Muslim must know that the Islamic spirit dominates his culture and that the historical processes of his society, as well as its moral codes, have all been shaped by Islam. To fail to understand this, as the majority of our "intellectuals" have, limits and restricts a person to his own irrelevant which are useless to the masses anyway- a Muslim enlightened person should engage himself in discovering, extracting, and refining t he life giving and powerful spirit of his society. He exists in the context of a dynamic culture and society as well as in the conscience of his people.

One characteristic of this spirit is that, unlike other religions which justify poverty, Islam condemns it. A great student of Islam, Abudhar, says, "When poverty enters a home, religion exits from the window." The prophet of Islam and the founder of that religion declared: "Whoever is not able to provide for himself will not have a good life in the hereafter." These are contrary to the contemporary understanding of Islam which claims that "one who is caught in poverty and misery has a cleaner and humbler heart and is, thus, more amenable to receive unseen inspirations." An empty stomach lacks everything. A society which has economic problems also lacks spiritual wealth. Whatever is called ethics in a poor country is nothing but deviant customs and habits, not spirituality.

Islam pays attention to bread, its eschatology is based on active life in the world, its God respects human dignity and its messenger is armed.

An enlightened person should obtain the raw materials from his contemporary society and social life. There exists no universal type of enlightened person, with common values and characteristics everywhere. Our own history and experience have demonstrated that whenever an enlightened person turns his back on religion, which is the dominant spirit of the society, the society turns its back on him. Opposition to religion by the enlightened person deprives society of the possibility of becoming aware of the benefits and the fruit of its young and enlightened generation.

An enlightened person should start with "religion." By that I mean our peculiar religious culture and not the one predominant today. He should begin by an Islamic Protestantism similar to that of Christianity in the Middle Ages, destroying all the degenerating factors which, in the name of Islam, have stymied and stupefied the process of thinking and the fate of the society, and giving birth to new thoughts and new movements. Unlike Christian Protestantism, which was empty-handed and had to justify its liberationist presentation of Jesus, Islamic Protestantism has various sources and elements to draw from. Such a movement will unleash great energies and enable the enlightened Muslim to:

1- Extract and refine the enormous resources of our society and convert the degenerating and jamming agents into energy and movement;
2- Transform the existing social and class conflicts into conscious awareness of social responsibility, by using artistic, literary and speaking abilities and power as well as other possibilities at hand;

3- Bridge the ever-widening gap between the "island of the enlightened person" and the "shore of the masses" by establishing kinship links and understanding between them, thus putting the religion, which came about to revive and generate movement, at the service of the people;

4- Make the weapon of religion inaccessible to those who have undeservedly armed themselves with it and whose purpose is to use religion for personal reasons, thereby acquiring the necessary energy to motivate people;

5- Launch a religious renaissance through which, by returning to the religion of life and motion, power and justice, will on the one hand incapacitate the reactionary agents of the society and, on the other hand, save the people from those elements which are used to narcotize them. By launching such a renaissance, these hitherto narcotizing elements will be used to revitalize, give awareness and fight superstition. Furthermore, returning to and relying on the authentic culture of the society will allow the revival and rebirth of cultural independence in the face of Western cultural onslaught;

6- And finally, eliminate the spirit of imitation and obedience which is the hallmark of the popular religion, and replace it with a critical revolutionary, aggressive spirit of i ndependent reasoning (ijtihad). All of these may be accomplished through a religious reformist movement which will extract and refine the enormous accumulation of energy in the society, and will enlighten the era and will awaken the present generation. It is for the above reasons that I, as a conscientious teacher who has risen from the depth of pains and experience of his people and history, hope that the enlightened person will reach a progressive self-awareness. For whereas our masses need self-awareness, our enlightened intellectuals are in need of "faith."

[This article is based on Dr. Shariati's articles on Modernization and Islam, Refinement of Cultural Resources and From where should we begin?]

Appendix II
Americanization of Islam:
Revamping of Islam in the image of Neocons

"Direct confrontation and military conquest are now secondary tools to dominate cultures and markets. Habits and lifestyles are primary targets of change in order to guarantee an open market based on a free consumer who has an open mind."

This premise sets the tone of the agenda-driven study of Rand Corporation, a Washington-based think tank, about Islam and Muslims. The study, titled "Civil Democratic Islam: Partners, Resources, and Strategies," is written by Cheryl Benard, a sociologist and fiction writer.

As US Deputy Defense Secretary, Paul Wolfowitz, a leading newcon, confided on the eve of the U.S. invasion of Iraq in March 2003: "We need an Islamic reformation and I think there is real hope for one." The Rand Study, released on March 18, 2004, apparently unveils the newcons' plan for global revamping of Islam.

Author of the study, Cheryl Benard, arguing that Islam is not necessarily a very "accessible" religion, arbitrarily compartmentalizes the 1.5 billion Muslims into four categories depending on their degree of affinity for Western values and concepts:

1. Fundamentalists, who reject democratic values and contemporary Western culture.
2. Traditionalists, who want a conservative society. They are suspicious of modernity, innovation, and change.
3. Modernists, who want the Islamic world to become part of global modernity. They want to modernize and reform Islam to bring it into line with the age.
4. Secularists, who want the Islamic world to accept a division of church and state in the manner of Western industrial democracies, with religion relegated to the private sphere

Although Benard arbitrarily divides all Muslims into four categories – fundamentalists, traditionalists, modernists and secularists – but pay attention to what's there, but not spelt out. For her objectives all Muslims, except modernists, are virtually the same.

Benard says that though the secularists should be our most natural allies in the Muslim world because Western democracies are premised on the separation of church and state but the problem has been, and continues to be, that many important secularists in the Islamic world are unfriendly or even extremely hostile to us on other grounds. "Leftist ideologies, anti-Americanism, aggressive nationalism, and authoritarian structures with only quasi-democratic trappings have been some of the manifestations of Islamic secularism to date."

Therefore, Benard suggests that Moderanists are our allies in the Muslim world. This group is most congenial to the values and the spirit of modern democratic society.

With the goal of selectively ignoring or rejecting elements of the original religious doctrine of Islam she also defines parameters for Muslim modernists:

- Modernists believe that Islam is responsible for the underdevelopment of the Muslims because prosperity and progress depends on modernity and democracy.

- Modernists believe in the historicity of Islam, i.e., that Islam as it was practiced in the days of the Prophet reflected eternal truths as well as historical circumstances that were appropriate to that time but are no longer valid.

- Modernists do not regard the original Islamic community or the early years of Islam as something that one would necessarily wish to reproduce today.

- Modernists believe that some verses (suras) may have been falsely or inaccurately recorded in the Quran.

- Modernists believe that the Quran is legend.

Benard questions the authenticity of the Qu'ran itself.

In the chapter on "The Hadith Wars" she says that two verses were lost in the process of recording of the Quran after the death of the Prophet. To authenticate her argument, she quotes from chapter 11 of an eminent scholar of Islam, Allama Ghulam Ahmed Parwez's book entitled: *The Status of Hadith . . . The Actual Status of Hadith - Holy Quran According to Our Traditions.* Ironically, this chapter is written to refute the premise that the Quran was recorded after the death of the Prophet. The references of Hadith in this chapter were given for argument's sake which Benard misquoted to prove her argument. Allama Parwez points out that the Quran was recorded in its present shape during the lifetime of the Prophet. He questions the authenticity of collections of Hadith which were collected by the Persian scholars more than 200 years after the death of the prophet.

Benard's "research" on Quran is the latest attack on the authenticity of the holy book of Islam. In July 2003, Newsweek launched a similar attack with an article entitled "Challenging the Qur'an." The punch of the article was that in the West, questioning the literal veracity of the Bible was a crucial step in breaking the church's grip on power—and in developing a modern, secular society and the Muslims should follow this. The Newsweek article referred to the "research" of a pseudonymous German scholar Christoph Luxenberg who claims that the original language of the Qur'an was not Arabic but something closer to Aramaic.

Practical guide to create a defanged version of Islam:

A close reading of Benard's work indicates that the main thrust of the study is to create a defanged version of Islam - to develop a Western Islam, a German Islam, a U.S. Islam, etc.

Now how to achieve this objective?

The daunting and complex task of religion-building (or revamping Islam in America's image) will include the necessity to depart from, modify, and selectively ignore elements of the original religious doctrine of Islam, Benard argues.

After establishing her case against Islamic tenets as practiced or accepted today by almost all the Muslims Benard provides a Machiavellian formula to achieve the goal of creating a defanged version of Islam acceptable to America and the West:

Support the modernists first, support the traditionalists against the fundamentalists, confront and oppose the fundamentalists and selectively support secularists.

The focus will be on education and youth, since "committed adult adherents of radical Islamic movements are unlikely to be easily influenced into changing their views. The next generation, however, can conceivably be influenced if the message of democratic Islam can be inserted into school curricula and public media in the pertinent countries."

It may not be out of place to mention that efforts are already underway to eliminate Quranic verses from school text books in Muslim countries. In Pakistan, Musharraf government is trying to eliminate Quranic verses from school text books amid mounting opposition from religious and non-religious political parties. In 1990s Kuwaiti Education Minister, Dr. Rubai, was forced to resign when he ordered deletion of the Quranic verses from the school text books. To many Muslims deletion of verses from the school text books is an endeavor to open a window for editing the Quran that survived 1400 years of distortion attempts.

Benard advocates another strategy, that will be promoting Sufism - which she includes in modernism - in the Muslim world. "Sufi influence over school curricula, norms, and cultural life should be strongly encouraged in countries that have a Sufi tradition, such as Afghanistan or Iraq. Through its poetry, music, and philosophy, Sufism has a strong bridge role outside of religious affiliations.....Encourage countries with strong Sufi traditions to focus on that part of their history and to include it in their school curricula. Pay more attention to Sufi Islam."

Apparently, she is suggesting to use Sufism now to counter Wahabi doctrine as Americans used Wahabism in 1980s to launch "Jihad" against the Soviet troops in Afghanistan and also to counter Shiism after the Iranian revolution of 1979.

The fact of the matter is that historically Islamic fundamentalism or the so called "Militant Islam" has not posed a threat to Western interests (corporate, oil, and geopolitical interests) but rather been exploited to serve those interests. Remember Lawrence of Arabia? What was his objective other than to forge a British alliance with the Hashemites during World War I? Later, the British boosted the Saudi royal family, patrons of the Wahhabi school of thought, into power. The U.S. inherited Saudi Arabia as a client state after World War II, and we all know how well U.S. oil companies have done there ever since. Aramco alone, prior to its nationalization in the mid-1980s, yielded some $ 3 trillion from the Arabian reserves. (Challenging Ignorance on Islam: a Ten-Point Primer for Americans by Gary Leupp, an Associate professor, Department of History, Tufts University and coordinator, Asian Studies Program. (August 2002)

The U.S. helped create, recruit, and finance the fundamentalist Mujahadeen, including some 30,000 young volunteers who came from throughout the Muslim world to fight "godless Communism" in Afghanistan in the 1980s. The U.S. encouraged them to view their war as a jihad "Holy War," and put many in contact with young Osama bin Laden, then a US ally. The Reagan administration was in love with fundamentalist Islam, so long as it served its purposes. On June 16, 1986, President Reagan told four Afghan Mujahideen who were invited to the White House: "I feel I am in the company of the founding fathers of this country."

The California-based company Unocal was cordially negotiating right up to Sept. 11 with Afghanistan's Taliban for an oil pipeline through Afghan territory, State Department official Zalmay Khalilzad, now US ambassador to Afghanistan, was arguing up through 1998 that the Taliban were friendly, potential business partners who did "not practice the anti-U.S. style of fundamentalism practiced in Iran.

Benard's study completely ignores that cause of anti-American and anti-West attitude and violence in the Muslim world. She holds Islam and Muslims responsible for this. While ignoring the root cause she made a passing remark on this critical issue: "a number of authors believe that fundamentalist hostility to the United States and to the West primarily reflects anger over some aspects of our foreign policy or discomfort over the more-liberal aspects of Western culture. It is important to be aware that, while such concerns play a part, fundamentalism represents a basic and total rejection of democracy and of the core values of modern civil society."

What she suggests is that Islam and Muslims are against democracy and civil society norms.

As a final thought, the release of the Rand study coincides with the formation of "Islamic Progress Institute" (IPI) by Daniel Pipes, an anti-Muslim and anti-Islam scholar, to articulate a moderate, modern and pro-American viewpoint on Islam. Pipe says: Islam in America must be American Islam or it will not be integrated (read accepted). The Rand Corp. study provides an ideological ground for creating an American version of Islam while IPI hopes to serve as a vehicle to implement that agenda in America.

Within the United States, "all Muslims, unfortunately, are suspect", Pipes wrote in a recent book, which called for the authorities to be especially vigilant towards Muslims with jobs in the military, law enforcement, or diplomacy. Last year, he cited as evidence of this insight the arrest on suspicion of espionage of Muslim chaplain Captain James Yee at the Guantanamo Bay detention facility that houses hundreds of prisoners from Bush's war on terrorism. The Army later withdrew charges against Captain Yee. In his grant proposal, Pipes writes that he is working on launching the IPI with "a group of anti-Islamist Muslims", whom he does not identify. (US Neo-Cons: From Nation-Building to Religion-Building by Jim Lobe Inter Press Service, April 7, 2004)   **April 10, 2004**

Exploiting Sunni, Shiite and Arab, non-Arab divides to promote the US policy objectives in the Muslim world

In December 2004 the Rand Corporation issued another study which suggested that Sunni, Shiite and Arab, non-Arab divides should be exploited to promote the US policy objectives in the Muslim world.

The new Rand study - titled "The Muslim World After 9/11" – was conducted on behalf of the US Air Force. One of the primary objective of the study was to "identify the key cleavages and fault lines among sectarian, ethnic, regional, and national lines and to assess how these cleavages generate challenges and opportunities for the United States." The research brief was issued by the Rand Corporation under the title: US strategy in the Muslim World after 9/11.

"The majority of the world's Muslims are Sunni, but a significant minority, about 15 percent of the global Muslim population, are Shi'ites..... The expectations of Iraqi Shi'ites for a greater say in the governance of their country presents an opportunity for the United States to align its policy with Shi'ite aspirations for greater freedom of religious and political expression, in Iraq and elsewhere," the study said.

The study pointed out that with the moves toward rapprochement between Tehran and Riyadh, there are reports that Saudi Arabia's Shi'ites are now turning from Iran and placing their hopes on the United States. "Their expectation is that any move toward democracy in Iraq would give the Shi'ite majority a greater say in the politics of that country and increase their ability to help their brethren in Saudi Arabia. Such expectations could present an opportunity for the United States to align its policy with Shi'ite aspirations for greater freedom of religious and political expression and a say in their own affairs in countries controlled by others."

On the division between the Arab and the non-Arab worlds, the Rand Study pointed out: "Arabs constitute only about 20 percent of the world's Muslims, yet interpretations of Islam, political and otherwise, are often filtered through an Arab lens. A great deal of the discourse on Muslim issues and grievances is actually discourse on Arab issues and grievances. For reasons that have more to do with historical and cultural development than religion, the Arab world exhibits a higher incidence of economic, social, and political disorders than other regions of the so-called developing world."

"By contrast, the non-Arab parts of the Muslim world are politically more inclusive, boast the majority of the democratic or partially democratic governments, and are more secular in outlook. Although the Arab Middle East has long been regarded (and certainly views itself) as the core of the Muslim world, the most innovative and sophisticated contemporary work in Islam is being done on the "periphery"—in countries such as Indonesia and in Muslim communities in the West, leading some scholars to ask whether Islam's center of gravity is now shifting to more dynamic regions of the Muslim world."

The Rand Report holds the post independence political and economic failures responsible for the current political environment of the Muslim world in general and the Arab world in particular. "Many of the ills and pathologies that afflict many countries in this part of the world and that generate much of the extremism we are concerned about derive from—and contribute to—economic and political failure."

This situation, the study argued, leads to the concept of structural anti-Westernism (or anti-Americanism). "This concept holds that that Muslim anger has deep roots in the political and social structures of some Muslim countries and that opposition to certain U.S. policies merely provides the content and opportunity for the expression of this anger."

According to the Rand study, "outside the Arab Middle East, Islamization has involved the importation of Arab-origin ideology and religious and social practices—a phenomenon that we refer to as *Arabization.*" The Rand study said that a number of critical or catalytic events have altered the political environment in the Muslim world in fundamental ways. "Catalytic events include the Iranian revolution, the Afghan war, the Gulf War of 1991, the global war on terrorism that followed the September 11 terrorist attacks, and the Iraq war of 2003."

The Palestinian-Israeli conflict and the Kashmir conflict, the study said, are not catalytic events per se but rather chronic conditions that have shaped political discourse in the Middle East and South Asia for over half a century, the study said.

The Palestinian-Israeli conflict and the Kashmir have retarded the political maturation of the Arab world and Pakistan by diverting scarce material, political, and psychic resources from pressing internal problems, the study added.

The Rand study called for madrassa and mosques reforms in the Muslim world and suggested that US should "support the efforts of governments and moderate Muslim organizations to ensure that mosques, and the social services affiliated with them, serve their communities and do not serve as platforms for the spread of radical ideologies." In chapter on Islam & Politics in Pakistan, the Rand Study even suggested that there should be government appointed and paid professional imams in all mosques to promote "civil Islam".

"While only Muslims themselves can effectively challenge the message of radical Islam, there is much the United States and like-minded countries can do to empower Muslim moderates in this ideological struggle," said Angel Rabas, RAND senior policy analyst and lead author of the report. "The struggle in the Muslim world is essentially a war of ideas, the outcome of which will determine the future direction of the Muslim world and profoundly affect vital U.S. security interests," he added.

The Rand Study also calls on the United States and its allies to support efforts in Muslim nations to:

- Create a strong and vocal network to unite the fractured voices of moderate Muslims. This can provide moderates with a platform for their message and provide alternatives to extremist movements. An external catalyst may be needed to give life to this goal.

- Support Muslim civil society groups that advocate moderation and modernity. The United States may have to assist in the development of civil society institutions where they do not currently exist.

- Disrupt radical networks. Engage Islamists to participate in the political process, and strengthen relations with the military in Muslim nations. In the war against terror, the U.S. should demonstrate that its efforts are meant to promote democratic change.

- Reform Islamic schools. Educational systems have long been a vital component of radical Islamic indoctrination and recruitment. The best way to counter this is to help Islamic schools ensure they are providing modern education and marketable skills for future generations.

- Create economic opportunities in Muslim nations, particularly for young people. Economic assistance programs will not guarantee an end to extremism or terrorism, but could reduce the perception that the U.S. relies solely on military instruments. Creating jobs and social services would also give young people an alternative to radical Islamic organizations.

In March 2004, the Rand Corporation released a report - titled "Civil Democratic Islam: Partners, Resources, and Strategies" – that called for supporting the modernists Muslims against "fundamentalists and traditionalists" and promoting Sufism to formulate a market economy version of Islam.

Angel Rabasa, RAND senior policy analyst, is the lead author of the 567-page new study. Other authors of the study include Cheryl Benard, author of "Civil Democratic Islam: Partners, Resources, and Strategies" and Christine Fair, formerly of RAND and now at the U.S. Institute of Peace heading by Daniel Pipes.

December 24, 2004

Rand Corporation's new recipe
to handle the Muslim World

In March 2007, the semi-official U.S. think tank, Rand Corporation, issued another study suggesting creation of networks of the so-called moderate Muslims to promote US policy objectives in the Muslim World. In its new report, titled "Building Moderate Muslim Networks" the Rand Corp advocates that the building of moderate Muslim networks needs to become an explicit goal of the U.S. government policy, with an international database of partners and a well-designed plan.

Just as it fought the spread of Communism during the Cold War, the United States must do more to develop and support networks of moderate Muslims who are too often silenced by violent radical Islamists, according to the report.

Lead writer of the report Angel Rabasa says that the United States has a critical role to play in aiding moderate Muslims, and can learn much from the way it addressed the spread of Communism during the Cold War. "The efforts of the United States and its allies to build free and democratic networks and institutions provided an organizational and ideological counter force to Communist groups seeking to come to power through political groups, labor unions, youth and student organizations and other groups."

The report defines a moderate as a Muslim who supports democracy, gender equality, freedom of worship and opposition to terrorism. This looks an amplification on its two previous reports - "Civil Democratic Islam: Partners, Resources, and Strategies" (March 2004) and "US strategy in the Muslim World after 9/11" (December 2004) - which also suggested supporting moderate Muslims and exploitation of inter-Muslim religious differences.

In the December 2004 study Rabasa had suggested to exploit Sunni, Shiite and Arab, non-Arab divides to promote the US policy objectives in the Muslim world. Echoing this theme, the latest report recommends reaching out to Muslim activists, leaders and intellectuals in non-Arab countries such as Turkey as well as in Southeast Asia and Europe. The report recommends targeting five groups as potential building blocks for networks: liberal and secular Muslim academics and intellectuals; young moderate religious scholars; community activists; women's groups engaged in gender equality campaigns; and moderate journalists and scholars.

The report warned that moderate groups can lose credibility – and therefore, effectiveness – if U.S. support is too obvious. Effective tactics that worked during the Cold War include having the groups led by credible individuals and having the United States maintain some distance from the organizations it supports. "This was done by not micro-managing the groups, but by giving them enough autonomy," Rabasa said. "As long as certain guidelines were met, they were free to pursue their own activities."

To help start this initiative, the report recommends working toward an international conference modelled in the Cold War-era Congress of Cultural Freedom, and then developing a standing organization to combat what it called radical Islamism.

The recent summit of *"Secular Islam Conference" in St. Petersburg,* Florida, almost coincided with the release of the latest Rand Report. A small group of self-proclaimed secular Muslims from North America and elsewhere gathered in St. Petersburg for what they billed as a new global movement to correct the assumed wrongs of Islam and call for an "Islamic Reformation."

The St. Petersburg conference, held on the sideline of the Intelligence Summit, was carried live on (Islamophobe) Glenn Beck's CNN show. Some of the organizers and speakers at the convention were well known thanks to the media spotlight: Irshad Manji, author of "The Trouble With Islam," and Ayaan Hirsi Ali, the former Dutch parliamentarian and author of "Infidel," were but a few there claiming to have suffered personally at the hands of "radical" Islam. One participant, Wafa Sultan, declared on Glenn Beck's show that she doesn't "see any difference between radical Islam and regular Islam." Other participants were the now public ex-Muslim Ibn Warraq and self-proclaimed ex-terrorist Tawfiq Hamd.

Surely, the "moderate" Muslim agenda is promoted because these ideas reflect a Western vision for the future of Islam. Since the Sept. 11 attacks, everyone from high-ranking officials in the Bush administration to anti-Islam authors have prescribed a preferred remedy for Islam: Reform the faith.

The Rand Reports about Islam appear to be part of a grand strategy to "change the face of Islam" as revealed by the *US News and World Report on April 15, 2005. The report entitled - Hearts, Minds, and Dollars:* In an Unseen Front in the War on Terrorism, America is Spending Millions...To Change the Very Face of Islam - reads: "From military psychological-operations teams and CIA covert operatives to openly funded media and think tanks, Washington is plowing tens of millions of dollars into a campaign to influence not only Muslim societies but Islam itself."

According to the well planned leaks to the *US News and World Report,* this strategy for the first time stated that the United States has a national security interest in influencing what happens within Islam. The report also confirmed that it is, in fact, the US which has been funding an American version of Islam, called "Moderate Islam."

The Rand reports try to create a fictitious vision of Muslims and of Islam, where it is antihuman, uncreative, authoritarian, and intrinsically against Western societies. It is an ethnocentric view of Islam that dominates current representations of Islam that are reductive, predominantly negative, and encouraging a culture of Islamophobia.

The complexities of the so-called fundamentalism and extremism in the past 100 years or so, whether it be Christian, Hindu, Jewish or Muslim, need to be understood in the context of modernization, the process of secularization, the changing nature of religious institutions, the post-colonial experience in developing countries, globalization, the divide between wealthy and poor, contesting political power, and the impact of totalitarian regimes on civil society.

What is not mentioned in the RAND reports is that the reason for the alienation of Muslims from the West, is the issue of "double standards" the West so brazenly practices when dealing with Muslim nations. America already has a very tarnished image in the Islamic world. It has already alienated a great majority of Muslims throughout the world through its misguided foreign policy. Who in the right mind will believe that this asinine assault on Islam and Muslims will win America friends in the Islamic world?

Now a word about the Washington-based semi-official think tank – the RAND Corporation. Among other government departments, the Rand Corp conducts studies for the Office of the Secretary of Defense, the Joint Staff, the Unified Commands, the defense agencies, the Department of the Navy and the U.S. intelligence community. Obviously, writers of the three under discussion reports on Islam may be considered as neo-Orientalists with clear intention to belittle Islam.

When the European nations began their long campaign to colonize and conquer the rest of the world for their own benefit, they brought their academic and missionary resources to help them with their task. Orientalists and missionaries, whose ranks often overlapped, were the servants of an imperialist government who was using their services as a way to subdue or weaken an enemy. The academic study of the *Oriental East by the Occidental West* was often motivated and often co-operated hand-in-hand with the imperialistic aims of the European colonial powers. The foundations of Orientalism were in the maxim "Know thy enemy". This equally applies to the modern day Orientalists of such semi-official think tanks as the Rand Corporation.

Rand Report on Islam revisited

March 18th 2005 marked the first anniversary of formal release of the Rand Corporation report on Islam, entitled Civil Democratic Islam: Partners, Resources, and Strategies.

The report has two fold agenda:

1. Try to create a version of Islam that suits the post 9/11 western agenda.
2. Creating divisions in the Muslim society at home and abroad.

The Rand Report recipe to achieve this objective is to encourage and promote the so-called modernist Muslims and play one section of the society against another to split the Muslim society. In another report released in December 2004, the Rand Corporation elaborated on the second point and recommended playing the two major Muslim sects Sunnis and Shiites against each other to achieve policy objects.

We are not sure what impact the Rand report has on the 1.5 billion Muslims living in 57 independent Muslim countries as well as minorities in many other countries.

However, we can see some reaction in the American Muslim community where the so called progressive or modern Muslims are trying to benefit from the current atmosphere of fear and siege caused by the arbitrary arrests, FBI interviews, racial profiling, surveillance of their mosques, closing down of Islamic charities and constant anti-Islam and anti-Muslim propaganda in the mainstream media.

We are experiencing the re-emergence of Orientalism of the 19th century aimed at forcing the Muslims living in US to abandon their basic tenets of belief. This neo-Orientalism is coming in the shape of such research documents as the Rand Report which questions the authenticity of Islam's holy scripture, the Quran. Even a fake version of Quran is now available in print. It was distributed in a private school in Kuwait in 2004.

At the same time, we see cropping up of some Muslim groups such as Free Muslims Against Terrorism, Progressive Muslim Union of North America (PMUNA) and Center for Islamic Pluralism which are not only challenging the basic tenets of Islam but also challenging the established Muslim organizations.

Free Muslims Against Terrorism, established by Kamal Nawash who ran for Virginia State Assembly in November 2003 as a Republican candidate. One can well understand his political ambitions and hidden agenda of his organization. Just one example, how it is working against the American Muslim groups. In January this year the Executive Director of Free Muslims Against Terrorism, wrote an e mail to Enver Masud of an Islamic website, Wisdom Foundation, saying: We are very disappointed in your site and it should be taken down.... I will recommend to our extremist watch committee that we place your site on our list of extremist sites or sites that support terrorism. Here is the website address of Wisdom Foundation where one can see what kind of message Enver Masud has: www.twf.org

The Progressive Muslim Union of North America (PMUNA) was formed on November 15, 2004 by some professed moderates who embrace the simple proposition that "you are a Muslim if you say you are a Muslim -- for whatever reason or set of reasons -- and that no one is entitled to question or undermine this identity."

The PMUNA is now forcing mainstream Muslim organizations to take positions on even non-issues in order to put them at odds with their own community, and if don't take a position they would be considered as the "bad or extremist" Muslims. Sarah Eltantawi, one of its co-founders is demanding the major Muslim groups and organizations to take position on a non-issue, i.e. if a woman can lead Friday prayers. It is not an uncommon knowledge that the status of woman in Islam is now being used by the West to defame Islam.

"I demand to know where the Muslim Public Affairs Council (MPAC), and the Council on American-Islamic Relations (CAIR) stands on this issue. I demand to know where the Islamic Society of North America (ISNA) stands on this issue. And KARAMAH, the American Sufi Muslim Association, Women in Islam, Azizah Magazine, and other groups who speak for Muslims and Muslim women," Eltantawi asks.

The PMUNA is not alone in working against the major American Muslim organizations. The first goal of Center for Islamic Pluralism established by Stephan Shwartz, a Muslim convert, is the removal of CAIR and ISNA from monopoly status in representing Muslims to the American public because, according to CIP, as long as they retain a major foothold at the highest political level, no progress can be made for moderate American Islam. By the way, Shwartz claims to be a Sufi

Muslim and the Rand study recommends promotion of Sufism in Islam for US policy objectives.

The Rand Report is silent on the reasons of discontentment in the Muslim world. The report does not address any of the core issues that are central in developing the perceptions of the Muslim world like; Palestine, Kashmir and Chechnya issues and the exploitative political systems supported by the American or European elites. No reference is made to the West's support for totalitarian secular Muslim regimes, Israel 's endless pogroms against the Palestinians and ethnic cleansing perpetrated against Muslims in Eastern Europe and Chechnya.

A number of recent studies have reaffirmed that the reason for anti-American sentiments in the Muslim masses is because of American policies. Pentagon advisory group, Defense Science Board, in its November 2004 report pointed out that Muslims do not hate our freedom, but rather they hate our policies. "American direct intervention in the Muslim World has paradoxically elevated the stature of and support for radical Islamists, while diminishing support for the United States to single-digits in some Arab societies."

To give a helping held in the daunting task of countering the anti-American sentiments in the Muslim world some 'moderate' Muslims established the American Muslim Group on Policy Planning (AMGPP) on December 13, 2004. "The AMGPP is willing to play a very active role in helping improve US image and counter the tide of extremism and anti-Americanism in the Muslim World, the AMGPP founder explains. Now one may ask does this group supports Bush administration's policy objects such as the occupation of Iraq, the war against Afghanistan, torture in Guantanamo Bay, Baghram and Abu Ghraib and support of undemocratic Muslim governments.

In this context, I would like to refer to a report "Understanding Islamism" issued earlier this month by the Brussels-based International Crisis Group: "The failure to address the Palestinian question and, above all, the decision to make war on Iraq and the even more extraordinary mishandling of the post-war situation there have unquestionably motivated and encouraged jihadi activism across the Muslim world."

The quotation of the report does not mean its endorsement.

According to the report , Sunni political Islamism, is definitely modernist in most essential respects, favoring non-violent over violent strategies, open to dialogue and debate and interested in democratic ideas. The report adds: that the West can encourage this evolution. But should it choose to do so, it will need to drop or at least moderate its more activist and interventionist impulses where Muslim countries are concerned, display greater respect for their sovereignty, understand their ambition to renegotiate their relations with it over a range of issues and come to terms with and take account of their viewpoints on the most controversial questions in the current relationship, notably the Israeli-Palestinian conflict, Iraq and the modalities of the "war against terrorism" in general.

The report warned that if "moderate" is defined to mean "co-optable", it can only really refer to groups and tendencies which fail to articulate the frustrations and expectations of the mass of "ordinary decent Muslims", have little or no purchase on their political reflexes and will prove unable to promote either significant reform in Muslim countries or a substantive modernization of their cultural and ideological outlook. "Rather than reducing the appeal of extremist currents, the patronizing of "moderates" in this sense by Western governments risks reinforcing it, while undermining the modernist tendency in Sunni Islamism to the benefit of fundamentalists and jihadis," the International Crisis Group report concluded.

Returning to the Rand report, Civil Democratic Islam: partners, resources, strategies, the suggestions of its author, Cheryl Benard, are nothing more than a Machiavellian manifesto that seeks to enforce Western hegemony and cultural imperialism through the policy of "divide and rule." The type of Islam that Benard espouses is a passive and weak Islam that can be easily penetrated and hence reformulated to suit the West's agenda.

The report may be seen as the latest in a long series of policy papers by the "embedded intellectuals" dedicated to further the military and economic objectives of the West as well as cultural onslaught on the Muslims.

In a briefing – entitled Taking Saudi Out of Arabia - given on July 10, 2002 [Washington Post August 6, 2002] to a the Defense Policy Board, former RAND analyst Laurent Murawiec described Saudi Arabia as the "kernel of evil, the prime mover, the most dangerous opponent" to US interests in the Middle East. He argued that Washington should demand that Saudi Arabia stop supporting "terrorism" or face seizures of its oil fields and its financial assets in the US.

Murawiec urged a multi-stage Grand strategy for the Middle East, beginning with Iraq as the tactical pivot, continuing to Saudi Arabia as the strategic pivot and finally to Egypt as the prize. **March 18, 2005**

Neo-Orientalism in USA

It will not be too much to say that for centuries European Orientalists have been working to defame and ridicule Islam through their 'scholarly' enterprises and the Neo-Orientalists in Europe and America are now following their footsteps. Alarmingly, such semi-official US think tanks as the Rand Corporation, in their "scholarly" enterprises, are demeaning Islam and Muslims while suggesting to exploit Sunni, Shiite and Arab, non-Arab divides to promote the US policy objectives in the Muslim world. Not astonishingly, the American neo-Orientalists are asking for the subordination of Islamic/Middle Eastern study in universities to American foreign policy interests.

According to Mucahit Bilici [1] of the University of Michigan, in the aftermath of the 9/11 the decades old media habit of association of Islam with terrorism found its eternal justification in the attacks of 9/11. Islam is perceived to be an inherently violent religion and approached to within the reductionist framework of security.

"Groups and individuals who have a vested interest in the demonization of Islam and Muslims in the United States have also seized the opportunity to attack Muslims and Islam. A phenomenon reminiscent of anti-Semitism is emerging and Islamophobia finds expression in the multitudes of ways without being subjected to anti-discriminatory measures.

"One theoretical aftershock of 9/11 has been the return of Orientalism as a veteran body of perspectives on Islam and Muslims. Advocates of Orientalist framework such as Martin Kramer took the opportunity to popularize their critique of not only postcolonial theory but also the entire discipline of Middle Eastern Studies in America. Neo-Orientalism has a large spectrum of participants from academia to the media. The neo-Orientalists fighting back are asking for the subordination of Middle Eastern scholarship to American foreign policy interests and certain brands of American patriotism. Even veteran Orientalist scholars such as Bernard Lewis made a return to the popular corners of American public sphere where he explained "the crisis of Islam" or answered "what went wrong" with the Muslims. According to Danny Fostel of *The Chronicle of Higher Education* return of Orientalism have already found some echo in new generation academics.

"Return of Orientalism is currently taking place more in popular literature than in academic works. The shock and impact of 9/11 has created a fertile ground for the proliferation of what can be called an alarmist literature. This growing body of popular literature on Islam simply demonizes Islam and Muslims. A representative sample of titles would include the following: *The Crisis of Islam, What Went Wrong, American Jihad: The Terrorists Living Among Us, Militant Islam Reaches America, Islam Unveiled: Disturbing Questions about the World's Fastest Growing Religion, Sword of the Prophet, The Terrorist Hunter.* Among the known alarmist writers and, in some cases, Islamophobes are journalist Steven Emerson, the author of *American Jihad: The Terrorists Living Among Us,* and the Middle East analyst Daniel Pipes, author of *Militant Islam Reaches America.* There has been a vicious war of images between such ideologically motivated critics of Muslims and the Muslim advocacy groups in the United States.

Reference

[1] "American Jihad:" Representations of Islam in America After 9/11" by Mucahit Bilici, University of Michigan, Ann Arbor. This paper was delivered at the 32nd annual conference of the Association of Muslim Social Scientists of North America, held at Indiana University, Bloomington, Indiana on September 26-28, 2003

INDEX

www.ingramcontent.com/pod-product-compliance
Lightning Source LLC
Chambersburg PA
CBHW030004290326
41934CB00005B/221